W9-DBN-025

RUDI COLLOREDO-MANSFELD

The University of Chicago Press
Chicago & London

The Native Leisure Class

Consumption and
Cultural Creativity
in the Andes

RUDI COLLOREDO-MANSFELD is assistant professor of anthropology
at the University of Iowa.

THE UNIVERSITY OF CHICAGO PRESS, CHICAGO 60637
THE UNIVERSITY OF CHICAGO PRESS, LTD., LONDON

© 1999 by The University of Chicago
© 1999 Drawings by Rudi Colloredo-Mansfeld
All rights reserved. Published 1999
Printed in the United States of America

08 07 06 05 04 03 02 01 00 99   1 2 3 4 5

ISBN 0-226-11394-9 (cloth)
ISBN 0-226-11395-7 (paper)

Library of Congress Cataloging-in Publiation Data

Colloredo-Mansfeld, Rudolf Josef, 1965–
    The native leisure class : consumption and cultural creativity
in the Andes / Rudi Colloredo-Mansfeld.
        p.   cm.
    Includes bibliographical references (p. 225) and index.
    ISBN 0-226-11394-9 (cl: alk. paper). — ISBN 0-226-11395-7(pa:
alk. paper)
        1. Indians of South America—Ecuador—Imbabura—Economic
conditions.   2. Quechua Indians—Ecuador—Imbabura—
Economic conditions.   3. Imbabura (Ecuador)—Economic
conditions.   4. Otavalo (Ecuador)—Economic conditions.
I. Title.
    F3721.1.I3C65   1999
    330.9866'12074—dc21   99-28259
                                                            CIP

To Chesca

◢ CONTENTS ◤

◢ ILLUSTRATIONS ◣

Photos

Gallery of photographs follows page 162

Maps

Drawings

◢ PREFACE ◣

"*Mingachiway,*" I called out.

It was early November 1994, and I was heralding my arrival at a weaver's house in the upper part of Ariasucu. The household had participated in my time-allocation study since the project's inception the previous February. Used to my unplanned visits, the weaver no longer rose from his loom to greet me and instead beckoned me into the interior where he worked. I stepped over the threshold and waited briefly, giving my eyes a chance to adjust to the dimness of this cluttered, windowless space. Holding his shuttle and resting his feet on the pedals of the loom, the weaver also paused. He then broke the silence with a question that he had evidently been waiting a long time to ask of me: "*Chay Macgyverca na armasta minishtin. Nachu?*"

He wanted to know whether MacGyver, the lead character in the eponymous television drama from the United States, ever needed to use weapons to get out of the predicaments he got into each afternoon. I told him I did not think so. I could not be sure, though, as the only time I had really watched the show was with him and other weavers whom I had visited while the show was on. In some houses, this U.S. production had become quite popular. In others, artisans tuned into Japanese cartoons. Still other weavers had no real interest in what was on; they just liked the dialogue and images as distractions from a long day at the loom. While the weavers may not have had the same tastes in programs, they did share the same routines. In 1994, the most commonly used object in an Ariasucu home was a loom; the second most common thing was a television.

Far from being awkwardly juxtaposed—a mismatch between traditional and modern—loom and TV exist in a symbiotic relationship. Each makes the other possible in this belt-weaving, agrarian sector. The earnings from intensified weaving allowed the purchase of a TV; the entertainment provided by the TV distracts weavers from the drudgery of their work and allows them to intensify production. Taken together, this mix of preindustrial technology and twentieth-century consumer electronics form a well-integrated economic whole. They also unite to create a powerful cultural symbol. The image of an eclectic material culture—new commodities in traditional settings, traditional handicrafts in a modern context— has come to stand for the interrupted modernity of Latin America (Garcia-Canclini 1995a). Within Ecuador, such blends assume narrower ideological meanings, representing for some the failures of native culture and national development policy. For others though, this scene, the weaver and his TV, signals a peculiar Andean success story: the triumph of the Otavaleños and their weaving economy.

This book explores the myths and realities of Otavalo; I center my examination on economic practice in general and the social power of material culture in particular. The study of commodities as symbols and consumption as cultural action has opened up new lines of inquiry in modern ethnography. The turn to material practices represents an effort to "work within the present"—to develop concepts that make sense of a globally integrated world (cf. Fox 1991). In the case of Latin America's rural peoples, the loss of shared occupational identities and, indeed, a more general cultural fragmentation, characterize this new world. Under these circumstances, consumption becomes a rare forum of common practice. Further, consumption directly engages questions of the "modernist" present—the rupture of traditions, market integration, community dispersal, and the pursuit of a better life through superior technology and products. In exchanging, displaying, using up, and talking about material culture, Otavaleños contribute to a specific Andean modernity. The racial ideologies, class cultures, and ethnic identities defining the Ecuadorian social landscape achieve an everyday potency through goods and their associated imagery.

The book's core chapters examine the farming, weaving, and textile-dealing occupations that have made both the economy and culture of the region unique. The chapters' ethnographic descriptions rest on four types of data: (1) quantitative data from household inventories and a nine-month time-allocation study; (2) extensive interviews with individuals from a core sample of thirty-two households; (3) historical information from the archives of provincial newspapers; and (4) forty hours of videotaped family gatherings, weddings, daily meals, and other primary social (and consumption) activities. Further, I include observations from my experiences of living in the community of Ariasucu and becoming compadres of two families. Finally, during my research, I have used pen, brushes, and ink to record the community's material culture—everything from chili-pepper grindstones to new blenders. Working as an artist, I open new opportunities for others to relate to my work and express their interests or respond more explicitly to my own.

While trying to capture the distinctive flair for cultural creativity that Otavaleños have exhibited in the 1990s, I also outline organizational regularities that may relate this case to other instances of indigenous communities in Latin America and elsewhere that have experienced something of a "renaissance." Among these, four factors seem notable. First, racism and ethnic discrimination continue to shape nationalist ideologies and devalue indigenous economic and social forms that fail to conform to modern ideals. Second, by exploiting some aspect of location or historic skill at a pivotal moment of economic integration, a single occupation, community, or ethnic group may leverage some initial advantage into significant and enduring long-term payoffs. Third, the large payoffs offered by an expanded market ultimately reduce the range of occupations people pursue. Following the example of the greatest successes within their ethnic group, talented women and men shun subsistence employment and ignore other potential avenues of advancement for uncertain payoffs in competitive markets. Fourth, as production becomes more specialized, consumption grows in cultural importance for demonstrating collective identity and obtaining stature.

As a whole, these conditions contribute to a process that could be called cultural concentration, resulting not in a uniformly enhanced culture but in the potential for a new division. On one side are the prosperous who creatively express indigenous culture and use distinctive cultural expression to intensify the bonds of their community. On the other side are those members of the community who have not reaped the benefits of the expanding economy. They are the "quick-change artists" (Kearney 1996) who shift among jobs and cultures according to economic opportunity and social circumstances and therefore develop a more fractured cultural identity. While the signs of such fragmentation exist, Otavalo has yet to split categorically in this way. Tastes for clothes and food and practices ranging from fiestas to *mingas* (collective work parties) breech emerging boundaries of class and occupation—at least for the time being.

Some prefaces conclude with a few brief lines in which the author thanks a small core of loyal informants, advisors, and readers for making the work possible. This is not one of them. This book is a while in the making and my debts of gratitude are correspondingly large. My interests in material culture and the Andes began at the

University of North Carolina, Chapel Hill, where I launched my anthropological career under the influence of Bruce Winterhalder and Norris Johnson. At UCLA, graduate seminars with Nancy Levine, Louise Krasniewicz, and Karen Brodkin (Sacks), as well as conversations and regular meetings with Tim Earle, helped to transform general ideas into a concrete project on architecture and economic change in Ecuador. A grant from the department of anthropology— enough funding for a one-way ticket—got my research going.

During that first fieldwork season, numerous individuals and groups supported my efforts. Jeannet Silva at the Instituto Nacional del Patrimonio Cultural del Ecuador provided me with all the relevant information that her institution had, then ushered me across Quito and introduced me to the Fundación Ecuatoriana del Habitat (FUNHABIT). Bolivar Romero and the other architects and engineers of FUNHABIT provided me with critical support and encouragement as I found my bearings during my first weeks of research as did Mary Weismantel, who met me in Quito for a very timely consultation. The success of that first work was due in large part to the help offered to me by Ariasucu residents Luis Antonio Castañeda, Elena Chiza, Pedro Vasquez, and Zoila Arias.

The doctoral research was funded by grants from the National Science Foundation (Dissertation Improvement Grant #SBR9318289), a Fulbright Award from the Institute of International Education, and an award from the UCLA Latin America Studies Center Small Grant program. To all of these institutions, I am very grateful, as I am to Madelyn Gianfrancesco in the UCLA Department of Anthropology who managed many of these resources. Helena Saona of the Fulbright Commission in Ecuador likewise helped not only with the administration of funds but also with the intricacies of immigration bureaucracies. Her office in Quito provided a cheerful refuge for weary travelers arriving from the countryside.

During my doctoral work, I received immediate and enduring support from my compadres and their families in Imbabura. More broadly, residents throughout Ariasucu, especially those who participated in the time-allocation study, helped in innumerable ways. The extended fieldwork would also have been unthinkable without the involvement of my wife Chesca. From helping me analyze the numbers of the time-allocation study to insuring that we fulfilled our *compadrazgo* functions at weddings, she played a pivotal role that year. During that time, the two of us benefitted from the companionship of a changing community of scholars, including Lynn Meisch, Linda D'Amico, Elizabeth Marberry, Mark Rogers, Linda

Belote and Jim Belote. The linguist Rafael Cotacachi helped with the transcripts from community meetings. My parents Susanna and Ferdinand Colloredo-Mansfeld not only unfailingly supported us from afar but also came down to visit and drink a few "little cups" with our compadres, as did my father-in-law Jeremy Varcoe and my sister-in-law Lucy Varcoe, who graciously let me use some of her wonderful photographs. Finally, I thank Hernan Jaramillo of the Instituto Otavaleño de Antropologia for his support and involvement.

The complications and culture shock that came with the return to Los Angeles diminished thanks to the administrative skill and sympathy of Ann Walters. Cristina Fernandez Carol followed up the logistical support she provided during fieldwork with the generous offer of a quiet place to write. And the active participation of Leland Burns, Alessandro Duranti, Nancy Levine, Mary Weismantel, and especially Tim Earle made for as smooth a dissertation-writing experience as I could have hoped for. In rethinking and refining these ideas for the book, I benefitted from discussions with colleagues at Occidental College, especially those who participated in the faculty seminar on conflict organized by Movindri Reddy. Completion of the manuscript was made possible through the writerly support of Susan Phillips, the cartographic skills of John Steinberg, the enthusiastic backing of T. David Brent at the University of Chicago Press, the careful editing of Kathryn Kraynik, and the infinite patience of Chesca.

Portions of chapters 2 and 4 were originally published as "Dirty Indians, Radical Indígenas, and the Political Economy of Social Difference in Modern Ecuador" in the *Bulletin of Latin American Research* 17, no. 2: 185–205, with permission from Elsevier Science, and "The Handicraft Archipelago: Consumption, Migration, and the Social Organization of a Transnational Andean Ethnic Group" in *Research in Economic Anthropology*, vol. 19 (1998), pp. 31–67, published by JAI Press, Inc., Stamford, CT.

Ultimately, this work of the past seven years would not have been as rich and rewarding without the support of my compadres and collaborators in Ariasucu. I remain profoundly grateful for (and in awe of) their kindness and generosity.

◢ PROLOGUE ◣
Andean Livelihoods in a Global Economy

◢ Of Pigs, Peasant Economics, and Politics ◣

Imagine the smell. By the end of the summer, the two pigs had doubled in size. The stench of their feces and urine drifted from their sty on the edge of the recently paved patio and permeated the five rooms of the tidy, white-washed, concrete block home that bracketed the opposite two sides of the patio. My wife Chesca and I lived closest to the animals in an L-shaped room that we had added onto Galo and Monica's house ten months earlier. We got whiffs of the pigs whenever we opened the door. During the days, the smell dissipated as Monica took them off to tether them in the stubble of nearby fields or on the grassy borders of the paths in our densely settled neighborhood. At nights, the swine scent strengthened when Monica or her boys again confined the two 150-pound animals in their pen.

The smell was only part of the problem. Household routines had warped to accommodate their hunger. Before dawn, Monica dressed speedily and hurried down the wide dirt path in front of the house to fetch water at the neighborhood's overused, weakly flowing standpipe. Rather than take the time to fill up all four of her plastic, twenty-liter water jugs, she settled for just a couple containers' worth so that she could get home and mix up the pig meal. As her daughter Clara swept the dust, chaff, and chicken droppings from the patio and her husband Galo turned their gas stove on to heat up a brew of sweet chamomile *café* for the family, she churned up a beige, lumpy breakfast of water and bran for the hogs.

After her two, late-rising, teenage sons José and Luis had drunk their *café*, combed out their hair, and bound it into loose ponytails, they took charge. They grabbed frayed, nylon lines and fixed them to each pig's ankle. Pulling hard, they hauled the animals out and tethered them away from the house. The pigs, however, rarely stayed put. Often, just as the men got down to their weaving and the women to cleaning the seed maize for the upcoming planting or some other task, the animals would break free of their stakes. Monica would have to leave Clara to put away the grain sacks and to prepare the soup for their mid-morning meal, while she went off to resettle the animals.

Sometimes, after she had eaten, Monica had to run errands in the middle of the day. Taking the bus from our small community of Aria-sucu into the market town of Otavalo, she would buy bread, bananas, or eggs for her small shop. Other times, she would walk down the cobbled road below the house, cross over the gully, and visit her par-ents—maybe to arrange to borrow their oxen for fieldwork, but more usually to check on the health of her elderly father. The pigs ex-ploited these absences. When they broke free, they scrambled back to the house, across the patio and plunged into the grain sacks on the edge of the *corredor*, the covered porch where the household worked throughout the day. They ransacked the place until Galo, José, or Luis could swing their legs out of their treadle looms, cross over to the animals and beat them away with a stick.

About 4:30 in the afternoon, Monica would have to prepare a sec-ond meal for the hogs. To the pig food she would add the long twists of potato peels she saved from the morning's meal or occasionally some leftover *buda*, a thick soup of milled grains that she brought back from a recent baptism or new house party. She also enlisted Chesca and me into the never-ending struggle to feed the pigs. After breakfast, we would dutifully scrape the cold Quaker oatmeal (that we purchased from her store) out of our pot and into her slop bucket. She sloshed this concoction into a stone trough and then sent José and Luis to retrieve the pigs.

Grabbing two short single-stranded whips and carrying them be-hind their backs, they went out to where the pigs were tied. Yanking the tethers off the stakes, the boys cracked the whips across the ani-mals backs, then raced them home, the four of them kicking up a thick plume of dust in the parched field. After eating their dinner, the pigs settled in for another night of grunting and farting under the tin roof in the corner of their pen outside our kitchen window. Only then could Monica return to her kitchen and finish preparing the soup for dinner.

This aggravation had been mounting over the past month, putting it into Monica's mind to sell these animals. Now, in early September, several other factors forced a decision. First, Ecuador's chronic in-flation had driven up the price of pig feed, making it costly to keep large animals with growing appetites. Second, in a few weeks, people would begin planting maize, the main subsistence crop of the region. The grazing areas would correspondingly diminish and households had to confine their pigs and sheep to the paths or their pens. Thus, a great hog sell-off seemed immanent, setting prices to plummet in early October. Third, the fiesta of Yamor would begin in a few days in Otavalo. This annual event, backed by the white-mestizo dominated municipal government, drew thousands of participants from around the province as well as from Quito, 100 kilometers south, on the Pan American Highway. The crowds would spur demand for roast pork, a popular Ecuadorian dish. Monica thought prices might be strong right now.

Beyond these market conditions, Monica also had to consider the shape of her household's economy. Her second daughter Celestina had married in June. Now she and her new husband Pedro have decided that Pedro should follow the lead of his cousin and thousands of other indigenous Otavaleños and go to Europe to sell handicrafts. To afford the plane ticket, the young couple would need to borrow money from Monica and Galo. Meanwhile, Galo and the boys earned less and less with their looms. As recently as nine months ago, they could sell the *fajas*, a narrow, multicolored belt worn by indigenous women, for a good profit, allowing Galo to buy sacks of pig food for Monica's animals with his earnings. Now his sales do not even cover the price of the acrylic threads he needs to keep his looms in production. A successful sale of her two pigs would restore her cash reserves and put Monica in a position to help out her husband and her daughter.

Taking all of this into account, Monica decided to sell the two pigs during the first Saturday market in September. Clara told us of the decision on the Friday afternoon before. We had been planning to go and videotape the market anyway and asked if we could come along. Clara had her doubts. We would have to get up at 4:00 A.M. and we would have to walk, she pointed out. We said we did not mind. To Monica's amusement, we all shared in some *café* at 4:15 on Saturday morning as her son José wrapped tethers around the pigs' ankles.

Already burdened by the complexity of Ecuador's rural economy, the pig sale had now become an anthropological event: something to be documented, questioned, replayed, and thought about. Otavaleños and other indigenous groups have become used to such attention. Over the past five decades, both national and foreign anthropologists have analyzed the many elements of Quichua culture, from saints' day fiestas and compadre relations to healing ceremonies and cuisine. In much of this research, writers have taken the very continuation of distinctive native culture in a modern nation-state as problematic and dedicated themselves to cataloging the ritual, economic, and linguistic processes which sustain indigenous societies

(Malo Gonzalez 1988; cf. Whitten 1981a). Recently the scrutiny has intensified as *indígenas* have more than reproduced their culture. They have radicalized it. Over the past decade, peasant leaders have tapped into indigenous cultural identity to mobilize tens of thousands of protesters for mass strikes and marches.[1]

Ecuadorian indigenous political activism first made international news in June of 1990. Native peasants throughout the highlands rose up and invaded *haciendas*, occupied churches, blocked highways, and marched on government offices. Seeking swift action on stalled land claims, indigenous organizations rallied their constituents to challenge government's institutionalized neglect of native peoples. Nina Pacari, an indigenous woman from the province of Imbabura—where Monica and Galo lived—and a leader of CONAIE, the Confederation of Indigenous Nationalities of Ecuador, called this *Levantamiento* (Uprising) a "sacrament of dignity" (Pacari 1993: 186). Describing the unfolding of the events, she emphasized that the indigenous woman participated in the uprising as if it were part of the daily routines like those described above—an extension of her work gathering firewood, pasturing animals, carrying water, and caring for children (Pacari 1993: 180–81).

The breadth of the uprising alarmed urban Ecuadorians, not simply because the strike halted much of daily life, but because it revealed the political will of indigenous society (Almeida Vinueza 1993). Natives were not simple peasants, "guardians of the earth," living according to timeless values and rituals outside the concerns of the twentieth century. On the contrary, indigenous life had a sharp political and economic edge. Its routines could switch abruptly into acts of protest. The prior decade of the 1980s not only saw invasions for land but also marches for potable water and sit-ins for proper bus service. In Otavalo, the fight for expanding local bus routes drew politically indifferent merchant-artisans like Galo into a violent strike against an unpopular, racist transportation cooperative in 1986. This grassroots, culturally rooted activism set the precedent for participation in subsequent strikes in 1992 (protesting the Columbian anniversary) and again in 1994 (against new land reform legislation).

Rallying to the demands of *"Tierra, Cultura, y Libertad"* (Land, Culture, and Liberty), Ecuador's national indigenous movement fore-

1. See, for example, the works of Andrés Guerrero (1993; 1994), León Zamosc (1993; 1994), and Nina Pacari (1993) for background and an analysis of the 1990 *Levantamiento*, or uprising. More recently, Whitten et al. (1997) have offered a broader symbolic analysis of the indigenous movement that has unfolded since 1990.

shadowed the more telegenic and violent uprising of the EZLN or Zapatistas that took place in Chiapas, Mexico, in January 1994. As in Ecuador, the movement in Chiapas drew its most committed supporters from native peoples, who demanded: "We want our culture to be respected, our languages, our way of life, and, especially, our land."[2] Seeking national legitimacy, native leaders in Mexico, Ecuador, and other Latin American countries have presented central governments list of demands for constitutional recognition of a "pluricultural" nation and of officially empowered native institutions. Peasant economic issues, once the substance of rural politics, have now become a subset of holistic cultural demands.[3]

Nonetheless, the shift to a broader ethnic agenda does not so much replace economic demands as fit the realities of the new native economy. Having migrated to cities for at least two generations, native peoples must have the cash and commodities of the marketplace to reproduce the *runa kawsay* (native Andean life). To be sure, subsistence farming, livestock keeping, creating extensive, kin-based networks of mutual support, and other facets of indigenous production matter as much now for most families as they ever have. Yet, such practices now achieve their value in relation to state development policy and must adapt to widespread and often disjointed circulation of people and goods. Exporting Andean handicrafts, importing Italian fedoras for men, shipping locally made sweaters to Colombia (goods made according to U.S. Peace Corps designs), bringing English tweed cloth back from Europe for women's skirts, migrating to Quito's construction jobs, settling back into Imbabura's farming routines, departing for the summer tourist season in Prague, returning for a child's baptism are the large and small acts producing Otavalo's social world. In all this flow, culture materializes not so much in fixed institutions and symbols but in rhythms of accumulation and consumption and in arrivals and departures.

2. *Excelsior,* 23 January 1994, p. 4A.

3. Scholars and politicians have debated the relative importance of ethnic and economic issues in Latin America's rural rebellions. Some writers have suggested that focusing on ethnicity ignores "fundamental economic debates and problems" (Powelson 1996: 6). Certainly, getting more land motivates many of the participants in both the Ecuadorian and Mexican uprisings (Field 1991; Harvey et al. 1994). Further, the economic dimension of native struggles draws support from across ethnic boundaries (Collier 1994). On the other hand, the movements' leaders themselves argue that their fight is a cultural upheaval, not just class-based, peasant struggle for land (Pacari 1993). In contrast to a "pure" peasant politics, the indigenous struggle is a spiritual movement challenging the exploitative values of the dominant culture (Hale 1994).

This mixture of agrarian practice, artisan commerce, migration, and working-class careers has contributed to the complexity of basic tasks such as selling a pig. It also feeds the political urgency of Andean culture. Demanding "Land, Culture, and Liberty," native peoples seek not separation from the nation and the modern economy, but rather justice for those trying to succeed within it. Whether Monica tries to raise livestock or Galo and his sons weave belts or their daughter Celestina transfers her textile-dealing operation from Ecuador to Holland, they are pursuing a social and material advancement—mostly—within the wider economy. In this effort, not only is the distance between daily life and political action getting smaller, but the gaps between the provincial, national, and international economic activities gradually disappear as well.

◢ Ecuador, Indígenas, and the Global Economy ◣

Straddling the equator, the nation of Ecuador covers about 284,000 km² (in U.S. terms, about the area of Oregon) and has a population of about 10,600,000.[4] While estimates of the number of indigenous people (Spanish: *indígenas*) vary widely according to criteria— language, residence, or work—several sources figure that about 35 percent of the national population or approximately 3,600,000 people are indígenas.[5] The bulk of these live in the highlands, speak Quichua as a first language, as well as Spanish, and maintain some connection to rural communities and the subsistence economy. Overall, Ecuador is the most densely populated country in South America, with a settlement pattern keenly influenced by the natural landscape. Two high, parallel *cordilleras* or ridges of the Andes run the length of the country from its northern border with Colombia to Peru in the south (map 1), splitting the nation into three regions, each having a distinctive political and economic identity (Alexander Rodriguez 1985). Each has also been drawn into the global capitalist economy in different ways.

Between the high, western *cordillera* and the Pacific Ocean lie the

---

4. *Statistical Abstract of Latin America*, 1994, volume 30, part 1, p. 102.

5. See, for example, Whitten et al. (1997: 357) or the *Statistical Abstract of Latin America*, 1994, volume 30, part 1, p. 140. Developing a comprehensive quantitative portrait of highland ethnicity, León Zamosc (1995) uses three lines of evidence: (1) linguistic indicators; (2) agrarian, demographic, and social statistics for peasant *cantóns* (rural administrative districts); and (3) statistics on peasant organizations. While his analysis corroborates many of the earlier statistical projections, he includes an indication of changes through time. In particular, he shows the faster population growth rates in "predominantly indigenous areas."

Map 1: Ecuador, the Highlands, and Cities where Ariasucu Craft Dealers Work

dry hills and humid plantations of the coastal or littoral plain. The region, known as the *costa*, supports close to half of Ecuador's population, its largest city, Guayaquil, and many major industries. Its economy has linked Ecuador with international capital and the world's commodity markets since the early years of the republic.

Beginning in the mid-1800s, coastal merchants and plantation owners marketed *kapok* (a cotton-like substance used to pad things), qui-
nine, and rubber internationally. Around 1860, Ecuador became a
leading exporter of cacao and stayed so until the 1920s.

With the Liberal Revolution of 1895, the economic dynamism of
the coast found political expression in the highlands. General Eloy
Alfaro challenged Ecuador's traditional oligarchic power structure
with the backing of the emerging middle class. Pursuing such liberal
ideals as freedom of expression, freedom of religion, the expansion of
primary education, and a restriction of the influence of the Roman
Catholic Church, Alfaro's administration passed new constitutions
in 1897 and 1906. The reforms, however, had little consequence for
the daily lives of the historically dispossessed—women, Indians, and
Afro-Ecuadorians—who remained excluded from politics and mar-
ginalized within the economy (Becker 1999). It was not until the
presidency of Alfredo Baquerizo Moreno, for example, that a law was
passed in 1918 "freeing" indigenous people from a brutal institution
of debt peonage known as *concertaje,* which bound them to the *haciendas* or large private estates in the highlands. Beyond their desire
to abolish an archaic and iniquitous labor system, politicians had
hoped Indians would migrate to the coast and work in the expanding
plantation economy (Barsky 1988). The political change, however,
had little social effect (Guerrero 1991: 47). By the early 1900s the
landed elite, or *hacendados,* had so cut off their laborers from the
wider society that few left their own settlements, much less the highlands (Casagrande 1971: 364).

Through the expansion of export-oriented agriculture, the coast
has continued its economic dominance of the country throughout
the twentieth century. Four of Ecuador's five top exports–bananas,
shrimp, cocoa and coffee–are grown there. Indeed, since getting into
the business in the 1950s, Ecuador has become the largest exporter
of bananas in the world. The coastal city of Guayaquil depends on
these exports as well as the bulk of Ecuador's manufacturing operations to support a population of close to two million inhabitants.
Becoming ever more cosmopolitan, the business elite of this city
continue to pursue their interests in liberalized trade, not just in Ecuador's capital but also in Washington, DC, and Brussels. In so doing,
coastal advocates of neoliberal policy in the 1990s step into roles
pioneered by the liberals in the 1890s. Their efforts to grow markets
for their goods lead them to push for the restructuring of Ecuador's
internal economy. By lobbying for reductions in tariffs and the pri-
vatization of communal property, they become a force for change in

highland communities that otherwise have no direct connection with coastal society.

The coast's economic antipode lies in the upper Amazonian region on the other side of the mountains. Known nationally as the *oriente*, the east, the area has a much lower population density than either of the other two sections of the country, with only about 3 percent of the national population (Whitten 1981b). Despite the paucity of inhabitants, the *oriente* has loomed large in the nation's imagination. Since the country's inception, Ecuadorian leaders have been preoccupied by the development potential of the rain forest. After losing half of this territory to Peru in a war fought in the 1940s, the state has only intensified the ideological place of the Amazon, carving the phrase "Ecuador has been, is and will be an Amazonian nation" into building facades and printing it in school texts. Although they agreed to new boundaries with Peru in the Protocol of Rio de Janeiro signed in 1942, Ecuador later repudiated the treaty and sporadic fighting continues in the region. Regardless of the current state of national boundaries, five different native peoples live in Ecuador's *oriente:* Quijos Quichua, Canelos Quichua, Achuar, Shuar, and Waorani (Whitten 1985). A mixed population of indigenous people and mestizos inhabit the towns of Puyo, Tena, and Coca. For most of the history of the upper Amazon basin, this human population sustained itself skillfully in the delicate medium of the forest.

Two decades ago, though, the highland population's need for land, North America's appetite for crude oil, and the central government's drive for dollars destroyed the ecological balance. Between 1970 and 1973, a consortium of national and international oil companies boosted Ecuador's crude oil production by 5,600 percent.[6] For the next thirteen years, these operations annually pumped an average of 12 million metric tons of oil out of reserves below the forest. The influx of people, machines, roads, pipelines, animals, and plants that has accompanied this new industry simultaneously killed the forests and ruptured the societies living in them. This destruction spurred local peoples to political action. Creating new federations and suing to get legal title to their land, Amazonian indigenous groups not only fought for their own rights but gave national and international legitimacy to native activism throughout Ecuador.

Political action, whether native marches from the *oriente* or trade negotiations for the business interests of the *costa*, inevitably takes Ecuadorians back to the *sierra*, the densely populated central Andean

---

6. *Statistical Abstract of Latin America*, 1994, volume 30, part 2, p. 663.

valley, and Quito, the nation's capital. The city had its origins in the ethnic polities and complex chiefdoms of the pre-Colombian *paramo* Andes. In the late fifteenth century, it became a key administrative district of Tawantinsuyu (the Inca Empire). After the Spanish invasion, imperial elites continued to use Quito as an ecclesiastical and political center. From its Andean base, the government sponsored the creation of a maritime link from the coast to other Spanish holdings, the opening of the Amazon to European explorers, and the reconstruction of the highland indigenous society as a labor reserve. Quito remained the capital after independence, becoming the site of national political authority of the large estate-owners of the Andean central valley.

The political clout of the *hacendados* (large landowners) did not translate into economic dynamism. In the years after independence, highland elites consolidated their social and political power by reinforcing the almost feudal economy of the central Andean Valley. They expanded their landholdings—often through the seizure of the common lands of indigenous peoples—and strengthened their control over peasant labor through various labor institutions of debt peonage that continued even after the abolishment of *concertaje*.

The concentration of assets persisted well into the twentieth century. In 1954, just 6 percent of the population owned 80 percent of the land. The vast majority of the rural population—90 percent of landowners—farmed holdings that averaged about two hectares and accounted for only 16 percent of the land (Barsky 1988: 43). The social problems caused by the *haciendas*, moreover, went beyond land distribution to the pernicious state of labor relations. To be sure, *concertaje* had been legally prohibited and the residents of Ariasucu and other "free communities" owned their own land. Nonetheless, within the same province, many indígenas had to earn the right to farm steep, remote, and marginal fields by working for several days a week on the *hacienda* lands in a labor system called *huasipungo*. While only 7 percent of indigenous families continued to work as *huasipungueros* in the early 1950s, the brutal *huasipungo* experience motivated peasant militancy and shaped the outlook of indigenous leaders, many of whom came from the poorest communities of the rural highlands.

Finally, in 1964, the government passed a reform law intended to eradicate serflike labor conditions, improve distribution of land, and provide a mechanism for the colonization of "uninhabited" land in both the rainforest and the *paramo*. Liberal political pressure or altruism alone did not bring about these changes. Indeed, in many ways, reformist measures mark the beginning of the highland's integration into international markets and capitalist production methods (Barsky 1988). The call to end *huasipungo* dovetailed with the large landowner's push for new economic efficiencies. Rather than maintain personal ties with an impoverished, peasant labor force, landowners looked for ways to rationalize their operations: reduce costs, modernize machinery, and produce high-value products such as milk and cheese.

As Ecuadorians searched for agricultural profits, multinational corporations like Nestlé became prominent actors in the agrarian economy. In the 1980s and 1990s, capitalist relations on the haciendas expanded further. Some Ecuadorian landowners struck deals with Chilean companies to clear-cut eucalyptus forests on their land. Others linked up with Colombian capitalists in a burgeoning cut-flower industry, which by 1994 exported US $50 million worth of roses, carnations, and other flowers to the United States. In short, rather than eliminating *haciendas,* land and labor reforms pushed them to develop into profitable enterprises along the lines of coastal plantations. Investments, labor allocation, and products in the sierra came to reflect capital and consumer markets in Bogotá, New York, London, and Madrid.

The public and private responses to Ecuador's integration into the global economy now demonstrate the limitations of national unity and a centralized state. Over the past two decades, hundreds of thousands of Ecuadorians—both white-mestizos and indigenous peoples—have left Ecuador's fickle labor markets and migrated to the United States. In the early 1990s, they made up the largest illegal immigrant population in New York.[7] Marking this dramatic population movement in a 1994 constitutional referendum, Ecuadorians voted for the first time in favor of allowing dual citizenship. Meanwhile, in an effort to control inflation and attract foreign investment, the government of President Sixto Durán Ballén forged ahead in the mid-1990s with a host of neoliberal reforms. His ministers tried to privatize everything from the national telephone company to the Pan American Highway. Alienating many indigenous communities (and prompting an extended national strike), they sought to eliminate restrictions on the sale of communal lands.

In sum, whereas in the 1970s the government used oil revenue to embark on an ambitious effort at national integration (Whitten

7. New York City Department of City Planning. Cited in *Harper's Magazine,* vol. 288, no. 1724, January 1994, p. 13.

1981b), twenty years later, Ecuador appears to be in the same predicament of other nation-states who are "retreating before, adapting to, being absorbed, dislocated by, the new supranational restructuring of the globe" (Hobsbawm 1990: 182). A unified citizenry, never true in fact, becomes increasingly hard to support ideologically as state institutions shrink, international financial institutions gain influence over government policy, and Ecuadorians, including thousands of native peoples, look abroad to pursue careers.

◢ Imbabura and Otavaleños ◣

Of all Ecuador's indigenous peoples, those in the province of Imbabura have probably prospered the most through circular, transnational migration, the exporting of handicrafts, and other features of a global economy. Like native society throughout the highlands, Imbabura's Quichua speakers divide into distinct ethnic groups. Differences in dialect, clothing, and occupations all contribute to social boundaries among peoples separated by mountainous geography. In the eastern part of the province, native communities have developed their political identity and social institutions through an extended struggle against the province's largest haciendas. A second group, the Natabuela *runa* live near the provincial capital of Ibarra. Losing arable land to urban development, many of the Natabuela women earn their living selling produce in nearby markets while men migrate to Guayaquil or Quito to look for jobs (Tobar Bonilla 1985). Finally, in the market town of Otavalo and the sixty or so neighboring rural communities in the south of the province live a third group of indígenas, who now number about seventy thousand. Since the 1940s, these Otavaleños have dispersed widely from their cultural homeland, with approximately five thousand living in a trade diaspora that spreads throughout Ecuador, Colombia, Venezuela, and on to Europe and the United States (Meisch 1987).

Native Otavaleños hold a special place in the national imagination and ethnic politics of Ecuador. The political scientist and former president Osvaldo Hurtado (1980: 52), for example, has written that Otavaleños "constitute the indigenous groups in which some of the traditional values of the 'native' tribes tend to be found in more or less pure form." While Hurtado's view may be oddly atavistic (tribes?), it illustrates the tendency to stand Otavaleños against other groups, declaring the Otavaleños as "typically indigenous" and "genuinely national" (Whitten 1985: 222). Glowing ethnographies with detailed descriptions and photographs, from John Collier and Anibal Buitrón's *Awakening Valley* (1949) to Lynn Meisch's *Otavalo:*

Weaving, Costume, and the Market (1987) and on to this work, institutionalize Otavalo's special ethnographic place. These accounts
offer foreigners greater access to Otavalo culture than to any other
Ecuadorian indigenous group and, ultimately, increase Otavaleños
access to foreign tourists.

Two aspects of Otavaleño society in particular have captured outsiders' attention: their appearance and their entrepreneurship. Otavaleño clothes have a quiet dignity to them. Even as she led two pigs
down a dirt path in the dark, Monica carried herself with a deter-
mined elegance. Like most other Otavaleña women going to market
that day, she wore an ankle length, straight, navy blue, woolen *anaku*
or skirt, bound tightly around her waist with two belts called *chum-
bis* (in Quichua or *fajas* in Spanish). As she walked along, the slit in
her skirt parted to flash a second, spotless white *anaku* underneath.
Her white polyester blouse, trimmed with a lace collar, and embroidered with light blue thread shimmered slightly in the occasional
brightness of the streetlights. Over her blouse, she knotted a thick
dark *chalina*, or shawl. Her hair reached to her waist wrapped stiffly
in a single long ribbon. On her head, she wore another *chalina* tightly
folded into a peaked cloth cap.

While she had taken care to look her best for the market, Monica's
outfit differed little from what she usually wore. Most Otavaleña
women continue to use the basic elements of traditional clothing as
daily wear. Men, on the other hand, have adopted blue jeans, windbreakers, and sweaters for regular use. However, for weddings, baptisms, and other fiestas as well as for important business or government dealings, they still wear white *alpargatas* (cloth sandals), white
pants, and a white dress shirt covered by a dark, navy poncho. On our
pig walk, though, Galo left his poncho behind, completing his white
outfit with a nylon jacket instead. Regardless of clothing style, Galo,
like other men of his generation, habitually wears a stiff, narrow-
brimmed fedora over his long braided hair.

Crafts as well as clothes set Otavaleños apart. They have historically specialized in weaving and textile dealing. Even before the Inca
invaded in the 1400s, the inhabitants of the valley, an ethnic group
known as the Caranqui, already included specialized weavers and
traders (Parsons 1945; Murra 1946; Salomon 1986). Over the centuries, weavers and merchants learned to adapt their trade to each
successive political and economic change. Products, raw materials,
and techniques changed to reflect the introduction of camelid wool
from the southern Andes, then sheep's wool and treadle looms from
Europe, and subsequently designs and products from Britain. Most

recently, the dominant influence has been the global demand for ethnic arts. As First World tourists search for authentic, nonindustrial artifacts, weavers oblige by turning their skills and wares to new tastes.[8] Otavaleños learned to produce over twenty-eight new products especially for tourists (Meisch 1987).

The market's growth in the 1980s and 1990s received an added boost from the men and women who lost their jobs in Quito in the wake of the 1982 fiscal crisis. As these migrants returned home, they channeled their energies and ambitions into artisan businesses. Their labor and ideas pushed handicraft manufacture to new levels of productivity (see chapter 5). Most important, unlike native artisans in other Latin American markets, like Chiapas, Otavaleño entrepreneurs have not ceded the role of middlemen to white-mestizos (cf. van den Berghe 1993). By building up their own retail and wholesale businesses, some native merchants have accumulated real capital and invested in other enterprises and assets, from hotels to bus cooperatives.

◢ Ariasucu and the Suburban Realities of Agrarian Life ◣

About a forty-minute bus ride from the town center, the sector of Ariasucu is one of the highest on Mount Imbabura's southern flanks (map 2). From the settlement's top houses, an uneven quilt of subsistence plots slopes up toward the mountain's angular shoulders and rocky gullies. Close proximity to *Tayta Imbabura* (Father Imbabura) and its scrublands (the *sacha*) engenders a special relationship between the people and the mountain. Upper residents pick wild fruit from the rocky drainages and water flocks of sheep at a high spring they call "the mountain's belly button." In past dry years a few older men have made their way up through the *sacha*, across the *paramo* (the high, grassy moor lands), and to the rocky ramparts of the upper mountain to leave an offering of a guinea pig and a chicken. They hoped to persuade the mountain to bring the rains. Growing up with these stories, children learn of the mountain's power and frequent indifference to those settled on its slopes. Often times when I showed children my first set of sketches, they asked me why I had no drawing of the mountain. In fact, one persistent eight-year-old boy pestered me each time I saw him, demanding that I draw the mountain, until I showed him my sketch (drawing 1).

8. Otavaleños join many other native or "fourth world" peoples in innovating and diversifying their craft production in the face of tourist demand (Graburn 1976). Indeed, constant turnover of products and design is now a hallmark of "traditional" craft production.

of textile entrepreneurs to look for similarities and differences between specialized artisans and others with a more diversified domestic economy. Thus, I chose all *faja* weavers with three or more
looms,[9] a total of seventeen households with ninety-one individuals
and compared them with fifteen households (that included another
ninety persons) drawn at random, for a total sample of thirty-two
households and 181 people.[10]

As I got to know the people in the study through interviews and
preliminary analysis of the spot sampling data, however, I learned
that craft expertise was not as socially significant as I had once
thought. While I found my detailed data on *faja* weavers valuable (see
chapter 5), I realized that the important differences in both economic
accomplishments and opinions about jobs, community politics, and
other matters correlated more with geography than with artisan specialization. Put another way, one could tell more about a person's material advancement, involvement in community matters, and values
by knowing whether they lived in the more suburbanized lower part
of the community or the poorer upper sector (see chapter 6 for a discussion of the growing internal cultural divides). Because both the
random and the artisan specialist segments of my sample draw
equally from upper and lower neighborhoods, I have aggregated them
to present a portrait of the community as a whole. This has the disadvantage of overstating the amount of time spent in manufacturing
but otherwise gives a more balanced portrait of farming, handicraft
dealing, and social activities.

As in other parts of the *cantón* or county of Otavalo, agriculture
affects every resident's life in some way. Local and regional festivals
coincide with planting and harvesting. The food, especially maize,
makes up the core of their diet. Even in an age of transnational textile
dealing, most people's sense of self-worth and economic security depends on maintaining one's land. Nonetheless, direct, in-the-field agricultural tasks take up less than 7 percent of the time for women

9. I chose three looms as the mark of a specialist for economic and organizational
reasons. Keeping a third loom in production introduces paid labor into an operation—
even when the third weaver is the proprietors' own child (see chapter 5 for a discussion of
Ariasucu's fledgling labor market). In order to keep a piecework weaver around, proprietors must maintain steady supplies of materials and embark on regular sales trips so that
weavers can be paid regularly. All these demands intensify artisan operations in a way not
experienced by a single weaver working on his or her own, even those who do not pursue
other major cash-earning activities.

10. I originally selected eighteen households at random. However, for reasons of migration (in two cases) and growing lack of co-operation (in the third case), my sample
dropped to fifteen households.

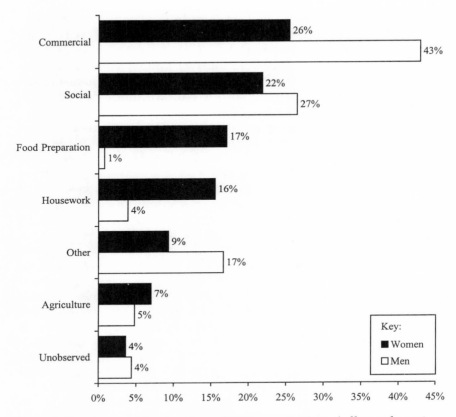

Figure 1: Percentage of daytime hours (7:00 A.M.–6:00 P.M.) allocated to primary activities in Ariasucu, February–November, 1994. (Percentages are based on 5,017 random spot observations of ninety-four females and eighty-seven males.)

and 5 percent of time for men. Increasingly, farming is little more than an interruption in routines dominated by commercial work, social activities, and domestic chores (figure 1).[11]

11. The study itself took place between February and November of 1994. I made my visits of randomly chosen households at randomly selected intervals, seven days a week, during daylight hours (between 7:00 A.M. and 6:00 P.M.). I had hoped to start earlier in the day, capturing people just after dawn, because I felt that many people tried to weed or begin harvesting first thing in the day. However, Ariasucu's electricity and other suburban features allowed people to stay up late and led to people sleeping in. I usually woke at least one household during 7:00 A.M. visits and inevitably would have woken up many

Subsistence food production, however, requires substantial commitments of skill and energy beyond the relatively few hours spent in the fields. Women, in particular, work hard to process home-grown food. From the start of the harvest, most women must dedicate a portion of their day to cleaning, drying, threshing, winnowing, sorting, and storing the family's crops. Throughout the year, they guard food against insects, rats, and other pests. Further, cooking their own foods takes much time as they mill, clean, soak, toast, or boil their grains to prepare them for a meal. These tasks, more than any other, distinguish women's work from men's work, accounting for 17 percent of a woman's day and only 1 percent on average of a man's day.

For their part, men work more intensively in the cash economy. Nonetheless, around Otavalo, subsistence and market spheres do not split along the same gendered lines as they do elsewhere in the Ecuadorian Andes (Weismantel 1988). Indeed, while cash-earning activities occupy almost half of men's time, they also take up a quarter of women's labor (see figure 1). For both the men and women of Ariasucu, textiles occupy the bulk of their commercial work.

Eschewing the relatively steady income of weaving, many residents prefer handicraft dealing for the potentially larger profits (figure 2). Textile sales often provide teenagers with their first business experience out of Otavalo and adults with their main chance for improving their standard of living. From the teenage girls peddling sweaters in Tulcan's rainy streets to the middle-aged couple commuting monthly between Imbabura and Cuenca with their Chevy Blazer stuffed with sweaters, bags, and tapestries, local residents spend much time selling goods to tourists. For more and more residents, that means moving away from this rural sector. In a small survey of thirty Ariasucu heads of households (all available participants in the time-allocation study at the time of the interview), I found that twenty-four of them had a close relative—sibling, parent, children, uncle or aunt—living outside the province in places like Quito, Cuenca (Ecuador's third largest city), Bogotá, Chicago, and Amsterdam.

While farming, weaving, and trading account for much of the community's economic activity, many Ariasucu residents search

more if I had started at 6:00 A.M. I did not want to jeopardize participants' commitment to the study by becoming the community alarm clock. In the end, I obtained 5,017 random spot observations of 181 individuals. Ages of participants ranged from three months to sixty-three years old; the sample included ninety-four women and eighty-seven men.

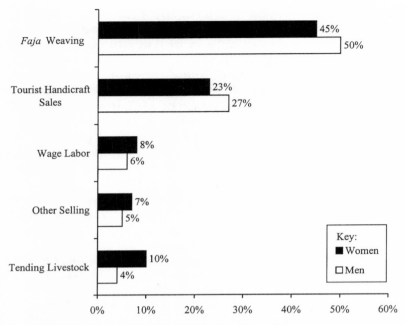

Figure 2: Percentage of commercial time allocated among top five cash-earning activities in Ariasucu, February–November, 1994. (Percentages account for 93 percent of 482 observations of ninety-four females and 93 percent of 661 observations of eighty-seven males.)

out wage work. Even with the uncertainties of 1990s economy, men still go to the cities to labor on construction sites, carry sacks of potatoes in the market, and sell baseball hats and used clothes in Quito (table 1). While women, too, find jobs—mainly as domestic servants—they are more likely to raise some livestock—cattle, sheep, chicken, and pigs—in order to make money.

The drive for material advancement, however, has not unduly squeezed the Otavaleños' active social life (figure 3). Men, in particular, enjoy their games and parties. Tellingly, aside from water taps and electric poles, Ariasucu's only public infrastructure is a concrete volleyball court. Beginning around three o'clock in the afternoon, men of any age gather to play three-a-side "Ecuavolley," betting the equivalent of a day's wages on the outcome. The small sector also contains enough players to fill out the rosters of two separate soccer teams, *Argentina* and *Cinco Estrellas*. Women's social life concentrates more on the family. When they have finished up the chores at their own home, many women visit their parents, siblings, cousins,

Table 1. Nonweaving Paid Work,
Ariasucu, January 1994

Employment	Number of People
Construction laborer	9
Market porter	8
Wool trader/barterer	7
Cook	6
Thread-maker	5
Agriculture laborer	5
Begging	4
Maid	3
Glove knitter	3
Used clothes seller	2
Office caretaker	1
Construction site guard	1
Harp player	1
Curandero (shaman/curer)	1
Total	56

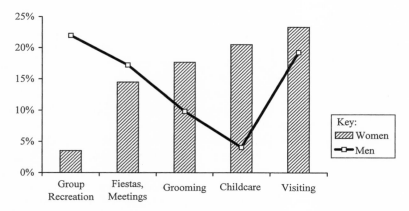

Figure 3: Percentage of time allocated among top five social activities in Ariasucu, February–November, 1994. (Percentages account for 75 percent of all social activities.)

or compadres, usually pitching in with some seasonal task as they do so. When it comes to fiestas, men and women participate more equally. People celebrate life's major events through lengthy parties for baptisms, confirmations, weddings, and new houses. With more money in the region, the occasions have multiplied. People now gather to mark the return of a trader from abroad, the construction of a new room, or the purchase of a new car.

⊿ Wealth and an Eclectic Landscape ⊾

Subsistence plots, wage work, craft sales, compadre networks, migration from the fields to the city and back again are all elemental features of the Otavalo economy. Not much new in this. Peasants throughout Latin America have long tried to protect themselves with subsistence resources, to embrace what opportunities were afforded to them in the wider economy, and to strike compromises necessary for operating in a dualized political economy (Wolf 1955). In Otavalo, though, something has changed: many have found a way to make it work. The Indians have money. The presence of indigenous controlled capital has led Otavaleños to expand their enterprises overseas and into the domains of white mestizos, from local real estate to hotel and restaurant businesses. New cultural expression flows from the influx of cash—as do class differences and cultural gaps among bordering native communities. The fragmentation of Otavaleño society and cultural form manifests itself in an increasingly eclectic landscape—something I was struck by the day we led the two pigs down from Ariasucu into town.

On that morning, the slow pace set by the animals and the commentary of Galo and Monica sharpened my awareness of the differences among the sectors. After leaving the house, we crossed over the gully, into the community of Agato, and walked by Monica's parents' house. A naked light bulb lit up the older couple's *corredor* and created a ragged fringe of shadows on the edge of their earthen patio. Monica's father, Alfonso Quilla, was packing up his *chalinas* to take to the market. Galo pointed to the scraggly trees that walled the patio off from the oxen pen. "With this tree, *Papasu* (Pop, Daddy) makes the colors," he said, referring to the older man's use of natural dyes and old-fashioned ways more generally. With a worm-eaten treadle loom, he still wove women's shawls out of threads that he occasionally dyed by hand. Tradition, however, rarely pays in this artisan economy. The wealthiest weavers have long since capitalized their operations, employing electric-powered looms to produce shawls and ponchos in large quantities. In a market flooded with machine-made wares, Papasu's products return the slimmest profits.

The next house over from Monica's parents was a modern, two-story cement-block home that belonged to her sister and brother-in-law. The adobe wall separating the patio from the street had been knocked down and smoothed over to make a driveway for her brother-in-law's new pickup truck. He rarely parked it there though since the family lived up in Tulcan on the Colombian border. Aside from periodic vacation stays, the house sat unused. Only recently has it gained new life. Ever since telephones lines were installed in lower Agato in 1996, this spacious, sparsely furnished home has served as a giant phone booth for the extended family.

After leaving Monica's old neighborhood, the next community we crossed into was Peguche, the richest indigenous town and source of many manufactured "native crafts." On any day of the week, the crowded, dusty lanes here echo with the clatter of machinery thumping out brightly colored textiles. Pickups come and go over Peguche's rough cobbles, gathering up sweaters, ponchos, and shawls by the hundred weight and transferring them to the *"mayoristas,"* the major wholesalers in Otavalo who sell them to market vendors or export them to customers abroad.

Walking downhill and out of Peguche, we picked our way over some railway tracks and arrived on a street in an outer neighborhood of Otavalo. At least, it was supposed to be a street. The department of public works bounded this avenue with two, raised cement sidewalks, incorporating it into a wide grid of suburban blocks. Rather than asphalt or cobbles, however, grass covered the road. The houses in this neighborhood showed a similar incompleteness. On some lots sat large homes with big windows, steeply angled roofs of glazed tile, and sturdy security walls topped with broken bottles. Nearby sprawled empty lots or mechanics shops sheltered under tin roofs and crowded by tires and broken-down cars. We made good progress through this eclectic landscape, as the terrain stretched out level and empty of people and dogs.

"That is my cousin's house," Galo said as he pointed up to a four-story building a couple blocks away. Peering at it in the darkness, he announced that the top floor had recently been finished. "He will have a party now, to celebrate the elaboration of the house. We went to his last party," he added, implying that he would go to this one too. Galo liked to stay in touch with his transnational relatives, especially this one, who seemed to be especially wealthy. "He has three houses, one here, one in Colombia, and one in Venezuela," Galo said. Like Monica's sister's house, this one seems destined for little use. Its mission seems to be to just get bigger. Like some slow-blooming plant, it periodically swells with a new floor, wing, or room; each addition arriving in a loud celebration of amplified music and free-flowing alcohol. Having successfully pollinated the event with their money, the cousins then depart for business elsewhere.

We left the darkened house and crossed out of the subdivision as a weak blue light soaked through the clouds on the eastern horizon. Our walk had brought us to the edge of the Pan American Highway. Even at dawn the road raced with traffic. Interprovincial buses sped down from the high fields north of town, gaining enough momentum to carry them up and around Otavalo on their way to Quito. Slower local buses motored in both directions to pick up people from rural sectors and deliver them to the market. Taxis wove amongst the traffic. As the two pigs panted at our feet, we stared at the headlights coming from either direction and tried to time our crossing so as not to be crushed by the streams of buyers and sellers rushing to the market. We sprinted to the weedy median strip, caught our breath, then charged over to the other side, leaving us with a short, uphill walk to our destination.

The animal market comes to life each Saturday on a muddy plaza on the western edge of Otavalo. The market loosely organizes itself into two sections. Vendors of pigs and sheep gather in the front half near the highway, while those selling cows mill around in the back. Buyers circulate among the crowd, inspecting animals and making offers. Upon closing a sale, people cross over the Pan-American Highway and head to the center of town to complete their business. The old part of Otavalo contains itself within five main streets that run north and south, cross cut by thirteen shorter streets that run east and west between a small creek and a hill that rises up behind the railway station. The main plaza in the center of town, the Poncho Plaza to the north and two food markets, one on the east side and the other on the west, provide the primary public spaces.

Like many provincial highland places, Otavalo transforms itself from a quiet country town to a noisy fair on market days. While *artesanias* (handicrafts) have made this market famous throughout Ecuador, the Poncho Plaza itself is often the quietest place in town. Too much competition among retailers keeps traffic light in any single stall. The action picks up with the produce trucks parked along the streets, where deep-voiced men and women sell fruit: oranges, bananas, pineapples, tree tomatoes, custard-apples, and wild *mora* (a raspberry similar to a mulberry). Indigenous women browse here, selecting treats for themselves and their family. Off on side streets other merchants hawk all manner of housewares from Chinese-made enameled bowls stenciled with flowers to big forty-liter plastic water jugs made down in Guayaquil. Although people can buy these items in stores during the week, most prefer to shop on a Saturday because of the better selection and prices—and the excitement of the fair.

At the intersection of an overburdened subsistence economy, provincial labor market, and global craft trade, Otavalo is shedding bits and pieces of its historic, white, Hispanicized mantel to exhibit a more mottled culture. In the 1940s, indigenous people abandoned the city after the market came to a close, avoiding the hostility of its white-mestizo denizens (Collier and Buitrón 1949). Now some white-mestizos talk of abandoning Otavalo in an Andean version of "white flight" as indigenous people modernize Otavalo. They buy more and more houses in and around town, building large town homes and opening hotels, retail outlets, restaurants, and even a health food store. Filling with the sounds of power looms and Quichua conversation, the smells of woolen handicrafts, the sights of shawls, *anakus*, white pants, and *alpargatas*, the city of Otavalo is going native. The reverse is also true. Native culture is getting urbanized—in addition to being suburbanized, proletarianized, capitalized, and revitalized.

◢ Otavaleño Modernity ◣

Emerging amidst these processes, Otavaleño culture and society seem to be diversifying to the point of irreversible fragmentation. A man who worked with a large electric loom in Peguche, for example, shook his head with disbelief when I told him that some Ariasucu weavers work by candlelight. More amazingly, I could not convince a young transnational merchant from Ariasucu that the houses five hundred meters up the path from her parents' home did not have electricity. Differences grow within the family, too. As Monica frets over the prices in the local market, her daughter Celestina worries about international exchange rates and the logistics of money transfers and craft shipments to Europe. In the long run, these intracommunity and intrafamily gaps in knowledge and experience may prove the greatest challenge in reproducing Otavaleño culture in a globalized economy. As Arjun Appadurai (1990: 18) writes, "generations easily divide as ideas about property, propriety, and collective obligation whither under the siege of distance and time." Migration and the expanding economy erode the commonalties of Otavalo's social world.

Modernization, of course, is predicated on such erosion. As a long string of writers on modernity have noted, the upsetting of traditional material, moral, and social unities is the essence of progress and the advancement of modern ideals (Habermas 1987; Berman 1981). Modern life unleashes several interrelated conditions: an increasingly individualized sense of self, alienation from one's inherited cultural forms, a new temporal sense of living in the present, and the secularization or disenchantment of the world (Miller 1994; Garcia-Canclini 1995b). These conditions arrive both painfully and promisingly, through acts of "creative destruction." As David Harvey (1989: 16) writes, "How could a new world be created, after all, without destroying much that had gone before? You simply cannot make an omelet without breaking eggs, as a whole line of modernist thinkers from Goethe to Mao have noted." Rife with contradiction, this "modernist project" works its way into the myriad cultural transformations taking place in Otavalo and elsewhere in the Andes in the wake of economic integration.

In Otavalo, though, a further dilemma inserts itself into this process of change: the problematic nature of indigenous affluence, defined narrowly to mean an influx of resources and material culture. In his novel *Gain*, Richard Powers (1998) writes, "ease upped the ante on the whole notion of existing." For an ethnic group that has toiled with looms, wooden plows, and back-packable inventories of crafts and has consequently defined itself through that toil, ease has upped the ante, if not on existence, at least on the specific notion of indigenous existence. Certainly, most Otavaleños do not own town houses, have much spare cash, or enjoy an easy life. However, they do experience incomes and consumption levels beyond what their parents had and such relative ease translates into greater creative license in the production of culture. Many Otavaleños not only can sample styles, tastes, and objects from more diverse cultures, but they also can invest more resources in reproducing native practice. This sampling and spending sets up the central questions of this book: What (and whose) values—understood broadly to include work ethics, moral obligations to family, ideologies of identity, race, and social difference—guide Otavaleños' economic development? Second, by what means do Otavaleños reconcile conflicting value systems? More narrowly, how do Otavaleños use material culture as a social medium to produce networks of identity and power? [12]

In the following chapters, I answer these questions by pursuing the interconnections between the general properties of consumption as a social process and specific historical transformations of modern Otavalo. In chapter 1, I provide theoretical background on the prob-

12. While it is a far more politicized example of indigenous cultural development, Pan Mayanism in Guatemala likewise illustrates issues of indigenous economic mobility and the social, cultural, and political consequences of what Kay Warren (1998) refers to as the development of a "parallel middle class"—a term she borrows from Jeffrey Himpele's work (1995) on identity and ethnicity in La Paz.

lems of affluence and culture change in general and the social role of consumption in particular. Going beyond models of change that emphasize either cultural dependence or cultural enhancement, I offer an alternative: the notion of cultural improvisation. Drawing on both practice theory and new consumption studies, I argue that the process of change is economically contingent, sensual, and ephemeral—dependent on constant regularizing activities rooted in material practice.

In chapters 2 and 3, I outline moral and cultural principles about economic action that shape Otavalo's social landscape. I begin by describing how the white-mestizo middle class has long used images of "dirty Indians," soiled possessions, and lowly houses to denigrate indigenous people as backward and degenerate even as more and more indigenous merchant households have largely given up a peasant livelihood. Nonetheless, white-mestizos continue to imagine new signs of disease and corruption in native society, discriminating against even the richest indigenous people. This "hygienic racism" operates as a form of "structural power" (Wolf 1990), shrinking the potentiality of native culture and careers.

Chapter 3 covers how poorer indigenous people invert racist ideology. Rather than believing that they live a "dirty life," peasant farmers speak of the *yanga kawsay*, or the humble/fruitless life. From their perspective, the problem is not hygiene but class: toiling for years with nothing to show for it but tired bodies and a roomful of worn possessions. Otavaleño peasants dwell upon the "worthlessness" of their goods, drawing repeated attention to the objects' circumscribed economic and social power in the broader economy and, in so doing, endow mundane things with a discursive force. People refer to them in conversations and use them during interactions to assert the continued importance of subsistence practices for household unity and indigenous identity, even in these transnational times.

In chapters 4 and 5, I move from ideals to specific instances of "cultural improvisation" by examining the institutionalization of transnational, kin-based trading networks and the commercialization of *faja* weaving. Borrowing from scholarship on earlier Andean economic practices, I explain in chapter 4 how Otavalo society has taken the form of a "global archipelago" with expatriates pursuing economic strategies among international market niches. While the search for better economic opportunities has drawn traders farther away for longer and longer stays, the circulation of commodities and the ritualized consumption at family fiestas has kept the institutions of this archipelago anchored in Otavaleños' Andean homeland.

In chapter 5, I return home with the migrants. Examining the lives the men and women who returned to Ariasucu after Ecuador's economy collapsed in the 1980s, I focus on how they invented the modern craft of commercial *faja* weaving. As these operations expanded, their proprietors created economically, socially, and morally hybrid spaces. Furnishing and using their home for intensified commercial enterprises, weavers have attempted to reconcile profit maximization with their moral obligations to their piece-workers, many of whom are godchildren, nieces, nephews, or other family members. In the social complexity of these shops, even the thinness of the proprietors' body becomes an ethnic and moral benchmark. The trajectory of *faja*-weaving careers underscores both the contradictions of modern indigenous life and the material, linguistic, spatial, and culinary means Otavaleños employ to reconcile them.

Finally, in chapter 6, I examine the separate, yet decidedly indigenous, class cultures emerging in Otavalo. Charting the rise of an indigenous "leisure class," I explore the paradoxical ways that consumption practices intended to show commitment to indigenous culture wind up undermining the importance of Otavalo as a homeland. The architecture, the expensive parties, and even the fat bodies of rich migrants threaten to displace native, agrarian values and usher in a more economically and spatially divided society.

◢ Closing the Sale ◣

Back on that late summer's market day with the two pigs, the most nerve-racking part had arrived: closing the sale. The negotiations began even before Monica got the pigs to the livestock plaza. A pickup truck with high, wooden-paneled sides swerved off the road and cut us off. A short, energetic man in a padded blue jean-jacket leapt out of the driver's door, came around, and jammed his fingers into the shoulder of the nearest pig. He turned and grabbed a handful of hindquarter flesh on the other animal. The exhausted pigs twitched, but held their ground. The man then turned to Galo who nodded at Monica. The driver went over and stood closely behind her. With his chin almost resting on her shoulder, he muttered a number in her ear. She stared straight ahead and shook her head. He glanced over at the animals and sweetened his price. Monica's eyes narrowed to a squint and she shook her head again. With that, the white-mestizo middleman jogged back to his truck and went on to the market. Monica reported that his best price would have meant selling the pigs at a loss. She needed to get at least 300,000 sucres (about $150; 50,000 more than he offered).

The encounter concentrated attention on the task at hand. Galo broke off and ran up the hill ahead of us to scout things out. The pigs trotted behind Monica, their heads bobbing from side to side as they labored up the rise to the crowded plaza where people bought and sold the *canton's* livestock. After Monica took up her position, Chesca and I wished her good luck, set up a time and a place to reunite with her and Galo in the main market, then headed off. We did not want to complicate her negotiations with our presence. After taping some of the other bargaining taking place, we shot the arrival of a trickle of tourists, mostly gaunt budget travelers in worn hiking boots looking for a more "authentic" experience than the tourist handicraft market could provide. As the crowd thickened, we lost sight of Monica and Galo. We shut off the camera and went into town for a *café con leche.*

Later that morning, we wrapped up filming other sections of the market and made for our designated meeting spot in the plaza. Monica and Galo were there already, staring stoically at the passing crowd. "Well, what happened?" we asked. Finally, Monica's smooth face relaxed and a brief smile crinkled her eyes. They got 300,000 sucres for the pair. It was not a huge amount, but enough to make it all worthwhile. The earnings would go to buy some fish for dinner, a sack of sugar, and two *quintales* of potatoes (two large sacks—each about 25 kilos). She planned to spend a few days next week selling dishes of cooked potatoes seasoned with a spicy, light peanut sauce to the tourists who came to town for the Yamor Fiesta. Right then, though, she had to take care of some other business. Disappearing into the throngs in front of us, she rushed off to sell two chickens and a vicious, bloodthirsty rooster that Clara brought down from the house on the bus. But that is another story.

◢ ONE ◣
Affluence, Consumption, and Cultural Improvisation

◢ Beyond Enhancement and Dependence ◣

Cash infusions and indigenous cultures mix in unpredictable ways. A relative rise in market resources sets some groups on paths to lively cultural expression and others to apparent dissolution. In India, for example, a tribal group known as the Muria Gonds was rich in forest lands in the last century (Gell 1986). As Hindus came into the area, the Muria sold them land which the Muria could no longer profitably cultivate. The sales generated earnings they spent to participate in village feasts. Buying finery for public ceremonies, villagers celebrated clan solidarity with distinctive assemblages of turbans, loincloths, short saris, and massive silver and brass bracelets—all of which were imported or patterned on objects from elsewhere.

In North America, the Osage escaped the poverty afflicting many Native American groups, in part, because their reservation in Oklahoma sits atop one of the largest concentrations of oil in North America (Thompson et al. 1984). Through leases and royalties, the tribe has earned more than $500 million since 1907. The money enables participation in both white and Indian culture. Osage have earned advanced degrees at Harvard, Oxford, and other universities. At the same time, Osage consistently travel from Colorado, California, and elsewhere in order to participate in the main tribal ritual, the *Inlonshka*. They have even found a way to preserve the central element of a warrior's funeral, the formal dedication of an enemy scalp. Instead of the traditional swatch of skin and hair, mourners buy the hair of white women as a symbolic replacement. Speaking of his tribe's commitment to its own traditions and rejection of either assimilation or Pan-Indianism, Chief Sylvester Tinker said in 1980: "The Osage got money. All them other Indians got is their ass and a hat" (Broad 1980: 35, cited in Thompson et al. 1984).

In the 1990s, the Kayapo of the Brazilian Amazon got money, too. Unlike the Osage case, though, wealth proved far more divisive. Beginning in the late 1970s, Kayapo chiefs granted mining and logging concessions to outsiders interested in the large quantities of gold and rich stands of mahogany and other hardwoods in Kayapo territory (Turner 1995). The younger chiefs who came into power in the 1980s exploited these contracts for personal gain, moving from forest villages into private town homes in Rendencao, where they kept cars, trucks, airplanes, and Brazilian servants. Eventually, young villagers and older chiefs revolted against their urbanized leaders and forced an end to the concessions. The Kayapo have subsequently built on village-based political organization to pursue a more sustainable, environmentally sound, and co-operative form of economic development.

While their histories and settings differ markedly, the Muria, Osage, and Kayapo confront a similar problem: adjusting to an influx of market wealth. The advent of relative affluence—the new opportunity to live without fear of poverty—raises fundamental questions about cultural survival, consumerism, and the agency of local groups in a global marketplace. Surveying scholarship on the subject, Richard Salisbury (1984) identifies two approaches to affluence. On the one hand, anthropologists describe how ethnic groups use new money to elaborate selected cultural forms, even as they neglect others, a process Salisbury (1984: 3) calls *cultural enhancement*. The Muria, whose investments in rituals and exotic goods reinforce local corporate identities, offer one example. The Sherpas of Nepal, who earn high wages in the tourist trade yet remain culturally rooted in the remote Khumbu region and devoted to Buddhist doctrine and ritual, offer another (Fisher 1990: 139–40). More generally, under newly wealthy circumstances, cultures with elaborate rituals of ceremonial feasting and exchange often intensify traditional symbols and stature associated with their leaders (Codere 1950; Strathern 1971).

On the other hand, ethnographers have recorded how a rise in earnings induces many people to forsake their culture for the products of industrial society. More than homogenization, such consumerism in nonindustrial society creates *cultural dependence*, a continuing need to earn money to buy the fashionable products of dominant metropoles (Salisbury 1984: 3–4). Keen to demonstrate modernity, groups such as the villagers of Erakor in Vanuatu tie "their identity to the ownership of object-signs that they can ill afford and that they are unable to produce . . . asserting their cultural identity according to a code that they do not control" (Philibert 1984: 92). Along with losing local meanings, historically egalitarian groups stratify socially, thus producing conflicts between haves and have-nots.

As alternative models, cultural dependence and cultural enhancement underscore the diverse outcomes made possible by affluence. Yet taken together, they reflect the same premise. Both assume that people will invest new resources in pre-existing cultural models, either embellishing past practices or imitating the lifestyles of urban or foreign elites. Such an assumption, however, falters on two accounts. First, rather than enhance shared cultural values, new money may bring latent rivalries into conflict and elevate the position of once-marginal groups within a culture. Thus, for example, in Chiapas, Mexico, gender relations have become more contentious as Maya women in some communities capitalize on the international demand for ethnic arts. In Amatenango del Valle, wealthy female potters "are becoming caught up in the contest of envy and competitive personal advancement that was restricted to men" (Nash 1993b: 141). In so doing, they place themselves in mortal danger. Two successful potters have been murdered as a consequence of trying to achieve the public legitimacy and stature long enjoyed by men. Any cultural group, even apparently "traditional, native" ones like the Maya or the Otavaleños, contain a diversity of interests and values. Gendered, generational, occupational, and individual variations in worldviews may be more forcefully expressed in the midst of affluence and have the potential to rupture institutions trying to cope with new points of view.

Second, a rise in earnings rarely results in a systematic transformation toward any single model of living. The hallmark of Latin American modernity, in fact, is the way that it hybridizes the modern and traditional (Starn 1994). As Néstor Garcia-Canclini (1995a: 46) writes:

> Latin American countries are currently the result of the sedimentation juxtaposition and interweaving of indigenous traditions (above all in the Mesoamerican and Andean areas), of Catholic colonial hispanism, and of modern political, educational, and communicational actions. Despite attempts to give elite culture a modern profile, isolating the indigenous and the colonial in the popular sectors, an interclass mixing has generated hybrid formations in all social strata.

In Otavalo, people commit themselves simultaneously and partially to multiple cultures, from Andean to an international consumerist culture. Like the Osage, Otavaleños travel great distances to participate in community rituals and will return from abroad to attend baptisms and weddings. Yet, like the people of Erakor, they sometimes seem to celebrate these events with "a code they do not control." My wife Chesca and I participated in one wedding in which the hosts continually came up to us for instruction on how to write the invitations to favored relatives, release the corks on the ersatz champagne, cut the three-level wedding cake, and cope with other accoutrements of their wedding. The event was simultaneously (and awkwardly) Andean and "Americanized." Such an occasion offers a specific, concrete example of Arjun Appadurai's (1990: 5) broader contention that the "central problem of today's global interactions is the tension between cultural homogenization and cultural heterogenization."

This tension calls for a more dynamic model of affluence-driven change. Rather than focus on a narrow set of outcomes, such as enhancement or dependence, we need to develop a model that emphasizes the complexities of "regularizing" social processes (cf. Moore 1975). That is, we need to consider *how* people establish the conventions and meanings that structure a community's relationships during an era of economic change and rising resources. Such an analysis would link two key concepts, organization and improvisation. By organization, I mean not the fixing of static, formal institutional structures. Rather, I refer more simply to creating consistency in interactions among individuals, a consistency that not only gives rise to certain distributions of material rewards but also to "mutual recognition of intent and significance" (Watanabe 1992: 13). Like John Watanabe, I consider such organization to be a fundamentally moral act, dependent on shared standards of conduct, beyond personal volition, for its success. Willful misuse or disregard of established conventions invites not only sanctions but unintelligibility as the meanings of new or utterly transformed conventions are no longer sensible to others (Watanabe 1992: 14).

Despite these moral and communicative constraints on individuals, people take charge. The cultural ordering that accompanies an expanding economy creates opportunities for exerting power and influence. Such initiative, though, operates less through overt coercion than through construction of new contexts of action. As Eric Wolf (1990: 586; cf. Wolf 1994) puts it, organizational power works "through the settings in which people show forth their potentialities and interact with others." It is a matter of tactics and allocation that concentrates the means of cultural participation in specific enterprises, rituals, and places, thereby accruing social and political benefits to those with access to such means. Indeed, for its connotations of consolidating power, "cultural concentration" may be a more apt term to describe the organizational process linked to rising incomes than "enhancement" (Salisbury 1984) or "intensification" (Fisher 1990). These other terms give a sense of the cultural growth taking place but not of the unequal participation that often accompanies it.

The term "organization," then, covers durable dimensions of change—regularity, morality, and power. In contrast, "improvisation" calls attention to the immediacy of this process (Jackson 1995). Cultural structuring occurs in and through the ongoing actions of people interacting in concrete situations, as Pierre Bourdieu (1977), Anthony Giddens (1979), and other advocates of "practice" theory have exhaustively argued. In explaining the role of social practice in historical transformations, Marshall Sahlins (1981) and Sherry Ortner (1984, 1989) emphasize how cultural schemas guide action in the present as people work to reproduce their culture under new circumstances. In the course of such practice, past symbols are revalued "because the 'objective' world to which they are applied has its own refractory characteristics" that disrupt expected systems of meanings (Sahlins 1981: 70). My approach similarly acknowledges the disruption of meanings and intentions due to "objective" circumstances.

In contrast to other perspectives, however, I argue that such disruptions do not signal either an unraveling culture or the missteps of shortsighted actors but, rather, moments of real agency. At times, Sahlins and Ortner describe a world in which people have shared knowledge of cultural schemas, yet partial understanding of the material, social, and political realities in which they operate. Often, though, historical circumstances are the reverse: people have a partial, situated understanding of cultural meanings and a pretty good grasp of the possibilities of and limitations for their actions. An Otavaleño teenager growing up in Bogotá may or may not share the same sense for the capricious powers of *Tayta Imbabura* that her cousin in Ariasucu has. Yet, each will be versed in the practical implications—tourist fascination, ethnic discrimination, indigenous solidarity, and rivalry—of exhibiting a native Andean identity linked to *Tayta Imbabura*'s homeland. Otavaleño culture comes from the ways these cousins, their families, and others act on these implications and assert their particular meanings as general models for the wider group.

Improvisation, thus, does not mean salvaging traditional cultural schema within new circumstances. It is not about *enacting* a culture, but *acting* it (Roseberry 1994: 10). Certainly, "acting culture" entails drawing on learned schemas, but it also means learning from new experiences, working in the moment, making do with the resources at hand, playing off the people who are present and, ultimately, devising something new. The terms "acting" or "improvising" conjure up the creativity immanent in a social world like that of Otavalo in the 1990s.

In his analysis of Maya society, Watanabe (1992) argues that the conjunction of people, place, and premise—"existential sovereignties" he calls them—guide the creation of culture as both locally rooted and part of the modern world. Otavaleño culture reflects such a "localized engagement with the world," yet its production is more open-ended than what he describes for the Maya. Migration and money undermine the sovereignties of place. The trappings of transnational artisan entrepreneurship casually intermingle with the conventions and artifacts of a subsistence economy. Long-distance phone service, VCRs, and other novelties join *uchurumnis* (chili-pepper grindstones), *anakus* (straight, wrap-around skirts), and looms to the influence of other societies and challenge the cultural primacy of any single locale. As the economy diversifies and Otavaleños disperse to growing expatriate communities, this eclectic material culture has become a primary means through which people work out their relationships with others and the ideals they hold in common.

◢ Consumption as Symbolic Action ◣

The study of material culture in general and consumption in particular has flourished recently within anthropology (Miller 1995a). This current interest in the cultural and social significance of the material world owes much to the work of Mary Douglas and Baron Isherwood (1979) and Pierre Bourdieu (1984) who illustrate the ways consumer goods serve as signs in the production of cultural categories and social dispositions. Following their lead, anthropologists have demonstrated how the traffic in objects becomes a process of signification, substantiating kinship, religion, status, class, and the other traditional categories of anthropological analysis. Thus, tiny, Japanese-made ceramic plates sold in Cairo yield clues about a changing Muslim faith (Starrett 1995). Or the Papua New Guinean television show *Pepsi Fizz* provides evidence of new concepts of personhood and national identity (Errington and Gewertz 1996). The creativity of this scholarship has put to rest older anthropological biases. Drinking Pepsi or buying mass-produced religious souvenirs can no longer be dismissed as the loss of authenticity or the tragic mystification of workers by commodity producers. Rather, these and other acts of consumption have been shown to be "the main arena in which and through which people have to struggle towards control over the definition of themselves and their values" (Miller 1995b: 277).

Consumption studies, however, have promised something more than symbolic explorations of identity. Scholars examine the distribution and consumption of commodities to understand problems of power and poverty. Daniel Miller (1995c: 21) puts the case succinctly: "The acknowledgement of consumption need not detract from the critique of inequality and exploitation, but this critique is foundering precisely because the enormous consequences and attractions of consumption are left out of the analysis." Sidney Mintz's (1985) historical work on sugar and global capitalism, Mary Weismantel's (1988) ethnographic analysis of bread and barley in a peasant economy, and Catherine Costin's and Timothy Earle's (1989) archaeological examination of consumption changes in the wake of Inca conquest all demonstrate the centrality of consumption in the constitution of political and economic privilege.

Despite the promise of these studies, the dominant anthropological approach to consumption remains one of symbolic analysis. Researchers frequently reduce consumption to communication and commodities to signs through which people work out their relationship to the world (see, for example, the contributors to Friedman, ed. 1994). In treating goods as signs, however, writers have divorced objects of their most obvious property, their materiality.[1] The weight, shape, flavor, odor, coarseness or fineness of things that require us to interact with them in specified ways has faded from many anthropological descriptions. We learn all about the brand-name marketing of biscuits as items of "traditional" identity in New Guinea, for example, and the predicament of connecting cultural identities with corporate marketing strategies (Errington and Gewertz 1996). Yet, we get little about what the biscuits taste like or how they are purchased, stored, served, and eaten. The meanings of goods seem to be endowed in opposition to other goods in some sort of generic, textual context, having little to do with the actual existence of biscuits.

Missing are the concrete movement of goods in a shop, kitchen, or other setting of social interaction. In Otavalo, for instance, the meanings of biscuits or crackers emerge from their place on the dusty

---

1. Timothy Burke (1996) makes a similar point in his analysis of commodification and consumption in Zimbabwe. While he singles out Douglas and Isherwood (1979) as the source of the problem, Jean Baudrillard (1981) has been an even more zealous advocate of the textual, ephemeral nature of "commodity signs."

shelves of little stores scattered throughout rural communities, the crinkle of the plastic wrapper when they are unpacked, their dry crunchiness, and their "pocket-ability" all of which distinguish them from boiled, homegrown grains coming out of a family's kitchen or the bulk raw foods bought at the market. Certainly, color posters showing who eats what can bestow important new meanings on both the eaten and the eater; however, advertisements do not erase other cultural meanings due to physical encounters with goods (see Miller's article "Coca-Cola: A Black Sweet Drink from Trinidad" [1998b] for a similar point).

In advocating the inclusion of material properties in the analysis of consumption, I am not arguing that the physical dimension precedes and ultimately determines the cultural one. Material and conceptual realms relate dialectically; cultural categories enable perception of physical forms, while "form itself is employed to become the fabric of cultural worlds" (Miller 1998a: 6). These interconnections do not spring from some universal meaning of objects or their properties but, rather, relate to specific practices of interpretation. More concretely, the physicality of "object-signs" introduces three properties that shape the construction of meaning: economic contingency, sensuality, and ephemerality. I take up each in turn below.

◢ Economy, Sensuality, and Time ◣

Along with the physicality of consumption, economics seem to have dropped out of recent studies. Such an omission threatens to make consumption studies an inchoate pursuit that adds little to textual approaches to society and culture (Carrier and Heyman 1997). Indeed, the implicit and sometimes forgotten premise of analyzing such disparate activities as buying a Coke, watching a music video, eating roast guinea pig, and furnishing a house within a common analytical frame called "consumption" is that they all fit into cycles of production and exchange.[2] While we need not elevate these other economic contexts as the "real" source of meaning, we can not ignore them either. The effort required to make, buy, or replace goods both substantiates economic value and affects people's interpretation of the meanings of things.

An important contribution of Arjun Appadurai's (1986) oft-cited analysis of commodity exchange lies precisely in the connections he

---

2. Colin Campbell (1994) has even questioned the utility of the gathering of such diverse activities and objects and grouping them together within a single amorphous, symbolic category such as "consumption practices."

makes among consumption, value, and the contexts of exchange. The meaning of things and the constitution of society happens in a continual motion of goods entering commodity contexts, becoming acquired and consumed by individuals, and later leading to other commodity exchanges, either of the same good or the same type of object. Within this model, exchange provides the forum in which politics, economics, and the sociality of things come together: "[i]t is exchange that sets the parameters of utility and scarcity, rather than the other way around, and exchange that is the source of value" (Appadurai 1986: 4).

An exchange perspective, however, has its own limitations. The emphasis on commodity transactions should not obscure the social and economic importance of display, possession, and consumption. During my initial research in Otavalo, I examined the links between economic and architectural change (Colloredo-Mansfeld 1994). As I interviewed people about the cultural and social meanings of house forms—from the most traditional straw-roof home to the newest cement-block concoction—respondents inevitably discussed costs. People appraised homes for the amount of cash spent or the size of the voluntary work party employed before they would tell me anything about cultural meanings. Houses, like all consumption projects, put a public face on economic accomplishments, as Thorstein Veblen (1994 [1899]) noted long ago. One need not accept his arguments about emulation and conspicuous consumption to acknowledge how resources shape the significance people attribute to object forms.

In a mixed economy like that of Otavalo, people study homes, meals, and fiestas for information about both the quantity and type of resources—subsistence or cash—that possessors control. Far from always offering a clear picture of someone's economic stature, conspicuous displays often raise questions about his or her priorities, in particular, and about shared definitions of appropriate economic activity, in general. Costly houses and big parties get neighbors talking. They spawn imitators, or prompt others to make a show of alternative tastes. Examined over time and across a community, these consumption activities form what Richard Wilk (1994) has described as a "dialogue about development," which, in Otavalo's case, frequently relates to the future of the subsistence economy.

By insisting that economics be taken into account when studying the meaning of consumption, I mean that we need to follow such dialogues. The relationship between the economy and meaning is thus not direct and quantitative (big things do not necessarily mean more) but rather pragmatic. Economic experience provides a context for interpretation and a means of participating in a public discourse about work, accumulation, and the propriety of material wants.

Consumption activities, of course, not only engage us as cultural subjects and economic actors but as sensual beings as well. Consuming, as Jonathan Friedman (1991) reminds us, is a total human phenomenon. Indeed, tastes, sounds, textures, and smells bear importantly on how we "make sense" of the actions of others and the situations we find ourselves in. In his analysis of ritual action, Victor Turner (1967) emphasizes the interdependence of ideals and emotions by pointing out that the sensory *significata* of dominant symbols unite the social norms with strong feelings and desires. Current scholarship on the senses builds on these themes. Paul Stoller's (1989; 1997) ethnographies of the Songhay highlight the ways that cognition depends on emotion, movement, and a sensing body. Taken further, the turn to the senses in anthropology represents a rebellion against excessive concern with abstract conceptual categories (Ebron 1998). Shifting to sensory-based descriptions of social action allows writers to engage people's practical knowledge of themselves and their culture without positing the formal organization of a symbolic system.

My own concern with the senses, however, does not signify a turning from the systematic nature of ideals. Rather, I am interested in the way commodities and consumption rituals organize the meaning of Otavaleño social ideals through the recreation of "referential experiences" within new social and economic enterprises. Bourdieu's (1977) insights into socialization and household space offer a model here. He argues that the rhythm of daily routines in the cooking, sleeping, and work areas of a home instill in children a sense for the basic principles of their culture—sexual division of labor, domestic morality, cares, strife, taste, etc. Growing up in a Kabyle home, an individual masters his or her culture with and through the body, not through critical reasoning (Bourdieu 1977: 90). Ideals learned in this way endure because they are ingrained—in the experiences, social habits, postures, and intuition of individuals. Lying beyond conscious awareness, such habitualized cultural principles evade overt analysis. People sense what is right or wrong in the flow of action without always being able to discuss it openly.

Consumption can offer analogous circumstances for "experiential" socialization. As with movement through the culturally organized spaces of a traditional home, consumption practices—the midmorning *café* breaks in weaving workshops, the exchange of beer among trading partners during the "baptism" of a new car—marry cultural principles to physical tasks. To be sure, drinking orange Fanta together at a party that welcomes traders back from Europe may not have the same cultural pedigree as sweeping the ashes out of the *tulpa* (an open cooking hearth). Nonetheless, such new consumption rituals expand the scope of established ideals according to the same practical logic analyzed by Bourdieu. Rather than overtly asserting that, for example, proprietors and workers in artisan operations are bound by reciprocal ideals of mutual assistance, their shared material life implicitly encompasses them within those ideals. Consumption socializes wage-earners, loom-owners, and exporters into the morality of subsistence relations, even while production splits them into new economic classes. Through this logic of the senses, Otavaleños can try to legitimize their capitalist innovations within noncapitalist social conventions.

Physical experiences raise yet another element that divides consuming from other semiotic acts. Unlike words, commodity symbols have a "shelf-life"—the use of objects in communication is inseparable from their deterioration. When we consume, we break in, wear out, draw down, use up, or throw away something. Consumption both constructs and destroys, raising questions not only about what we create when we consume but about what goes away in the moment of use. Anthropologists have largely ignored the mutable, ephemeral side of consumption.[3] Arguing for the eternal nature of an object, Alfred Gell writes,

> But consumption as a general phenomenon really has nothing to do with the destruction of goods and wealth, but the reincorporation into the social system that produced them in some other guise. All goods, from the standpoint of sociological analysis are as indestructible as kula valuables—the valuables that circulate in the kula exchange system described by Malinowski for the Trobriands. (1986: 122)

This denial of destruction corrects older scholarly biases that denigrate consumption as a simple terminal point in a cycle of production and exchange.

3. Arjun Appadurai (1996: 83–84) discusses the significance of ephemerality and consumption, although he directs his analysis toward the impact of "the short shelf life of products and lifestyles; the speed of fashion change; the velocity of expenditure" and other features of consumption in postindustrial societies that have transformed the experience of time. While related, the ephemerality discussed in this book is less a product of the logic of capitalist (over)production and mass-marketing and more a function of the mutability of physical objects themselves.

Yet by denying the destruction that takes place during consumption, anthropologists miss the historicity inherent in using up value. Consumption may be about "conversion"—the manner in which people convert things to their own ends (Strathern 1994: x; cf. Lury 1996)—but this conversion differs from the conversion that takes place during production. It removes, rather than adds to, an object's value. Such removal takes place even when that value is almost intangible, like the purity of a brand-new thing used for the very first time. While this loss has obvious economic consequences, spurring production to replace used goods, it has equally important social ones. Such diminution in value aggravates other causes of social indeterminacy—the loss of continuity in meaning from one occasion to the next (cf. Moore 1975). Instead of reinforcing social routines and position, an ailing material culture may wind up betraying them. "Durable" symbols (architecture, religious relics, heirlooms, etc.) lose the luster they held on prior occasions and gain new, and not always desired, associations of recent use.[4] "Consumable" symbols (meals, drink, fashionable clothes, etc.) disappear entirely in use and can never be re-presented in precisely the same way again. The sociological analyst may treat all goods as indestructible but social/economic actors rarely can. The mutable property of goods forces symbolic as well as material investments to preserve cultural coherence.

Grooming, preparing, serving, and storing rituals all restore a measure of integrity. When an object's properties are perishable, owners lavish largely redundant time and energy grooming or "supercharging" the object, so "that it might, in turn, give special heightened properties to its owner" (McCracken 1988: 86). Many a man in Otavalo, for example, devotes special care to his heavy, double-faced poncho on the eve of a fiesta where he must perform special duties. Removing it from storage, he may drape it over a clothesline and minutely inspect the navy-blue nap for chafe or dust, pinching and stroking out impurities to restore the fabric's sheen. Meals achieve their own consistency, if not through the exact repetition of ingredients, then through the ritualized flow of preparation, service, and cleaning up. Requiring constant maintenance and cyclical routines, the physical world sets in motion regularizing processes, "the kind by which people try to control their situations by struggling against

4. In some cultures, the chips, scratches, and discoloring that an object picks up over the years actually adds social value. This patina testifies to the longevity of possessions and solidifies claims to ancient lineage (McCracken 1988). Rather than refute the importance of "using up" as a social process, though, objects with patina underscore how some wear and tear must take place—although at a glacial pace—in order to mark a family's social claims in and through time.

indeterminacy, by trying to fix social reality, to harden it, to give it form and order and predictability" (Moore 1975: 50).

Yet ultimately, loss occurs. Whether it happens in an afternoon, a lifetime, or over generations, objects yield their physical properties and potentially their associated symbolic power.[5] This depletion matters no less than the social action employed to stave it off. An object's physical decline sets the contours of its possessors' biography. Studying such a biography "can make salient what otherwise might remain obscure" in the history of a people (Kopytoff 1986: 66). By comparing an object's ideal "career"—what a good would be used for, by whom, for how long, to what effect—with actual uses, we learn about its owner and his or her triumphs, failures, and compromises. Pursuing such an analysis, the anthropologists have usually concentrated on a culture's most valuable objects or stylized goods. Sacred heirlooms and other manner of inalienable possessions monopolize accounts of life histories and group identities (Weiner 1992). However, for charting the breadth of cultural change and the minutiae of its workings, simpler, everyday objects may often offer clearer guidance.

◢ The Social Life of a *Faja* ◣

In Otavalo, women's belts or *fajas* serve as just such a tell-tale object, revealing individual and collective responses to the economic and social currents of the new handicraft economy. Approximately seven centimeters wide and 250 centimeters long, *fajas* are worn by indigenous women throughout the central Andean valley. Prior to the 1980s, *faja*-making was one of the last subsistence crafts as men wove them for their mothers, wives, and daughters on a backstrap loom. Nowadays, weavers churn them out for the market using upright, treadle looms. Patterned with hearts, suns, diamonds, these sashes appear in subtle shades of blue and teal, garish mixes of orange and silver, or trendy monochromes of black, white, or blue. Relatively inexpensive (they cost around U.S. $4), *fajas* provide an unmistakable sign of native identity. Most indigenous women would don them daily; white-mestizo women, in contrast, never would. More than differentiating indigenous from white mestizo, though, these belts also make real the economic divisions within Otavalo society.

Frequently, indigenous women purchase a *faja* for a special occa-

5. As Igor Kopytoff (1986) and Appadurai (1986) point out, the loss of value in one context often leads to the gain of value in another. Moving through new social contexts, goods undergo many such value transformations. While this examination of recontextualization illuminates how value gets created, it should not obscure the social impact of when value is used up.

sion, such as a wedding or confirmation. Among the general prosperity of the region, most women attend these social events wearing spotless outfits in fine condition. Thus, to achieve special status, wealthy women need something more. The ephemeral, crisp quality of unworn garments delivers it. A young woman I know became so preoccupied with showing off the success of her European trip that she felt compelled to wear new clothes not only to fiestas but to regular community work days as well. Other travelers similarly invested in sequences of *fajas, alpargatas* (cloth sandals), and blouses for each new event. Thus, before succumbing to daily wear, a *faja's* fleeting pristine qualities are consumed at parties and community meetings to signal achievement. Wealthy women have taken what was once a sign of a male relative's skill and affection and heightened its use as a status symbol.

In another twist, some younger, urban Otavaleñas use traditional sashes to adopt a more westernized body image. Older women wrap the *fajas* around their hips, a preference that, when combined with shawls and the large white blouses, flattens and broadens the appearance of women's bodies. Eschewing the squarish silhouette of this look, teenagers in the market town now wrap their *fajas* at the waist, especially when dressing up in their finest for public gatherings. They show off a "whiter" feminine figure accentuating hip and bust. Sticking with traditional clothes, these young women nonetheless produce a citified look that divides them from their "country cousins," especially when all have gathered for parties and fiestas.

After serving its time as special-event item, a *faja* rotates regularly through the daily wardrobe. Wrapping the multicolored sash around herself, cinching in the thick fabric of her *anaku* (skirt), an Otavaleña unifies both her morning routine and her own look with those of other indigenous women in her neighborhood and across the province. Woven with a supplemental warp pattern and acrylic or polyester threads, the belts stand up well to the rigors of rural life. When they do darken with dust and grit, they are taken to a washstand or the river and scrubbed with the rest of the clothes. The belts long remain an attractive ornament and contribute to the tidy, formal appearance that Otavaleñas present to each other and outsiders. Such grooming is more than a matter of personal style. The strength of their culture and the recognition they enjoy from others inheres in the sharp details of Otavaleño lives: the clean-swept patios, the creases in men's pants, and the brightness of a woman's *faja*, to name a few.

As it nears the end of its career, a *faja* takes on more eclectic roles. Stained from daily wear and frayed from washings, a *faja* loses its place in the wardrobe. Instead, it may bandage up a lose joint on a loom, suspend weaving implements in the rafters, or pad the handle of a grain mill. Like most possessions, a *faja* will not be thrown out, but rather it will be repaired and recycled through other tasks. This practice of using goods that have already been in some senses "used up" is an unavoidable aspect of Ecuador's peasant economies. Around Otavalo, they call these worn objects *"yanga cosas,"* meaning "humble," "useless," or "worthless" things. The quality of humility is not confined to the object itself. As the last bit of value is squeezed out of a faded *faja*, it has a way of humbling the tasks and people who pressed it into service. In fact, Otavaleños use the same adjective to describe both old tools and a hard life, *yanga*, as in *yanga cosas* and the *yanga kawsay* (humble life).

The *faja's* different guises—unworn fiesta outfit, item of clothes, utilitarian strap—help produce Otavaleños as a group and as classes within the group, from city trader to dirt-poor farmer. Inexpensive and ubiquitous, *fajas* say something about any woman's income while offering cultural signals at the personal and collective levels. Indeed, taken most broadly, the growing numbers of *"faja* wearers" permanently residing in the city culturally help to transform urban space itself. These symbolic and economic dimensions intersect in practical action: fingering through a rack of crisp new *fajas*, or absorbing the pressure of a *faja's* turns across the stomach, or smoothing the frizzy end of a worn *faja* out of view in the folds of an anaku. As they did for their grandmothers, *fajas* help women reproduce characteristic experiences of their culture and themselves, even if women are sporting them for work in Amsterdam and not on the slopes of Imbabura.

I have dwelt at length on *fajas* because they are locally produced and worn commodities and they appear in all contexts of indigenous life. Their ubiquity makes them something of an oddity, however. With the exception, perhaps, of hats, a similar item of men's wear could not be chosen. Most male Otavaleños have consigned their ponchos, white shirts, and white pants of traditional outfits to formal occasions and wear the jeans and shirts of Western fashion on a daily basis. Turning from clothes to other possessions reveals an increasingly diversified material world. I inventoried thirty-two homes and could not find one type of item that was common to all of them (the closest was the open hearth, which was in thirty-one of the thirty-two; two gas stoves were found in the exceptional home). As stated earlier, modernization has eroded the commonalties of Otavalo's physical universe.

The diversity of Otavalo material culture speaks to Otavalo's widening social gaps and returns us to the questions set forth at the end of the last chapter. What (and whose) visions of the "good life"—in both the moral and material sense of the term—guide Otavaleño cultural production? Second, by what means do Otavaleños reconcile conflicting cultural ideals and visions of themselves to materialize a distinctive transnational, Andean identity? In the chapters that follow, I spell out the entrepreneurial and subsistence ethics, racial biases, and migrant's imaginings that inform these visions. Throughout this chapter, I have raised points related to the second question. More particularly, I have laid out the power of consumption as social practice through which people improvise their culture.

While building on the burgeoning consumption scholarship, three things distinguish my approach. First, studying consumption requires economic analysis. People scrutinize goods for information about their peer's resources and construct objects' social meanings in reference to their own workaday experiences. Social analysts must follow suit or miss a pivotal context that shapes interpretive practice. Second, by enculturating individuals through sensation, ritualized consumption links symbols with feelings. It extends corporeal socialization beyond the settings and routines of childhood, as emphasized by Bourdieu and others, to the physical life of adulthood. Through rituals of eating, drinking, or breaking in new objects, individuals naturalize cultural innovations experientially, enveloping new enterprises in a sense of moral appropriateness, parallel to any effort to offer an explicit ideological discourse.

Third, even as one acknowledges the productive aspect of consumption, one must also confront the destruction of value that occurs. Controlling value-loss introduces grooming rituals, preparing rituals, and other regularizing practices that contribute to the broader effort to maintain continuity from one event to the next and throughout one's social world. As students of material culture, we must not let a preoccupation with the creation of new meanings for old goods distract us from social and cultural dilemmas posed by the deterioration of original value.

Having set out the case for using consumption and material culture as a way to understand cultural change during economic expansion, I want to introduce a pair of limitations to this perspective. In Otavalo, cultural improvisation proceeds on many fronts, in Quichua language practice, music, and beauty pageants to name a few (Mark Rogers 1998). Although they connect with material culture studies through matters of the senses, settings, and instrumentalities of discourse, these other expressive realms nonetheless entail their own structuring principles. They are not reducible to the analysis offered here, just as the study of material culture is not reducible to textual or linguistic analysis. Each offers a way to understand the cultural, racial, economic, gender, and moral processes at work in Otavalo. Of all expressive realms, in fact, the material world is perhaps the most constrained when it comes to representing new ideals and identities. Far from being a weakness, though, this relative inflexibility contributes to the object world's strength for mediating, masking, or foreshadowing change (cf. McCracken 1988). Material culture studies thus complement rather than replace other symbolic analysis.

Second, an emphasis on cultural improvisation highlights possibilities of local agency. Yet, I want to avoid overstating the case. Current anthropological writings have dwelt so much on agency that the power of individual action is in danger of being oversold. Although Ortner (1989: 12) and other proponents of practice theory have cautioned that "asymmetry, inequality, domination, and the like" are primary elements of person-centered analysis, ethnographic writing tends to endow agents with undue power.[6] Indeed, the very practices singled out as signs of agency often reveal the weakness of a group's capacity to act rather than its strengths (Fiske 1993; Spyer 1997).

In Ecuador, for example, the textile trade that has made Otavaleños famous signals the predicament of indigenous social power. Many weavers and traders from Ariasucu have tried pursuing different careers only to be forced home by unfavorable job markets or downturns in the nation's economy. When I asked one of Ariasucu's relatively successful migrant-turned-weavers what he would do if he won the lottery, he replied without hesitation, "I would live like a white-mestizo." He wanted to live the "clean" life of apartment-dwelling, modern appliances, and occasional meals out at restaurants that he started to pursue in Quito in the late 1970s. That he cannot testifies, in part, to a life hemmed in by persistent discrimination and deprived of regular wages.

The lack of material resources is only part of the problem. Whatever their practical motives, indigenous work and social habits may resist some elements of cultural domination while consistently reproducing many others. In her work on Zumbagua Ecuador, Weismantel

---

6. Noting the widespread emphasis on agency, Wolf (1994: 6) has complained: "[M]uch of the discourse about agency and construal strikes me as unduly voluntaristic, like the "little-engine-that-could" of American children's literature—the little locomotive that can accomplish feats of strength through the application of will and power." See Michael Brown's work (1996) for a related point about the notion of "resistance."

(1988; 1989a) shows that cooking and serving food can affirm specifically indigenous cultural beliefs—the importance of a daughter-in-law's obedience in the kitchen, for example, or the intrinsic value of homegrown products within a meal. However, the practices of the native hearth do not uniformly resist the values of white-society and the capitalist economy. When "the children cry for bread" and husband and wife squabble over whether they can afford to indulge their kids with purchased food, the conflict between rural/subsistence and urban/market values simmer within the home. By trying to accommodate conflicting demands, women's work in the kitchen and men's purchases in the market can become "objectively adapted" (cf. Bourdieu 1977: 72) to goals of capitalist production even as people contest those goals. Subjective opinions about the value of the land and the strength of family traditions alone cannot preserve subsistence values against myriad small, daily decisions to the contrary.

Even as they act within such material and ideological constraints, though, indigenous Ecuadorians do "make their history." With vitality springing from their kitchens, weaving porches, fax machines, oxen teams, Andean rock music, and merchant profits, Otavalo contains much that I want to celebrate. And much that I worry about, too, from the persistence of hunger in rural sectors to the rise of profound class differences within families and communities. Neither dependent on Ecuador's dominant culture, nor bound to enhance the agrarian world many grew up in, Otavaleños are creating an expansive and distinctly Andean culture rife with new contradictions—and excitement.

◢ Sketching as an Ethnographic Encounter ◣

I conducted the research for this book during four separate trips spread over five years. My methods ranged from structured, formal data-gathering to spontaneous participant observation. From the first days of fieldwork in 1991, I gathered information on community history and artisan work through discussions with a small group of key informants, several of whom became my compadres. During my first two trips, I relied on a collections of photos, sketches, and maps that I added to regularly, using the visual cues as prompts for questions about economic change and the social meanings of the architecture and material culture of the region. Core economic data emerged from the time-allocation study discussed in the prologue, a communitywide household survey, and career interviews with artisans, all of which took place in 1994. The sample of thirty-two households assembled for the time-allocation research became the core sample of four sets of other interviews regarding consumption priorities, personal possessions, migration histories, and opinions about the prestige of the handicraft trade.

Interviews, surveys, and spot-observations produced valuable information. They also threatened to lock my fieldwork encounters into the formal constraints and asymmetrical power relations of observer and observed. Turning the tables some, sketching releases my relationships from undue formality and my field data from an entirely anonymous objectivity. Like the other methods of image-making I employ—taking photographs and videotaping—drawing has two key elements. It is both an act of representation and of social intercourse. In each aspect, drawing offers unique opportunities. Unlike images dependent on chemical or electronic technology, pen and ink graphics invites a more complex relationship among observed, observer, and those observing the observer. This complexity opens up drawing as a medium for discussion and critique during fieldwork, while, for better or worse, undermines the scientific authority of the images brought home. I expand briefly upon these ideas below.

As presentation of data, drawing often suffers the stigma of trivialness and unnecessary subjectivity. In the academic enterprise of anthropology, the text is king; serious scholarship appears as a written essay (Bakewell 1998). Even those who have sought to displace the authority of objective, ethnographic writings have preserved the primacy of the scholarly text. The critique of the poetics and politics of ethnography urges a more self-referential, evocative, and critical ethnographic literary product—experiments in rhetorical form, not in the possibility of images (Clifford and Marcus 1986).

This is odd because image-making has been so important within anthropology. Along with scientists and writers in other disciplines, anthropologists select images in order to make subtle and perhaps idiosyncratic observations seem obvious and natural (Lynch and Woolgar 1990). Image "genres" differ in the authority they evoke. The simplest figures, such as graphs and histograms, connote the objectivity of scientific measurement and quantification. On the other hand, detailed images, such as drawings and photographs, make the subject of the image seem to have "an immediate contact with reality" (Myers 1990: 235). Such contact matters especially for ethnographers whose photographs index a lived field experience and imbue a written account with the legitimacy of having "been there" (Geertz 1988). Without images, texts seem to close in on themselves, breaking relations with other discourses, places and peoples.

In comparison to other images, drawings have their own strengths, both in terms of traditional concerns with ethnographic accuracy and current preoccupations with subjectivity. To draw an object or a scene, the artist must segregate the world in front of him or her, pull reality apart into visual details, and decide what is to be included or omitted from the composition (Wallis 1984). Short of attempting photographic realism (and even then), the illustrator must include only a limited amount of what he or she perceives. Such economy has its advantages. It produces clarity, often rescuing objects from the murky hues of black-and-white photographs. As Geertz (1988: 67) observed in his essay on Evans-Pritchard's writings, "[he] is one of the few modern ethnographers (quite possibly the only one) who seems to have grasped the fact that the photograph has not only not rendered the sketch obsolete, but as the film has for the photograph, has pointed up its comparative advantage."

Such selection of detail also highlights the subjectivity of drawing. The compositions I offer here may call attention to my perceptions, my hand, my attention to detail, and my feel for the visually important—in short, my presence—in a way that photos do not. Generally speaking, visual representation operates iconically; images hold some nonarbitrary connection to their referents (Maquet 1986). Although bound to capture something of the given proportions and textures of a scene, I am otherwise free to shape an image in idiosyncratic ways. "Icons," as Liza Bakewell (1998: 29) writes, "may deviate significantly from conventions without losing their communicative value (Bouissac et al. 1986)." In separate drawings of a spinning wheel (drawings 2 and 3), for example, I preserve the basic form of the implement. From there, though, the compositions diverge. In the first, I want to capture the clutter of the shop, the haphazard placement of the wheel (on top of some cloth), the lack of formal spatial organization dividing manufacturing activities from each other, or from domestic life. In the second drawing, I separate the wheel from any physical context, simplify it and smear the ink to suggest its active potential as a human-powered machine. In both sketches, I am guided by my sense of the object and its "social life." Departures from more conventionalized images of a spinning wheel reflect my own feel for the thing developed through afternoons of hanging out in shops with weavers.

Although perhaps not as apparent, the drawings throughout this book similarly follow my intuitions about subjects as well as my objective observations. In chapter 6, for example, I changed pens when I moved from the wealthier part of Ariasucu to the poorer one. The precise line of the crow quill that helped capture the power lines and clean house forms of the lower sector seemed less appropriate for rendering the crumbling agrarian realities of the upper region (see drawings 24 and 26 in chapter 6). I shifted to a worn calligraphic pen

Drawing 2: Spinning Wheel in Weaving Shed

Drawing 3: Spinning Wheel

that blotched my efforts to carefully crosshatch the tiles or dapple the adobe.

Despite the freedoms afforded by pen and ink, I generally kept my illustrations simple and accessible, avoiding too many sojourns into the angular, silhouetted, or smudged imaginary. That I did not stray farther from conventional images of the objects portrayed in this book reflects my desire for some visual accuracy—some faithfulness to the tactile details these goods presented to others and to me. The conservatism also grew from the social circumstances of drawing in Otavalo and my relations with informants who watched me work and reviewed my sketches.

Drawings have always offered Otavaleños and others a way into my research (Colloredo-Mansfeld 1993). In the first weeks of my initial fieldwork, I used to leave my hosts' home, take up a position on the edge of some public thoroughfare and try to get down a part of the scene in front of me. The task immobilized me. As I hunched over, developing an image in an exposure prolonged by my timid hand and the fussy medium, others came up to observe and interview me. Questions came first about what I was drawing, then why I was here, where I was staying, etc. While I spent the day getting information from weaving entrepreneurs, traders, and village council members, I spent the late afternoon sitting passively and drawing, allowing others to get basic information on me.

The process of sketching brought about this role reversal, with the sketches themselves often prompting the questions about and reactions to my research interests. I would turn my sketchbook over to someone so she or he could flip through at her or his own pace and ask me about the maps, drawings, or photographs I had included. People sometimes praised my skill or scolded me for omissions—missing objects that they thought belonged in a collection of goods or mountains left out of landscape compositions or the general lack of people. Prompted by what they had seen, some led me back to their houses to show me their own grindstone or loom or map. In some cases, they even insisted that I draw a favorite of their own possessions.

Through all these reactions, I learned how my own perceptions fit in with those of community residents. On two separate occasions, for example, two different children flipped through pages of the sketchbook, reciting the names of the objects as they went, "grain mill, blender, sewing machine . . ." Both children unhesitatingly called out "loom" when they came to an abstract composition of black lines (drawing 4). These two kids seemed to recognize, and perhaps share, my own view of multiloom weaving porches as a tangle

Drawing 4: Looms as Rectangles

of rectangles, an expansive wood and wire mechanism cutting up and encompassing domestic space. For their parents, though, neither this drawing nor my other less conventional sketch of a loom's silhouette (drawing 5) elicited much comment. Rather, a more straightforward picture of a *faja* loom (drawing 6) prompted observations about *faja*-making and "the indigenous man's tool."

Drawing 5: Loom Silhouette

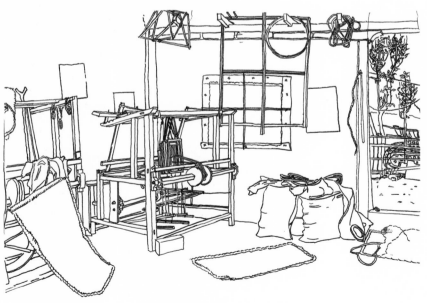

Antonio's Loom   Ariasucu, Imbabura '91

Drawing 6: Loom Set-up for *Fajas*

To open up discussions, therefore, drawings seem to need enough conventional elements to facilitate recognition. Yet, they also needed a "hook" of some sort. For instance, my misdirected attention to detail on "useless" objects (see chapter 3) or stripping away of a good's normal physical context engaged people's interest and invited commentary. Thus, rather than being an incidental distraction in the field (although often I valued it for just that reason), the social practice of drawing helped to constitute my role as an observer. Pen and ink mediated my perceptions and intuitions about Otavaleño routines and material world, while at the same time locally legitimized my effort to record it. More generally, the inclusion of drawings with writing, photographs, maps, and charts opens up possibilities for more personal and situated ethnographic representations that go beyond textual experiments. Although this work does little more than raise the question of opportunity, I hope that, as anthropology develops in a "postcolonial" world, the image experiments of ethnographers could blur the boundaries dividing artist and ethnographer and, perhaps more important, anthropological subjects and academic audiences.[7]

7. Transformations in the division of labor between artist and ethnographer have already begun (Krasniewicz 1993; Foster 1995). Yet such work seems to exist at the margins of the art world and beyond the pale of anthropological practice.

Outsiders' Wealth:
Race and Advancement, 1930–94

◢ The Water *Minga* ◣

Imbabura thirsts for water. Across the mountain's southern slopes, thousands of people depend on the flow of a few springs captured in a patched-together system of reservoirs and pipes. Cracked plastic tubes repaired with inner tubes deliver this water in thin dribbles to community standpipes. It is not sufficient. Women must continually put off more productive commercial and domestic work to babysit twenty-liter containers at trickling water taps.

In 1985, engineers from the national public health ministry drew up ambitious plans for a new potable water system. Work began on 13 July 1987 with a massive *minga,* or communal work party. Over five thousand men and women came together with shovels and picks and buried 7.7 kilometers of pipe in just two days.[1] Hopes ran high as people looked forward to receiving clean water piped into their homes for cooking, bathing, washing clothes, and preparing handicrafts. Within a year, however, funding dried up, leaving communities to expand the networks of trenches on their own in anticipation of the day that the money would be found for the pipes and pumps.

In the summer of 1991, work took on new urgency as cholera had spread from the coast into the highlands and the need for clean drinking water became painfully apparent to provincial officials. They arranged funds and revived the *mingas,* calling out a rotation of work crews from eight different communities. Thus, in late July of 1991, I found myself in the midst of a contentious water *minga.*

About one hundred men and women from Ariasucu hiked an hour from their homes to join others at the site of the water project's future pump station on the shore of Lake San Pablo. It was a rare co-operative action for local residents. Typically, people from richer households bought their way out of manual labor, choosing to pay fines rather than swing a shovel. On this day, though, the common

---

1. As reported in *Diario del Norte,* 16 July 1987, p. 8.

need for water united all residents. Thus to coordinate the *minga*, the current president of the council left his teenage daughter to run his sweater business up on the Colombian border while he stayed in Ariasucu. And the ex-president, Jaime Cuyo, took time away from his preparations for an upcoming trip to Europe to lay pipes with his neighbors. Before embarking for Amsterdam, he wanted to have water flowing into his home in Ariasucu.

The work had stalled, however, when women from the community immediately surrounding the springs protested that they would lose their only source of clean water. The *mingueros* (communal workers) stopped shoveling while the council and engineers entered into discussions with local residents. As the negotiations dragged on, people broke for lunch. Pots of hot, toasted maize and boiled beans poured out onto sheets spread across the grass. The workers sprawled next to their meals. Popping the salty kernels and beans into their mouths, they chatted about the water-flow rates and the cost of pipes. When Jaime saw that the engineer had nothing to eat, he invited him over to sit with his group. The engineer declined. Jaime insisted, pointing out that they had plenty. Saying something about the dirty ground and the dangers of cholera, the engineer curtly refused. Jaime, his sister, and his brother-in-law exchanged knowing glances and brief smiles and carried on eating. With the exception of one sympathetic official, urban professionals involved in the project shunned contact with native workers. Choosing to go hungry rather than to share a meal was just one small sign of their disdain.[2]

White-mestizos have long stereotyped native peoples as filthy, lazy, irrational, and backward (Stark 1981). Even as native entrepreneurs like Jaime Cuyo explicitly espouse an ideology of progress through rationality and pursue "clean lives," they find little unqualified acceptance. Despite their cash, commodities, and growing capital, Otavalo's merchant class continues to operate in a social landscape closed in by racist imagery. Like all racial ideologies, those of the Andean urban elite have dwelt on "allegedly biologically ascribed attributes that include morality, sexual behavior, and education" (de la

2. Later that afternoon, the *mingueros* resolved the dispute over the springs in one bold move. Ignoring the engineer's effort to carry on with the original plan, they invaded the neighboring fields of an absentee landowner. Spontaneously clearing the land around two springs tucked into some overgrown bushes, they insisted that the pumps be installed there. When I returned to the site three years later, I found that they had, indeed, set up the pump stations there. Community laborers, with whom the engineer could not bring himself to share a meal, had prevailed.

Cadena 1996: 144).[3] However, as social practice, "race" goes beyond abstract notions of genetic inheritance and the purity of bloodlines and becomes grounded in "natural" forms of bodies, homes, and food. Part cognitive system, part physical reaction, mestizo racism takes shape through the hostile aversion of the peasant sensory world—a mound of cooked beans on the ground, smoky, earth-walled houses, dirt-crusted tools, woolen clothes, and river-washed bodies. Social identities divide at boundaries marked in these tangible traces of class and livelihood, leaving weathered and poncho-clad peasants categorically split from showered and shampooed engineers.[4]

The materiality of racial practice helps account for social encounters like the one that occurred between Jaime and the engineer. Unreasoned, the interaction followed a script embedded in the sights and smells of peasant bodies and "humble" food. Yet, to understand racism as a structural force organizing the indigenous economy, we must go beyond daily interactions and physical signs. As the historian Barbara Fields (1982: 151) has argued, emblems which symbolize race—whether born of biology or occupation—"are not the foundation upon which race arises as a category of social thought." Rather, the foundation lies in the set of ideologies underpinning the dominant position of the urban middle-classes. The textures of rural life only become racial emblems as the white-mestizo elite establishes their claims on state power and economic privilege. Pursuing a slippery physical and moral ideal of cleanliness, the bourgeoisie constitute themselves masters of the nation's economic development while delegitimizing the rival claims of native peoples.

This preoccupation with hygiene and disease is not peculiar to urban Ecuadorians. As Foucault points out (1990: 125), the emphasis on the body—"on body hygiene, the art of longevity, ways of having healthy children and of keeping them alive for as long as possible, and methods for improving the human lineage"—all were linked to

3. In her analysis of the social position of mestizas in Cuzqueño society, Marisol de la Cadena (1996) argues for maintaining the analytical distinction of race and ethnicity. She notes that for Cuzqueños, the contrasting conceptions of race and ethnicity coincide with social position. Dominant groups have subscribed to racial schemes, while subordinate groups assert ethnic ones. Her analysis has important parallels to my explorations of Otavalo society. For another example of analysis that distinguishes between racial and cultural perceptions of difference see Kyeyoung Park (1996) on the relations between Koreans and blacks in Los Angeles.

4. See André Béteille (1990) for a discussion of the interpenetration of the physical world and racial categories and David Theo Goldberg (1992: 547–48) for an analysis of the various ways that the contemporary uses of "race" assume significance in terms of class.

the establishment of bourgeois hegemony in Europe and elsewhere. For the emerging middle classes, the destiny of the national body politic depended on the discipline and institutions that keep the nation's bodies healthy. Such concern with the body related to a new type of "racism." It was not the conservative racism that proscribed the dilution of aristocratic bloodlines in order to preserve class privileges. Instead, it was "a dynamic racism, a racism of expansion" (Foucault 1990: 125). As a practice, this racism depended on a broadening struggle against new signs of contamination and impurity in order to create a homogeneous, modern nation state.

Ann Stoler (1995) develops Foucault's ideas, describing how race, sexuality, and bodily discipline served as ordering mechanisms for the bourgeois order in European colonies. Especially in the tropics, colonizers elevated hygiene into a gendered and racial "micro site" of political control. It provided a context for appraising racial membership and designating "character," "good breeding," and proper rearing (Stoler 1995: 11). Similarly, in southern Africa, after the 1890s, white settlers characterized Africans as filthy and depraved and used those images to justify segregation. As Timothy Burke (1996: 21) writes, "such sentiments stand out as a distinctive aspects of colonial racism not merely because of their omnipresence, but because of their physicality, the manner in which they influenced whites to react with revulsion and avoidance in the presence of Africans." In Latin America, scientists and health officials co-opted the European science of eugenics and bound it to hygiene. The public health ministries of Brazil and Argentina linked genetic purity to sanitation, social and mental hygiene. State-sponsored "public hygiene was therefore viewed as a way of rescuing the country from racial and climatic degeneracy" (Stepan 1991: 89).

Thus, for white-mestizo Ecuador, ponchos stained with soil or a kitchen blackened by smoke and reeking of guinea pigs demonstrated not just the hard realities of peasant life but a moral and national failing. To turn indígenas into healthy citizens and integrate them into the economy, the government undertook comprehensive rural development programs, ranging from Mision Andina in the 1950s to the potable water projects of the 1990s. While these policies have often benefitted rural sectors, preoccupation with cleanliness can also skew priorities. As detailed below, the public health ministry wanted to begin an expensive sewage project in Ariasucu and other rural communities in 1994. Threatening a wasteful allocation of limited resources, the proposal had more to do with state fear of disease than with Otavaleños' own development needs. Even as Otavalo prospers, elements of dominant society identify new sources of physical and moral contamination, from cholera to drug trafficking.

The "discovery" of new sources of corruption renders native people's conduct perpetually suspect. In the face of such ingrained racial antipathy, many Otavaleños eschew integration into formal economic and political institutions and instead "defend themselves with their own work in their own homes." If rural Otavaleños do mobilize politically, it is often to fight for narrower issues: striking for bus service, occupying land, and organizing for water. Through these struggles, indigenous people create their own economic and cultural space for the expanding textile economy, reproducing indigenous wealth as outsiders' wealth (cf. Colloredo-Mansfeld 1998).

◢ Community Economies and Ethnic Divisions, 1930–50 ◣

Toward the end of my 1994 fieldwork, I asked one of my compadres, Santo Conejo, to work with his father and draw a map of Ariasucu as it was when the older man was a boy.[5] In comparison with maps of modern Ariasucu, several features of his historical reconstruction stand out. First, at that time (circa 1950) the sector had little more than half the number of homes that now sprawl along the paths. Second, houses seem more evenly scattered up the slopes. Without bus service and electricity to draw people down, families lived among their fields. Third, in two spots houses clustered together forming little neighborhoods, one at the crest of the hill and the other near the junction of two dry *quebradas* (gullies). Otherwise, the area had no central focus, natural boundaries, plazas, chapels, or any public structures.

Strolling across Imbabura in the early twentieth century would have revealed many such sectors. The terrain did not offer obvious routes among the houses. Narrow footpaths skirted fields, dropped into *quebradas*, and twisted along *zanjas* — great barriers of stones cleared from fields, piled one to two meters high.[6] Trees, bushes, and

5. Santo was adept at mapping. Indeed, we met in 1991 when, after glimpsing some maps I had made in my sketchbook, he invited me back to his house to see some maps of Ariasucu that he had done himself.

6. The use of the word *"zanja"* to refer to these stone barriers seems to be local. A more standard definition of *zanja* is ditch or trench. Perhaps such ditches once ran along the *zanjas* of these communities and have since been obscured through erosion and the overgrowth of wild plants. These stone walls define the various neighborhoods and sub-neighborhoods of upper Agato, Ariasucu, and La Compañia. See Joanne Rappaport (1994) for an interesting discussion of *zanjas* (trenches) in the history of individual landholdings in the southern Colombian Andes.

cabuya plants rooted into these *zanjas,* fringed the paths, and hid the houses. Although maps showed large communities called *parciali-dades*—Quinchuqui, Agato, La Compañia, Camuendo, Pucará—the actual social geography was more fragmentary. The slopes contained loose settlements of homes named for families—Santillan (Ucu) (meaning "inside Santillan's"), Cando (Ucu), Arias (Ucu). Likewise, people identified clusters of homes by natural features—Yaculoma (Waterhill), Chimbaloma (Facinghill), Yacupata (Riverbank).

The *parcialidades'* political power was as decentralized as the settlement patterns. Describing its organization, Frank Salomon (1981: 428) writes: "The *parcialidad* is held together largely by kinship and cooperation; its authority structures are few and not mandated to exercise control outside their narrow specialties. In no single individual are power and authority decisively combined." Elsewhere in Ecuador, the *hacendado* (landlord) was the most powerful, secular figure (Casagrande and Piper 1969). In many Otavaleño communities, however, he was absent or his power was restricted to specific land transactions. The parish priest and *teniente politico* (an official of the provincial government) tried to assert their own authority through appointed *alcaldes* (mayors). These officials, though, often received more contempt than respect when they tried to organize road-building or church-repairing *mingas* (Salomon 1981: 429).

The primary institution integrating peoples across the region was the market.[7] While settlements may have lacked clear political definition, they often had distinct economic specializations. In a broad survey of the area's economy, Aníbal Buitrón (1947) was able to divide over forty communities into thirteen occupational categories, including weavers of wool, weavers of cotton, weavers of reed, weavers of husks (for baskets and hats), merchants, laborers, market porters, wood gatherers, and *huasipungueros* (indentured *hacienda* laborers). Purchasing and selling raw materials and finished products of their trade, Otavaleños interconnected the *cantón* (county) economy at their weekly market. Already by midcentury, regular commodity exchange fostered the specialized skills of a competitive economy and concentrated resources in communities like Peguche and Quinchuqui that would experience impressive growth in the decades to come.

---

7. While only engaging agricultural production in a limited way, the market touched all facets of textile production from the sale of raw wool to finished products. Such horizontal exchange, as Stuart Plattner (1989: 203) explains, can foster regional economic integration and stimulates development.

While reaching out economically, Otavaleños largely isolated themselves socially and politically. Although most lived less than an hour's walk from Imbabura's main interprovincial road, few had contact with white-mestizos. As Santo Conejo told me, his grandparents' generation did not tolerate "*no-conocidos*" (unknowns) in their communities. The distrust of outsiders could have tragic consequences. One event, in particular, has scarred interethnic relations to this day. According to an account published by Moises Saenz (1933), three government revenue agents visited Agato to appraise property holdings in 1932. Fearing a new increase in their taxes, local residents attacked and beat up the officials, "leaving them half dead." The incident terrified townspeople who petitioned for help from the provincial governor. Armed forces were sent. "These approached the rebel natives, receiving their challenges and insults; they negotiated with and pacified the Indians" (Saenz 1933: 118).

In his summary of the conflict, Saenz did not seem to capture the whole story. In 1994, Santo gave me what I believe is the indigenous version of the same events.[8] He told it to me as he and I were scouting out water pipelines in Agato. When we got to the edge of a *quebrada,* he spoke of a bloody fight between soldiers and local families that his elderly mother had witnessed at this spot when she was a girl. The governor's forces had ridden up along the *quebrada* and ran into a gang of men and women armed with rocks and sticks. Santo said that the soldiers took flight. On the way down the hill, though, they met a *kuraka.* (Santo described this as a powerful "individual who more or less knew how to speak Spanish." He implied it was the *alcalde* [mayor, officially recognized leader].) This man told the soldiers that the local residents did not have anything that could kill them. The soldiers then turned around and started to shoot at their attackers. Some were shot in the face, others in the leg. They killed several women. According to the version heard by Santo, when they gunned down a pregnant woman the battle stopped.

Although it is not possible to prove the truth of either account, both illustrate the tension and distrust that pitted indígena against mestizo. Santo's story of violence underscores the animosity indígenas still feel toward their own people who co-operate with white-mestizo authorities. In his telling, the treachery of the office-holder,

8. Santo told me this tale unprompted and before I had read anything about the conflict. Although I cannot be certain that the two accounts refer to the same incident, the timing, location, and extraordinary presence of soldiers in Agato suggest that it was the same event.

the collaborator, brings misfortune to the community. With the exception of the avid marketing of textiles to customers in Otavalo, Quito, and elsewhere, Otavaleños tried to keep their communities, land, and homelife out of the reach of official Ecuadorian institutions. As Buitrón (1947) put it: "experience has taught [Otavaleños] for more than four centuries to distrust the white man, and we are not going to erase this only by offering not to deceive them from now on. The most urgent aid needed by the Indian, in our opinion, is to acquire land." For most Otavaleños, the development they sought would come as long as they could grow their own food, manufacture artisan commodities, and pursue "one's own work, in one's own home," without outside interference.

◢ Embodied Memories of the "Industrious" Indian's Home ◣

Set back in their fields and tucked behind a protective screen of eucalyptus, lechera, and capuli trees, rural homes in the 1940s enclosed the private worlds of farmers and weavers.[9] The houses took two general shapes. The wealthiest families constructed rectangular homes of packed adobe walls and tile roofs. Others lived under thatched roofs in small square houses. Whether living in large or small homes, Otavaleños spent their days outdoors, either in the patio or the *corredor*, an open porch spanning the front of the house. Indeed, while most women set up their *tulpacuna* (hearths) inside their home, not all did. Some households not only ground grain and wove on the *corredor* but also slept and cooked there as well. They turned the dark, cool interiors over to possessions, stored food, and *cuyes* (guinea pigs, which are raised to be eaten on special occasions and to be used in both religious and healing practices [Morales 1995]).

In the course of my 1994 fieldwork, I interviewed people about these old possessions that occupied earlier homes. I first got informants to sort through photographs of today's household objects and to rank them in order of current importance. Then I switched the topic to the past and asked respondents what their grandparents had had. Having set up the question with an explicit discussion of pots, pans, beds, looms, stools, and farm tools, I was not prepared for the responses: "wool," "oxen," and "grains." When it came to older

9. I have created the descriptions of home and countryside based on published reports (Buitrón and Buitrón 1945; Buitrón 1947), the excellent photographs found in Collier and Buitrón (1949), interviews and extensive walks with informants through the upper sections of communities, where I was told how paths used to look, where houses were, and what sorts of plants were found around homes.

generations they spoke not of furnishings, much less of consumer goods. Instead, the spaces of past houses held the raw materials and products of peasant life. Thus, asking what grandparents *possessed* inevitably got descriptions of what they *did.*

Frequently, people acted out their responses, conjuring old goods out of the air. During one interview, for example, a woman described her grandparents' possessions by working through the fourteen steps necessary for turning raw wool into woven cloth. As she spoke, her fingers twisted invisible sticks clumped with invisible wool, her hands spun imaginary wall-mounted spinning wheels, and her torso rocked to the rhythms of backstrap weaving. In another interview, a man described the earthen pots his grandmother had used. These had had four knobs around the top, he explained, and had to be picked up with two pairs of hands. As he spoke, he stood up and grabbed at the handles around the long-gone pot's mouth and then he rotated his hands 90 degrees and grabbed at the other two handles. Still others bound pretend yokes on absent ox with leather straps (drawing 7), ground barley on missing stones, and toasted maize on long-broken clay pans.

While for the most part, these objects and their owners no longer existed, they nonetheless left an indelible stamp on the next generation. Remnants of past kitchen life and weaving sessions now endured in experiential memories that could flicker to life in brief performances. As I followed people's hands and watched postures, I saw how a previous generation worked to transform raw grains into festive meals and rough wool into fine cloth. I also witnessed how my current informants—maids, transnational merchants, and construction laborers—have kept a part of their cultural legacy. "What is 'learned by body' is not something one has, like knowledge that can be brandished, but something one is" (Bourdieu 1990: 73). Trained in their grandparent's houses as youths, these middle-aged Otavaleño bodies carry the agrarian memories that used to unite them. Even if they no longer serve practical purposes, physical remembrances act as an archive of a culture's creative powers (cf. Seremetakis 1994).

More than just enacting skills, these informants expressed bodily their grandparents' ideals, their faith in hard work. Describing Otavaleños commitment to their jobs, Buitrón (1947: 52) wrote, "the Indians in their communities work all day. Rest for them consists in changing from one task to another." Such industriousness spoke of ambition, not desperation. Artisans wanted to increase their earnings to buy more land and spend more lavishly on religious offices and the celebration of local saints (Salz 1955). A moral virtue in

Drawing 7: Yoke and Whip

itself, hard work made the "good life" possible—economic independence, participation in religious and family celebrations, and the
presentation of self through fine clothes and a solid home. Pursuit
of these ideals turned old earth houses, with their built-in hearths,
looms, and spinning wheels into machines of production.

Dedication to their work and pride in their culture elicited glowing praise from outsiders. In the early 1930s, the Mexican anthropologist Saenz contrasted Otavaleños with other Ecuadorian natives

by saying that they had a reputation for being "extremely clean" while indígenas from central provinces are "ragged and dirty" (Saenz 1933: 37).[10] He elaborated, writing that in the market and in their own communities, they are "clean and tidy" as well as "robust and vigorous." He then went on to provide a physical description: "sharp nose, large eyes, and lips that are not too thick" (Saenz 1933: 37). With his comments on cleanliness, facial features, and skin ("it is not too dark"), Saenz situated Otavaleños somewhere in the middle of the supposed racial gap between the indigenous populations and the white-mestizo ones.

Ecuadorian anthropologists and writers also elevated the status of Otavaleños based on their combination of hard work and cleanliness. Buitrón claimed Otavalo to be "one of the most progressive and picturesque" regions of the province and Otavaleños the most industrious native group of the nation (Buitrón 1947). And the poet Ramon Serrano Cambert wrote:

> Not yet dawn and yet already full are
> The street, the markets
> With clean Indians, so clean
> That they could serve as a pleasing example
> For the rest of the Indians that we have seen
> In all the American continent.[11]

Health statistics corroborated the favorable impressions. Civil records in Otavalo from 1934 to 1944 testify to the general good health

---

10. Saenz was an important voice in the Mexican *indigenista* movement (although he himself was at times ambivalent about the label). He saw anthropology as meaningful only in its service to a well-defined goal: national integration. Indeed, he became the most fervent partisan for a politics of incorporation during the period when he was subsecretary of education in charge of the rural program (Aquirre Beltran 1970: xxvi). His work in Ecuador was criticized by Ecuadorian writers who believed Saenz had not ventured south of Quito and actually visited the peasants of the central provinces (see Monslave Pozo 1943).

11. The lines come from the poem "Estampa de Otavalo," which was included in an anthology about the region, called *Paisaje y Alma de Otavalo* and put together by Virgilio Chaves Valdospinos. The book carries no publication date, but the materials inside range from colonial days to the mid-1970s, with the majority dating from the mid-twentieth century. Another poem in the collection was titled "Indios de Otavalo" and included the lines:

> El indio es buen mozo
> y la "longa" linda
> El con trenza negra
> y camisa limpia.

of native peoples. The population categorized as "Indian" had lower infant mortality rates and higher life expectancies than those defined as "Mestizo" or "White" (Buitrón and Buitrón 1945). Children born and raised among the looms, spinning wheels, and clay cooking pots of peasant households lived longer and healthier lives than those who lived in town during the early part of this century. With low population densities, sufficient spring water, and homegrown foods, rural residents enjoyed some advantages over white-mestizos.

◢ Lowly Homes and Ragged Indians ◣

Despite facts and praise, though, Otavaleños could never escape the strong prejudices of the day. Seeing little that was virtuous in the worn implements and straw-roofed homes of native communities, urban Ecuador worried about the physical and cultural threats of the indigenous material world that stretched the length of the central Andean valley from Tulcan through Imbabura to Loja. The Ecuadorian writer, Neptali Zuniga, for example, condemned all native peoples for their farming ways in his book, *Fenomenos de la Realidad Ecuatoriana* (1940). After describing the national economy and society, he dismissed the indigenous population as hopelessly tradition-bound. The source of native degeneracy was their relationship to the land: "the Indian biologically evolved cultivating and loving the land. The Indian is son of agriculture and agriculture is mother of his race, his biological content . . . Indian and land confuse themselves" (Zuniga 1940: 189). All the ills of native society came together in rural homes:

> The Indian has put his temperament in the construction of his hearth . . . Their lowly, rustic houses with roofs of straw or tile enclose a miserable way of life. The Indian lives in an unhealthy tenement house, in a plane of reduced life, his biological development negatively influenced by food, the environment, the hygiene and the disorder. (Zuniga 1940: 191)

On the basis of their domestic conditions, Zuniga condemns indígenas to inevitable demise, and others agreed. Medical and public health professionals argued that "racial poisons"—alcohol, nicotine, venereal disease, and other infections—led to hereditary decline (cf. Stepan 1991). In a health assessment of native Ecuadorians, Dr. Luis A. Leon (1946: 260) wrote:

> The insufficient clothing, the lack of bodily cleanliness, the bad conditions of the hearth, the co-residence with domestic animals,

the absolute ignorance of alimentary hygiene, the witchcraft and curing are the principal factors that favor the propagation of infectious and degenerative diseases in the indigenous race.

In the context of these fears, Otavaleños' progress presented itself as an incomprehensible hybrid. The Ecuadorian social scientist Pio Jaramillo Alvarado (1949), for example, described his visit with a North American anthropologist to a weaver's home as follows:

And we could verify that in Otavalo the industrious Indian is intelligent and rich and consequently owner of magnificent arable lands. But, likewise, our astonishment was great when we visited a house of one of these industrious Indians and one could not differentiate his home life from that of the needy Indian. And we asked ourselves: if the Indian has been to school and is industrious and a property owner, what more is necessary to live at a level corresponding to his economic situation? Culture? With this word one says much, but in concrete cases it signifies very little or perhaps nothing.

While he does not describe the home other than to say it manifested the conditions of "Indian serfdom," I can imagine some of what he saw: an open, ash-filled cooking hearth with blackened stones supporting a large pot, rafters hanging maize cobs paired off and tied together with the loose leaves of their husks, and a floor littered with dried grass and small droppings, evidence of the guinea pigs that would have scurried off into the shadows at the entrance of strangers.[12] The merchants' large, new *tapial* walls still enclosed a world of farm tools, grain sacks, and hard-worn cooking implements.

Having condemned this homelife as worthy of a peon, Jaramillo Alvarado missed its distinctive modernity. The more the "industrious Indian" invested in magnificent lands, the more maize he had to cook, the greater the number of guinea pigs to feed, and the larger the hearth to prepare soup for bigger family fiestas. The new weaving economy allowed Otavaleños to revitalize the subsistence economy (Salomon 1981). Jaramillo Alvarado's shock arose from his mistaken assumption that some things—native farming and cooking practices—rightfully belonged in the past, while others—education, hard work, property ownership—were the exclusive domain of the present. Expecting Otavaleños to offer unequivocal signs of "cultural progress," the author labored to explain his disappointment at finding a mix of old and new.

12. See John Collier's (Collier and Buitrón 1949) wonderful photographs of Otavaleño homes, interiors that he shot in 1946, about the time of Jaramillo Alvarado's visit.

The Otavalo case troubled Jaramillo Alvarado because the obvious causes of lowliness had been removed; the indígenas enjoyed an improved economy and education. Yet, they still failed to meet expectations. Thus, the writer vacillated between indigenous culture itself and a native inferiority complex as the cause of their degraded homes. Either way, wealth that came clothed in subsistence practices and indigenous artifacts came across to authorities as pathological—crippled by its association with the farm life and desperate for a good cleaning up.

In very different ways, the writings of both Zuniga and Jaramillo represent a basic shift in attitudes that took place at midcentury. During the first 100 years of the Ecuadorian republic, the white-mestizo populace restricted its dealing with indigenous peasants to extracting labor, saving souls, and raising revenues through the Indian tithe and other taxes. Now they threatened to meddle more intimately. Jaramillo's struggle to explain "what is necessary to live at a level corresponding to his economic situation" implied a call to action. Social science needed to discover why Otavaleños had not "progressed" domestically according to modern ideals; the state needed to purge kitchens and *corredors* of their deficient practices. To borrow from Santo's violent tale, the state would no longer shoot at a pregnant woman but rather find new purpose in "developing" her: help her feed, educate, and nurture her child into a healthy citizen who is integrated into the nation. National legitimacy came down to the problem of well-ordered hearths.

◢ Expansion into Town and the Entrepreneurial Ethic ◣

While initiated in the 1930s, the national development effort did not gain momentum until the 1950s. In 1954, Ecuadorian officials formed Mision Andina in response to recommendations by a special United Nations council on indigenous Andean populations. It was the first major, secular development program targeted at the most populous indigenous areas of the sierra. With funds from such United Nations' organizations as FAO, UNESCO, WHO, and UNICEF, Mision Andina initiated demonstration projects and research in Chimborazo in 1956, then expanded to Loja in the south and Imbabura in the north in 1958.[13]

Mision Andina's two guiding principles were to overcome the lack

.

13. *Seis Años de Trabajo de la Mision Andina en el Ecuador,* n.d.; cf. Linda Belote's and Jim Belote's work (1981) for an account of Mision Andina's work and impact in Saraguro, in Ecuador's southern Andes.

of harmony between indigenous people and other groups and to promote the development of indigenous communities in the broadest sense (Mision Andina n.d. p. 2). Toward that end, the project's top three (of ten) goals were (1) organize the community, (2) create schools, and (3) improve the hearth (including improving nutrition and fighting against alcoholism). Other activities related to agricultural extension work, communal work and construction, rural industry, handicraft formation, rural health, and recreation. The state hoped to implement these programs and develop the countryside through strongly centralized community councils, agricultural cooperatives, and sports clubs.

Around Otavalo, though, people inverted the government's goals. Infrastructure projects received enthusiastic support, while community organization faltered due to apathy and health projects failed for lack of funds. Consequently, Mision Andina's lasting impact lay not in effective councils or better schools but in the new roads connecting rural *parcialidades* to Otavalo. Participating in regional *mingas*, community members widened footpaths, knocked holes in the earth walls around fields, and tore open the stonewalled, tree-lined *zanjas*. Santo Conejo reported that neighbors who lost land to the new dirt roads had protested angrily. The *mingueros* (communal workers), however, carried on, their loyalties secured by provincial officials who donated wheat flour, cooking oil, and canned chicken to those who volunteered.

In 1966, this road-building culminated in the construction of a new bridge over Ariasucu's gully. Its prominence led me to sketch the bridge early on in my fieldwork (drawing 8). Despite the drawing's crowded composition and the obscure vantage point from which I made it, people throughout Ariasucu and upper La Compañia instantly recognized it. When talking to people about this bridge, I was surprised to discover how little credit the state received for building it. Galo Ajala, for example, told me, "Chon Effe [John F.] Kennedy built this bridge. He was a good man. He was the last good president in the United States." Galo ignored the Ecuadorian government's expenditure of 56 percent of Mision Andina's $2,113,000 budget over its first six years. Instead, he and other's thanked the North Americans, who contributed only 3 percent of the budget. The state's history of broken promises kept people from recognizing when government action actually does work.

The greater mobility afforded by new highways in Imbabura and elsewhere shifted both economic horizons and work ethics. Otavaleños put the new roads to immediate use. In the 1960s, Otavaleño

Drawing 8: Mision Andina Bridge

textile entrepreneurs took more frequent sales trips, developed new products, and intensified handicraft textile production. Rather than expanding agricultural holdings and paying the rising costs of cargo fiestas (Saint's day celebrations), entrepreneurs channeled money back into their business and took their wares to more distant markets.

With new awareness of the returns on careful investments in the handicraft business, merchants and manufacturers developed a market-oriented habit of mind. Stressing the need to live cheaply, save money, and, little by little, build one's business, they sought their own advancement. More than saving against hard times— "ensuring stock for future uses" (cf. Gudeman and Rivera 1990: 84– 85)—these peasant-entrepreneurs wanted to accumulate profits and change their lives. According to Leo Ralph Chavez (1982: 130), the fundamental tenets of the Otavaleño entrepreneurial model were as follows: "Slow economic growth through gradual savings and investments in (*a*) equipment; (*b*) merchandise; or (*c*) some combination of the two." The commercial weavers emphasized how their progress came through rationality—the very quality white-mestizos said they lacked. They had to save and suffer—giving up not only the luxuries of new clothes and leisure time but also salt, meals, and other basic necessities. Chavez (1982: 138) quoted one entrepreneur's description of starting a business with his wife:

> My wife knew how to sew and I learned how to cut material for sweaters. But we suffered and worked very hard. We would work from six in the morning to about one in the afternoon. Then we would eat and sleep a little. Then we would work some more. Like that, we suffered until we had enough money to buy more machines.

While reflecting deeper market involvement, the rationality professed by Otavaleños was not reducible to a strict reckoning of profits and loss. Rather, the rational person is one who behaves responsibly toward others and one's work—keeping commitments, avoiding the distractions of drink, and staying respectful (Chavez 1982: 98). One man explained the concept of rationality to me by describing both the proper way to grow a business and the proper way to dance. In the former case, one must work at selling sweaters and tapestries day after day, taking the money from sales and buying a "a little more, a little more" inventory. When it comes to dancing, he told me that the rational man asks a woman to dance, "they dance respectfully, not like those from above [upper Ariasucu]. They are not rational. They have to drink before they dance—drink more, drink more—and then they fight." Working or celebrating, some Otavaleños found new ways to demonstrate their level-headedness. As economic and social experience broadened, Imbabura's traders adapted their moral ethos to match.

◢ The Fight for Humane Bus Service ◣

The faster links between rural communities and urban markets served as a catalyst for many of these changes. The transportation service not only encouraged interprovincial sales trips but also daily commuting between Otavalo and the surrounding rural communities (Buitrón 1974). To handle the rising demand, a series of co-operatives tried running scheduled service from the market up into rural sectors. After an indigenous-run co-op failed in the late 1960s, a white-mestizo-owned company took over the routes. The service became more regular. Unfortunately, so did the racial conflict.

Mestizo resentment of natives frequently became most bitter in that intimate public space of provincial life: the interior of local buses. Some passengers recoiled from the touch of an indigenous weaver's lanolin-smoothed hand or shrank from the kitchen smells of a peasant woman's blouses. The worst were the bus conductors, mestizos who found their economic and social position slipping relative to the rising native merchant class. They yelled at older passengers if they did not get on and off fast enough and they prohibited inebriated people (that is almost anyone who had been to a baptism or wedding) from coming aboard. On crowded market days, they refused service to the poorest riders, would not touch *kipis* (bundles that women carried), oversold the seats and aisles, elbowed their way through the crush of men, women, and children dressed in their finest outfits, and complained about *"indios sucios"* (dirty Indians).

Finally, in 1986, riders from rural sectors had had enough; they "made the definitive strike" according to Santo Conejo. The immediate cause was a substantial hike in fares. Although not uncommon throughout Ecuador in those days of hyperinflation, indigenous people believed the mestizos raised fares faster and higher for rural communities. On 22 July 1986, communities around the southern and eastern sides of the lake lodged a formal complaint with provincial authorities. They reported that the "drivers continued abuses against the users, do not respect the routes, carry an excess of passengers, and meet any complaint with impolite language."[14] The Federation of Indigenous People and Peasants of Imbabura (FICI) jumped on the bandwagon the next day and denounced the new round of fare hikes. Within a week, the communities around Ariasucu responded by digging up the roads and stoning the buses when they tried to enter. The drivers returned to Otavalo and sent the police into the communities to open them up. Galo Ajala remembered how the conflict escalated.

The police tried to use tear gas to disperse the protesters. Residents responded by attacking the police with poles, stones, and slingshots. Galo said he joined the strike in Peguche. His wife Monica interrupted his account to say he just liked to fight. He paused, scowled at her, then turned back to me and broke into a big smile as he said he nearly died when a tear gas canister hit a light post near him and exploded. The police carried the struggle into Agato where people fought "hand to hand." The newspapers reported that at least eighteen people were injured throughout all communities.[15] Locally, several strikers claimed that a policeman died after he had been hit in

14. *La Verdad*, 22 July 1986, p. 11.
15. *La Verdad*, 12 August 1986, p. 1.

the head with a rock. The police returned with sufficient reinforcements and arrested twenty men, including four or five from Ariasucu. When word returned to Agato that prisoners were being mistreated, dozens of people traveled to Ibarra and occupied the cathedral. They refused to leave until they gained the release of their comrades, secured lower fares on their bus routes, and had the definitive expulsion from Ecuador of the Summer Institute of Linguistics, a Protestant Bible group which had been banned in the early 1970s (this and other demands seem to have been articulated by FICI). The combination of the sit-in and the bishop's intervention finally resulted in the prisoners' freedom.

Years later, Santo had a simple explanation for these events. From his perspective it all came down to this: "The drivers were always calling us 'dirty Indians.' " The white-mestizo fear of contamination met its violent reflection in indigenous anger at mestizo racism. More than two decades after the government launched a comprehensive program to create harmonious relations among indígenas and mestizos, pernicious stereotypes about filthy bodies still divided them. The white-mestizos who have the most contact with indígenas often treated them and their possessions with the most disrespect. Notably, as frequent bus riders, Otavalo's merchant artisans regularly suffer such contempt. The very group who has taken to the market, made money, and professed faith in rational progress—all values espoused by the urban middle class—still felt driven to pick up rocks to fight the humiliation of racism. While the economy of Otavalo had changed a lot since 1932, politics had not.

⁌ Otavalo in the Time of Cholera ⁍

The myth of the "dirty Indian" and state efforts to clean up the countryside gained new strength in the 1990s. The catalyst was an outbreak of cholera in 1991. As with other diseases, most notably AIDS, a general public health problem quickly became a pretense for resurrecting boundaries between clean and "infected" populations (Farmer 1994; cf. Briggs 1997). In their analysis of a related public health crisis in Brazil, Marilyn Nations and Cristina Monte (1996: 1009) write, "Epidemics of particularly dreaded illnesses always provoke a popular outcry. When such adversity as cholera—a virulent, infectious agent which spreads capriciously and kills—strikes, people quickly incriminate: 'Shame, Shame, Who's to blame?' Finger pointing becomes a human passion." In places like Ecuador, where contagious illness feeds other stereotypes, such passion can fuel racism.

Cholera had reappeared first in coastal cities before moving into the highlands and rural provinces. Although the disease spread rapidly across the country, it struck at a narrow population. In Imbabura, for example, cholera left the market towns and wealthier native communities alone. Even in more remote, poorer areas, it targeted a small segment of the population. Four of the five victims said to have died from cholera in Ariasucu were men, older than forty, and living in a high neighborhood of sagging, straw-roofed homes. Both poverty and gender played a role in their deaths. I was told that men died because they do not know how to cook. On those occasions when their wives were away during the day, they did not bother to prepare a hot meal for themselves. Instead, in a fatal move, they would wave flies off cold leftovers and snack on infected food. Among the poorest households though, those with the right skills—that is, the women— could protect themselves by boiling their soup and toasting their maize in sizzling oil.

Despite both its urban origins and the narrow group of victims, cholera soon subjected all indigenous communities to suspicion and fear. In 1991, Otavaleño, hotel owners warned me not to go anywhere in the countryside. Some taxi-drivers refused to take indigenous people from the town back to their homes. Wealthy merchants who had flown in from Caracas or Amsterdam had to plead with drivers to take them just fifteen minutes out of town. When fares did convince drivers to make the trip, the cabs would rush back to the city. Residents in Ariasucu described how cabbies locked their doors and waggled their index fingers to reject anyone impertinent enough to seek a ride back. In the urban imagination, peasant communities once again seethed with filth and corruption.

These fears quickly translated into new development efforts, some of which had a positive impact on Ariasucu. Others, still under consideration, would be disastrous if they were ever carried out. The nongovernmental organization CARE, in conjunction with Ecuador's public health ministry, embarked on a regionwide latrine installation project. In Ariasucu, their efforts resulted in an increase in the number of outhouses from 21 in 1991 to 120 in 1994 (drawing 9). The center of the sector now bristles with little, cement-block structures vented with white, plastic pipes (drawing 10)—a sign of modernization that pleased many residents.

More critically, worries about cholera renewed commitment to the potable water project. As mentioned above, the engineers once again called communities out in regular *mingas* to lay dozens of kilometers of pipes. Antidisease efforts, however, veered toward the

Drawing 9: *Servicio Higiénico* (outhouse)

extreme. In 1994, the public health ministry proposed extending a sewage line out of Peguche and Quinchuqui, the most densely populated areas, and into more rural sectors like Ariasucu. They claimed that by beginning immediately communities could take advantage of the ninety kilometers of trenches they had dug for the water project, many of which had not been filled back in. They also could use money from an "emergency development fund" that President Sixto

Drawing 10: View across Center of Ariasucu

Durán Ballen had set up. The catch was that project planners wanted each household to contribute 50,000 sucres, tantamount to more than a month's earnings for the poorest residents. Leaders and residents from Ariasucu debated the merits of the project at a meeting held during their first *minga* in September.[16]

Opponents of the project balked at the price. In the course of the meeting one speaker got up and complained that they did not have enough money to pay fees to the water board for potable water, let alone for the materials of this new project. Speaking through a battery powered bullhorn, he said:

> . . . in vain do we look for 50,000 sucres or 5,000 sucres. They are saying contribute just 1,500 sucres to the water board; we cannot do it. Because we need to buy salt, a little cooking fat, we have hardly 1000 sucres left . . . we are poor people in little Ariasucu, we will not be able to make a contribution.

16. For other accounts of the bitter intracommunity politics that crops up during water projects and other development projects, see Susan Andrade (1990) for nearby La Compañia or Nicole Bourque (1997) for communities in the central Ecuadorian Andes. For an excellent historical account of intracommunity land disputes, see Elizabeth Marberry Rogers (1998).

The images of stark poverty captured the assembled's feelings of hardship. Even if he overstated the severity of their circumstances—most had little trouble shopping for basic needs—he spoke to people's frustrations. Few wanted to spend their meager cash on a dubious government project.

Others criticized the project's unfair distribution of benefits. Engineers wanted to concentrate the work in the lower, more populated neighborhoods. Once again, every household in the sector would have to donate labor, while those living in upper areas would receive nothing in return. As the president of the community said:

> The engineer wants that we do his project. Compañía, Agato, Aria-sucu, Yacupata, each and everybody, yes Pucará's side too, wherever a lot of people like to live. [But] here, there, wherever just a few people live, [the engineers] do not want to do it, "a lot of material is used; it costs a lot and has less users," they say. In vain, they would do it, they say . . . They are using up a lot [of the project] from Quin-chuqui up to Compañía and Pucará too. For those upper living *tay-tacuna* (fathers), middle living *taytacuna,* there will be no sewage system.

From a strict cost/benefit standpoint, the engineers had a case. People would have had to lay a lot of extra pipe to reach the upper-most houses. However, decades of restricting projects to the lower neighborhoods had created Imbabura's starkest zones of poverty and in fact contributed to the cholera problem. The places where the disease took a fatal turn had been cut off from the services delivered to lower areas: public standpipes for (relatively) clean water, electricity to see around windowless kitchens, and roads that connected sectors to emergency health services. Recognizing past iniquities, few wanted to sign onto a sewage project that left a large segment of the community out.

Others, however, favored the project. Some repeated outsiders' images of a dirty and disease-ridden countryside:

> Everyone is noting that you [people of Ariasucu] are not getting the project. "Where will the dirty water go, it will fill with flies," they are saying, right. "It will fill with flies and ugly sickness, ugly what-ever, piss will overflow, sickness is coming," they say.

These images of flies, urine, and dirty water had no relation to current reality. Further, even if the state delivered on its promise of potable water, few believed that the flow rates would meet established household need. No one entertained dreams of indoor plumbing, showers, toilets, and so much water that it could "overflow." This nightmarish fantasy of overflowing piss and sickness stems from white-mestizo water practices and speaks to urban paranoia, not Imbabura's hydrological resources.

More expressed concern about the political consequences of not participating. Rumors circulated that if Ariasucu did not sign onto the *mingas*, Agato and La Compañia, the large neighboring communities, would take over its official jurisdiction. The community would be split up. Losing their own council, they still would have had to participate in the sewage project. One man speaking for involvement put it this way:

> Following the comments we have heard, people are saying Ariasucu and Yacupata will disappear, I will have to turn to Companía, I will have to meet with Agato . . . for me that does not appear good because I am only one person. In vain do I meet with them about personal matters . . . in my respective community I cannot be denied.

The sewage project placed Ariasucu in a bind. The plan had every appearance of a boondoggle. It was expensive and would not serve much of the community. Since the public work ministry did not even have the money to buy the small pumps for the water project, they most certainly lacked the funding for any sewage treatment plant. Therefore, if the sewage lines ever went into service, they would most likely foul the river where hundreds of women went each day to wash clothes. However, turning their backs on the project risked political disenfranchisement for Ariasucu's residents. To avoid losing autonomy to neighboring councils, they were forced to support their own council's effort to organize *mingas*.

In an ironic twist, it seemed Ariasucu's political organization would be leveraged with sewage pipes and toilet bowls. They had avoided getting official jurisdiction for fear of the corruption and costs associated with a formally empowered council. Now, the combination of this project and the rivalries among rural sectors motivated members of the acting council to seek recognition from the ministry of agriculture as a legal peasant community. Not long after the meeting, the secretary of the council came to me to look at the maps I used during my research. Sitting at my laptop computer, the two of us reworked my maps' boundaries so that he could use them in a petition for *jurídico* (juridical authority).

The push for *jurídico*, however, remained half-hearted. Rather than get tangled up in this new project, Ariasucu's great majority wanted their leaders to pressure the public health ministry to finish the potable water project. As the ex-president Jaime Cuyo said on that day of the meeting:

> Good Afternoon *taytacuna, mamacuna* (fathers and mothers) for my part I thank you. As the president was saying, I am standing here a little bit. . . . to inform you from another viewpoint, *taytacuna, mamacuna.* As I was saying earlier this morning, you . . . have to come to an agreement. From my point of view, I want the water already finished then later let us get out the so-called sewage project . . . if you *taytacuna, mamacuna* are saying 'yes, let us just install it, let us just support it,' . . . then I must be able to do it, but from my point of view, I want to finish this water, then later let us do it.

In the three years since they had invaded the land by the lake to get at the springs, Jaime, his brother-in-law, and their musical group *Runa Causai,* had been on trips to Costa Rica and Europe. They had seen the world and made some money. Yet they still did not have running water in their homes. They did not want the government's preoccupation with filth to keep them from receiving it. Running into the opposition of this and other communities and facing budget shortfalls, provincial water authorities seem to have postponed the sewage project indefinitely.

Eventually, in 1995, the *mingas* laid the final links of the potable water project and officials turned on the pumps. After ten years of planning and hard work, a trickle of water now reaches some of Ariasucu's houses, a few hours a day, several days a week. Many residents, however, have not even bothered to lay the last few meters of pipe from the public lines into their homes. The weak flow rates do not justify the effort.

◢ "Walking with Drugs:" The Limits to Social Mobility ◣

Even as the threat of cholera subsided, elements of local white-mestizo society offer other images of native contamination. Sensing the passing of an era when all deferred to them because of their race and gender, white-mestizo males can be particularly nasty.[17] They insist that native money is "dirty money" coming from drugs, not handicrafts. Once, in a doctor's waiting room, I sat with three white-mestizos—a gaunt, gray-haired man in a worn suit, a pregnant

17. Indigenous informants said that younger men between the ages of twenty and forty could be the most hostile.

woman, and matronly middle-aged woman—listening to the suspicions they had about the textile dealers. The older man complained about the buses to Peguche, the wealthiest native town. He then said, "these *indios* almost do not need buses. They all have cars."

"Nice cars, big cars," the pregnant woman added.

"The Indians are all walking around with drugs, aren't they?" the man queried. The other woman heartily agreed while the pregnant woman said nothing. The older two then nattered away, enumerating all the signs of an illicit drug trade such as the large new houses up and down the Pan American Highway, all the parties, and the big imported pickup trucks. The pregnant woman tried to interrupt and say that the money actually came from handicrafts, especially overseas sales. I supported her position. The other two were not swayed.

Some white-mestizos pick over the minute details of indigenous life, pondering any possible signs of a hidden drug trade. The thousands of cement blocks needed for new houses are allegedly paid for with illicit profits. Natives buy new pickup trucks with plastic linings, the story goes, so they can smuggle drugs in the narrow spaces underneath the linings. Most oddly, they believe textile dealers sew packets of cocaine into the collars of the shirts they ship to Europe. As dedicated retailers, once they sell the drugs, they supposedly sew up the shirts and then peddle them, too (Meisch 1996b). These rumors stigmatize the "cleanest" Otavaleños, those who finally escaped the *yanga kawsay* (humble/fruitless life) as the most dangerous traffickers.

These spiteful rumors aside, Otavalo shows no sign of a drug trade. At a national level, Ecuador has been spared the insidious effects of the drug trade. Colonial and papal policy first eradicated the cultivation of the coca leaf as early as the sixteenth century (Bonilla 1993). Modern demand for cocaine has not significantly reintroduced it. In 1990, for example, growers cultivated 41,000 hectares of coca in Colombia and 121,300 in Peru, but only 150 hectares in Ecuador (U.S. State Department figures, cited in Eastman and Ruben Sanchez 1992). The problem in Ecuador is thus not one of production but of transit (Ortiz Crespo 1990; Riley 1996). Authorities charged with controlling the drug trade worry about the southern cities of Loja and Machala, near the Peruvian border, not about northern Andean provinces like Imbabura (Fundacion Nuestros Jovenes 1989). In short, while no one can be certain that any individual is not involved in drug trafficking, powerful national and international antidrug agencies have found no systematic widespread Ecuadorian, much less Otavaleño, involvement in the trade.[18]

Yet despite the lack of evidence of drugs in Otavalo, richer indígenas are branded as traffickers. Many white-mestizos tell elaborate stories that connect native peoples' houses, cars, clothes, and trade goods to powdery white cocaine, a (racial) "poison" threatening the health of the nation and the well-being of society. Racism rises again as mestizos have a new reason to spurn indígenas.

◢ Dirt Poor and Dirt Rich ◣

In the early twentieth century, most of Otavalo had a peasant-artisan economy in which farming came first, weaving second, and merchant activities third. Artisans lived relatively isolated lives in dispersed settlements, cut off from regular interactions with urban society. Reinforcing the divide between indigenous and white-mestizo social worlds, Otavaleños reinvested earnings in land and community ritual and reacted belligerently to outsider involvement in their lives. Paced by hard-worn, human-powered tools and long walks to weekly markets, economic enterprise grew slowly. Yet, it did grow. Led by entrepreneurs in Peguche, Quinchuqui, and Agato, artisans found more outlets for their goods. They opened the boundaries of their economy, acted on new opportunity, and embraced development programs that brought roads, electricity, buses, and water into their communities.

In working for their advancement, Otavaleños have pursued an "entrepreneurial ethic," grounded in the virtues of industriousness and independence (Chavez 1982). Seeking to weave and sell handicrafts rather than look for wage work, recent generations of artisans have tried to establish "their own work in their own home." While reflecting certain peasant ideals of self-reliance, the ethic contains a market rationality, too. Entrepreneurs express their ideals in stories of working hard, foregoing both luxuries and necessities, weathering

18. For some authorities, the greatest concern lies not with drugs themselves, but with money laundering. In August of 1989, the *Miami Herald* reported that as much as $400 million may be being cleaned through Ecuadorian banks, investments in agricultural operations, and elsewhere. That figure, though, does not seem to correlate with other numbers that show only $317 million in the whole banking system, a figure that includes a sizeable amount of remittances from the United States, tourist dollars, and other documented, legitimate earnings (Bonilla 1993). Needless to say, as individuals with no authority within or control over Ecuador's banks, Otavaleños would not be involved in this sort of drug-trade activity.

setbacks, and expanding their business little by little. In chapters 4, 5, and 6, I explore some of these stories in detail. Before getting into the complexities and payoffs of the handicraft economy, though, I wanted to describe a specter haunting indigenous economic accomplishment. During each phase of their advancement, Otavaleños have contended with the image of the "dirty Indian," a racist fiction that undermines the social and political legitimacy of their material progress.

Scholarship on the Andes has detailed the many forms that oppression of native peoples has taken. Marxist-influenced analysis reveals the inequalities of land distribution, skewed commodity exchange, and unjust labor markets (Mallon 1983; Smith 1989; Collins 1988). Cultural studies focus on symbolic domination of rural peoples and ritual resistance to white mestizo values (Allen 1988; Isbell 1978). Still other ethnographies combine political economy and symbolic analysis to show the ideological erosion of native values through the daily effort of provisioning and running a household (Weismantel 1988). In much of this work, writers explain the division of Andean societies in terms of class, ethnicity, or both. "Race," however, has recently been ignored or explicitly refuted as an analytical category (van den Berghe and Primov 1977).

For Andean peoples, however, race endures as a social fact (Gose 1994b; Weismantel and Eisenman, 1998; cf. Poole 1997). Ethnic theory alone, with its emphasis on culturally achievable differences, gives only a partial account of Ecuador's lasting social divisions. Attending to descent categories, boundary-marking activities, and other elements of ethnic analysis does help make sense of the politics of Otavaleños and other groups. However, it fails to account for white-mestizo fixation on the "dirtiness of the Indians." As Carlos de la Torre notes (1997: 8), such an obsession manifests a deep fear, "a terror that the 'dirtiness' of the Indians will infect and disgrace [Ecuador's] whites and mestizos" (cf. Kovel 1984: 81–90).

Connected to notions of sanitation, modern racial ideologies in the Andes dehumanize subordinate peoples, as they do elsewhere, by making reference to the body. In Ecuador, though, race means more than skin pigmentation, genetics, and blood; it relates to bodies in an expansive sense. The physical world of native peoples—the foods of their gatherings, the fabrics in which they are clothed, the private spaces of their homes, the products made and exchanged through their skilled labor—contains many "micro-sites" (Stoler 1995) where white-mestizo elites find signs of contamination. If dirt is "matter out of place" as Mary Douglas puts it (1966: 35), then "dirty Indians" have been bodies, homes, and material cultures out of place in a modernizing Ecuador. Casting their goals in universal terms of shared progress, government authorities, therefore, work toward a one-sided and self-serving transformation: national development through "cleansing" the society of peasant practices and indigenous culture.

This hygienic racism constitutes a central element of the elite, white-mestizo society's structural power. Such power, as Wolf (1990: 587) points out, "shapes the field of action so as to render some kinds of behavior possible while making others less possible or impossible." In this case, the protean nature of racism, its ability to fix upon new emblems of native practice, allows the continual reproduction of white privilege and invalidation of indigenous work.[19]

This discrimination endures in the face of important changes. Many white-mestizos in Otavalo, for example, have made their peace with the indigenous social and economic presence in the city and are willing to publicly challenge racist comments, the way the woman in the waiting room did. Development professionals at many NGOs (non-governmental organizations) do not press their own agenda upon native communities but work with community leaders on projects local residents have identified. And, in a national political movement, native peoples have forced the government to recognize the legitimacy of indigenous culture. Yet none of these changes, including the wealth amassed by native Otavaleño merchants, has translated easily into native political power, including the basic right to allocate state resources in the development of their own communities.

In this world polarized between the clean and the dirty, political discourse has often taken the form of confrontation. From the violent expulsion of revenue agents to the bloody struggle with the police-backed bus company, residents have fought against the unwanted intrusions of white-mestizos. Rather than use formal political offices or judicial processes, Otavaleños have taken direct action for specific causes. Such efforts have not always succeeded, but they have blunted some state meddling into the intimate affairs of daily life. Otavalo's peasant artisans have thus preserved something of

19. In this analysis, I have been inspired by the ideas of Peter Gose (1994a: 19) who suggests that the words "indio" and "blanco" persist in the southern Andes not as descriptive labels of modern life but as verbal indices of a violent encounter. They evoke the historical moment of conquest and produce a sense that the primordial encounter between Hispanic and Indian still goes on. The language captures the aura of violence, which underpins political rule in provincial Andean towns. I argue that the language of cleanliness has similar pragmatic force.

their own political and cultural space as they go about their business of making a living.

Spurned by the dominant sectors of provincial society, rich indígenas nurture the growth of native social institutions in their urban communities—fiestas, trade organizations, and churches that confer respect and prestige. However, external pressure alone does not explain the persistence of a distinctive Quichua culture among Otavaleños in general or among elite traders, in particular, who might otherwise "cut their hair" (as is said of decultured indigenous men) or give up their *anakus* (straight skirts) and pass into white-mestizo society. The complex moral and social relations of the Otavaleño economy develop their own forces for indigenous cultural expression. Many of these forces reflect the enduring cultural influence of a shared "subsistence ethic," a topic taken up in the next chapter.

◢ THREE ◣
"Useless Things":
Subsistence Ethics and Native Identity

◢ *Mingas* and *Gringos* ◣

Back in 1991, I heard about the water *mingas* within the first week of moving to Ariasucu and asked Galo Ajala if I could accompany him to the next one. "No," he replied. "It is only for indígenas." His answered surprised me. Already, Galo and Monica had invited me into their home, shared every meal with me, taken me to the market with them, and shown me around the area. Despite having included me in many private aspects of their lives, they nonetheless kept me from this public work party. I wondered whether the *mingas* represented some exclusive domain of indigenous sovereignty; a realm guarded from foreign intrusions. In the following weeks, I discovered their reticence had a simpler explanation. They did not think *gringos* would work.

Then I joined them to stack cornstalks my second week in their home. I had been writing up notes on a stool in the patio, observing their daughters Clara and Celestina and son José as they heaved bundles of stalks up to their father standing in the midst of a conical stack. As the pile grew, their throws began to fall short and stalks tumbled down in a shower of chaff. I put my notebook down, headed over, gathered up a bundle and handed it up to Galo. He paused, then laughed, joking with José about how I could reach up and over the edge of the stack. Eager for them not to turn me away, I rushed back to get another bundle. Galo greeted each of my armfuls with an uncertain "*gracias*" and a wide smile, as if he could not believe he had this big foreigner working with him in the field behind his house.

Not long afterwards, I joined Galo and others at a water *minga.* The *mingueros* had come together to dig a platform for a water tank. Although at least 120 people had come out from two communities, only thirty worked at a time within the confines of the site; most watched and chatted. I borrowed a hoe from an idle worker, stepped down into the hole and joined the line of workers. As I raised my hoe, everyone else lowered his or hers. Now the whole *minga* became observers. Panting in shallow breaths of self-consciousness, I carried on. I drew the hoe up over my head and swung it in a quickening curve. My right hand skidded down the shaft and gripped as the blade bit into the soil. Levering the tool out, I sprayed black soil across my ankles, raised the implement and swung again. People just watched. In my nervousness, I worked harder and began to suffer gas and heartburn. The shaft heated up my palms with each swing.

Finally, someone joked about how the *gringo* was the only one working. The line of workers came back to life in arcs of hafted steel and a shower of dirt. I kept at it until the young guy working at my side took pity on me and suggested that the two of us rest. I recognized him as our evangelical Protestant neighbor. (He wore a T-shirt of a screaming war eagle with a skull in its claws and the legend "Kill Them All, Let God Sort 'Em Out." I think his English extended only to the word "God.") For the rest of the afternoon, I matched my shifts to his. Trying to make my effort look genuine, I stuck with it until the end, even as the pads of flesh below my fingers bloomed into blisters, which burst and oozed muddy smears on the handle.

Days later, I found myself working at a third *minga*. This time, at Galo's invitation, I joined him at his compadre's new house construction party. Again, people took amused advantage of my 6' 2" frame and had me spend two days passing materials up to the roofers. In the course of the work and the celebration that followed, I fell in with a rowdy group of men, return migrants from Quito who now spent their time weaving. They made sure I was offered *chicha,* beer, Coca-Cola, and *trago* (a rough, bootleg alcohol) from each passing server and pushed me along with them as they danced the rough terrain of the construction site into the smooth floors of a new home.

The day after this third *minga* and the festivities of the new house party, both Galo and Monica came and stood before me asking to have a little talk. Their somber expressions alarmed me. The thoughts rushed through my head: "Oh no, I went too far. I blew it with all that partying; I knew they don't like drinking. They don't want some drunken *gringo* getting mixed up with their work here." Galo spoke, "My Monica and I have discussed it and we think you should no longer pay rent in our house."

"Oh God," I thought again, "they are kicking me out." Then I realized that the opposite was happening. They wanted me to live with them rent-free, as if I were a member of the family. In fact, such an arrangement would be far more costly than paying for my lodging. I now incurred lasting, unspecified obligations to them. Nonetheless, their offer made me happy. I had moved a little closer to fitting in with at least this family.

Anthropologists have recorded the heroic, mundane, and bizarre ways they have gained acceptance in their research communities. In perhaps the most famous account, Clifford Geertz (1973) describes bolting from the police along with other spectators at a Balinese cockfight. His flight signaled fellowship with the villagers and paved the way to more sympathetic treatment. In the Andes, many ethnographers have drunk their way past barriers of community suspicion. By trading shots of *trago,* they slowly shake the aloofness associated with foreigners. Describing her own anguished efforts to join in the Peruvian social world of Chuschi, Billie Jean Isbell reveals how much anthropologists are willing to put up with to be treated as equals. She writes (1978: 6) about visiting a funeral and uncertainly joining in the drinking along with two colleagues, Bill Isbell and Tom Meyers. Following the lead of an old man, the three of them drank shots of kerosene, mistakenly offered in the place of alcohol. When another woman was offered the fuel, she realized the error. She put an end to the nonsense, shouting at the old man for grabbing the wrong bottle and joking with Billie Jean Isbell for drinking kerosene. The North Americans' blind commitment to ritual form, though, advanced their effort to join community life. After receiving real shots of alcohol, they participated in the rest of the gathering and became regular visitors at future rituals.

Around Otavalo, drinking communally, becoming a compadre, and learning how to speak *Runa Shimi* (the people's language, Quichua) all helped to legitimize my presence in the community. Indeed, many people who speak Spanish and Quichua fluently prefer to talk to me in my bad Quichua. In conversations, they forsake better comprehension for the solidarity that the native language affords. Yet, for all the importance of language and fiestas, I find that the physical labor I did with people still makes the greatest difference when it comes to describing my connection with community members. People habitually refer to *mingas* that I have worked in when explaining my presence to others, with some calling me *ñuca minga gringo* (my *minga gringo*). Recounting my bond to her family, Monica always points out that I lived with them like a son before I married Chesca—sleeping, eating, stacking maize, and digging ditches with the family. In the long run, cut-up hands, muddy socks, and a dark band of sweat around the crown of a hat counts for a lot in creating a friendship.

Even in the era of international commercial travel, physical labor endures as a practical and symbolic feature of native life. For many, the work of *mingas* and *chagras* (cultivated plots) categorically divides indígenas from white-mestizos. The water project alone illustrates the burden Quichua speakers bear. With paid labor and back hoes, public health ministries have formalized and mechanized the tasks of tearing up the earth and laying pipes in urban Ecuador. In the countryside, though, water systems come down to the onerous, unpaid labor of indígenas, including those who have had exotic, international experiences.

◢ Deadheads and the Subsistence Ethic ◣

After yet another hiatus, work on the potable water project restarted in February of 1994. I had not been to such a multicommunity *minga* in almost three years and watched in amazement at some of the changes. In 1991, for example, people walked to the *minga* or caught the local bus; in 1994, dozens of people from other sectors drove up in their own pickup trucks. Many young women came dressed in bright, new blouses; some protected their shirts by wearing Patagonia sweatshirts. Young men attended in jeans and oversized button-down shirts, with their long, black hair worn in the new style of unbraided ponytails (down to the back of the knees in one teenager's case). Leaning on their shovels and picks, joking together, and checking out the women, these guys looked to me like trendy, Southern Californian undergraduate students on some kind of a cultural outing.

Indeed, the connection to U.S. fashion was not coincidental. I fell into conversation with one twenty-year-old man as we made our way from the meeting to the worksite. When he found out that I was from Los Angeles, he asked me whether I owned a car. His interest was not simply in my relative wealth. It turned out that he owned a van in Los Angeles and wanted to know where I had stored my vehicle. He and I shared a predicament; keeping a car is a constant problem when commuting between Ecuador and the United States for long stays. In fact, he had found a better solution than I had in having located a cheap storage place deep in the San Fernando Valley.

He later explained that he owned the van so he could tour with the Grateful Dead. Teaming up with a Guatemalan man, they sold crocheted hacky sacks and knitted sweaters to Deadheads. Business was pretty good, he confessed. After spending some time with his parents, helping out with the start of the maize harvest and representing their household at this *minga*, he planned to go back to California, load his van with more crafts and head out on tour again. Like many other wealthy dealers, his participation in *mingas* and the harvest would be short-lived. Later he would choose to pay fines rather than show up for work, and his parents would take in most of the maize by themselves. Yet, even his token effort came at price. The round-trip airfare, lost sales, and van-storage costs added up to a lot, not to mention the pants that were trashed and the shoes that were soiled in the pipe trenches that day.

Why bother? Two generations ago, rural resources offered a lot; a household could provide for most of its nutritional needs from its own fields. Now, a growing population, continued inequality in land distribution, and declining soil fertility make such self-sufficiency impossible. On the other hand, commercial success has become a real possibility. More and more people can earn high enough wages and profits to pay for what they want in the market. Under these circumstances, why invest labor and resources into ever smaller and more exhausted subsistence plots?

"The Indian must farm," Galo Ajala answered, when I put the question to him. "It is wrong to leave one's fields abandoned." Although he has been an enthusiastic merchant since the age of twelve, Galo's own loyalties are to his fields first. His priorities say a lot about the severe setbacks he has suffered in the textile markets. Were it not for the food that Monica and he raised, he would have been destitute after disastrous sales outings. His values, though, are not entirely idiosyncratic. Misfortune strikes in many forms in all occupations. Farmers watch their crops rot in the fields during wet years and whither during dry ones. Weavers forfeit profits and products to mechanized forms of production. Merchants lose their inventories to thieves. While many of the well-to-do have been able to overcome adversity, others who have worked diligently have not. Those who stay out of the textile trade can have it harder still as Ecuadorian labor markets, like all those in Andean Latin America, are "seasonal and erratic . . . marred by surplus labor and low wages" (de Janvry 1987: 402).

Coping with chronic economic insecurity, many households diversify their incomes and, most important, continue to farm. To be sure, agriculture's proportion of a household's income has declined steadily. In-the-field tasks now take up less than ten percent of the work week (see figure 1). Nonetheless, farming survives. Even as a younger generation tries to secure their advancement through new market niches in remote countries, some have painfully realized why their parents argue that "the Indian must farm" as part of "defending themselves." For the only thing certain about a profitable trade opportunity is that it will disappear. Some fade gradually with changing tastes. Others can collapse overnight, as my LA-based friend found out when Jerry García died and the Grateful Dead broke up.

Amid this instability, even the prosperous Otavaleños' worldview is grounded in a "subsistence ethic" (Scott 1976)—an obligation to utilize one's fields, help those who would help you, and be prepared to sacrifice earnings to insure the long-term economic security of the household.[1] In the effort to sustain a collective commitment (primarily at the immediate family level) to economic security, agriculture's importance goes beyond the stored sacks of grain, which cushion against lean economic times. The physical labor and rough implements of a rural hearth serve as an idiom of indigenous life and suffering. This idiom turns on the word *yanga*. Combining ideas of risk, poverty, and futility, *yanga* can mean *useless, in vain, worthless,* or *humble.*[2] Otavaleños use the word to contrast the expectations of indigenous people with those of dominant mestizo society. Many speak of their own language (*yanga shimi*), their core possessions (*yanga cosas*), and rural life (*yanga kawsay*) as being humble and worthless.

In so doing, members of this most prosperous of Ecuador's highland ethnic groups underscore their relative weakness within national society.[3] In such circumstances, the need to safeguard their subsistence security in an often racist economy becomes a cultural imperative, a defining obligation. Such an ethic is rooted in the practices of peasant farming. However, it differs from James Scott's (1976) characterization of a peasant moral economy that accepts a meager standard of living while mitigating significant economic inequality within the community of peasant producers. For most Otavaleños, a security ethic does not preclude making profits. It is neither a broad

1. The social, political, and economic significance of subsistence security in peasant society is a well-researched topic. A. V. Chayanov (1966) explained social differentiation in terms of peasant strategies that balanced subsistence resources with household consumer/worker ratios. Other researchers have argued that risk aversion figures highly in a peasant household's daily decisions as well as in long-term strategies (cf. Halperin and Dow 1977; Johnson 1971). In the Andes, cultural ecologists show how farmers frequently minimize risk by diversifying crops to exploit vertically arranged microclimates (a vertical archipelago of ecological niches [Murra 1972]), either with household labor or by building reciprocal relations among households (Masuda et al 1985; cf. Knapp 1991 for a critique based on the Ecuadorian case). The reliance on social ties to survive a bad-crop year raises an essential point. The pursuit of subsistence security is not just an economic strategy. It is, as James Scott (1976; 1986) argues, a moral ethic.

2. In their pedagogical grammar of Imbabura Quichua, Carmen Chuquín and Frank Salomon (1992) define *yanga* as "simple, simply, humble, ordinary, in vain."

3. Rainer Lutz Bauer (1992) offers an interesting comparative case in his description of Spanish Galicia. He describes how mountain peasants often portray themselves as marginal, degraded, and disadvantaged to powerful outsiders as part of developing their place within a centralizing nation-state.

cultural ideal of "shared poverty" (Wolf 1957) nor an Image of the Limited Good (Foster 1965). I met no Otavaleño who believed that one family's material success—if gained through hard work—threatened the livelihood of the community. Rather, Otavaleños try to balance agriculture and subsistence security with their drive to accumulate wealth. In the pages that follow, I describe how farming has evolved in the latter half of the twentieth century. Focusing on the lives of Santo Conejo's family, I trace the factors—from parental pressure to economic need to symbolic power of everyday goods— that make subsistence agriculture a vital element of Otavalo culture.

◢ The Politics of Household Farming ◣

Chapter 2 described how the rural home in the 1940s was an engine of subsistence production. Households built the technology of food preparation and textile manufacture into their *corredors* (open porches) and interiors. Grindstones, hearths, spinning wheels, and backstrap looms all fit into well-worn nooks within the house. According to Santo, the cultivation and preparation of grains not only dominated domestic space but time as well. Households had comparatively more land and grew a wider variety of foods. Santo told me that his father, Manuel Conejo, grew up in a household that extensively diversified its crops. For grains, they planted maize, wheat, and barley as well as three or four varieties of *quinua*, a native Andean cultigen. Further, in the household's upper holdings, they cultivated three types of tubers: potato, *oca*, and *milloco*. Rounding out their basic food, they intercropped their maize fields with beans, *habas* (fava beans), and *zambo*, a type of squash (drawing 11). All together, Manuel calculated his father and mother sowed twenty-two different crops, in addition to plants used as medicines and condiments.

The greater range of crops demanded regular visits to the fields. Using a precise, hand-drawn chart he made for my benefit, Santo explained how much work a rich diet required. Throughout July, August, and September, families plowed, leveled, and carved their soil into furrows in anticipation of the rains that arrived by the end of September. Planting began with the onset of the wet months and continued through December, when some crops required a first round of weeding. While the demands of farming slackened in January, they picked up in February when the first beans, aptly called *frijol matahambre* (hunger-killing beans), matured and could be harvested. In some years fresh maize could be gathered starting in early March, with the bulk of the harvest coming in April and May depending on how much moisture people wanted in the kernel at the moment of

Drawing 11: Intercropped Cornfield

picking. In June, households stripped their fields of cornstalks and put in a crop of peas before preparing the fields later in the summer for the next maize planting.

This general seasonal schedule often had to be adjusted to accommodate changing rainfall and the idiosyncrasies of the microclimates of individual fields. Maize planted up high, for example, ripened at slower rates than the plants grown at lower levels—unless it lay in some level basins near the upper *quebrada,* where maize seemed to grow at rates approaching crops planted down nearer the river. Faced with these variations, subsistence production, while conforming to a general pattern, differed from house to house.

Likewise, the transmission of land from parents to children varied according to family. As a general practice, Otavaleños followed principles of partible inheritance. Men and women retained separate ownership of their land and passed on an equal portion to each of their children. Even long-married couples identified each field by the spouse who owned it. Determining inheritance according to their own formulas of equity and affection, most people stuck reasonably closely to the norm and endowed their children with relatively equal shares.

Nonetheless, stories abound in Ariasucu of omissions, conflicts, and eccentricities in the passing of land from one generation to the other. In the upper community, for example, one woman inherited all the land of an old widower whom she cared for after that man's two children moved away and rarely visited. Conversely, Miguel Cando, who is universally known by his nickname "Chevrolet" and is one of the community's more successful textile entrepreneurs (see chapter 5), inherited no land. His own parents had several children and little land, so they gave Chevrolet away as an infant to a more prosperous neighbor.[4] The adoptive parents cared for him but reserved their fields for their other children. The stigma of being landless still haunts Chevrolet even as he has bought many parcels throughout the community. I find that half my conversations with him come back to discussions of who is selling what parcel and for how much.

In short, at midcentury, subsistence agriculture was a highly particular activity. People planted according to their tastes, cultivated to meet the needs of their parcels, and disposed of their land in step with filial duties and sibling rivalries.

The state set about to change all that. The ideology of national development placed a premium on rationalizing farm production. Streamlining agriculture became a central part of the effort to transform the indigenous population. In 1937, the government lay the cornerstone of this program with the Law of Communes and Statute of Jurisdiction of Peasant Communities. The law embodies three key political and economic principles informing state policy. First,

4. See Weismantel (1995) for an analysis of adoptions in rural Ecuador and how inequalities of generation and class shape these practices.

rather than acknowledge the cultural and social differences among indigenous peoples, the legislation homogenized the *sierra*'s disparate groups within a single rural class of peasants (Iturralde 1984). Second, it sought to circumvent the old elites by making the local community the smallest cell of a linear power structure passing from the community to the canton to the province to the national government (Villavicencio Rivadeneira 1973; Becker, forthcoming). Third, the law moved toward synthesizing collective units of production out of scattered indigenous households. Article 3 of the statute explicitly stated this goal: "the public power will adopt the necessary measures in order to transform the communities into production cooperatives" (1937 Law of Communes, my translation). Thus, by setting legal limits on territories, granting communal rights to land, and certifying locally chosen leaders, the state tried to replace household farming with modern collective production (Almeida Vinueza 1981: 218).

Indigenous communities largely ignored these efforts. By the early 1970s, three decades after the Law of Communes was enacted, only about half of the *parcialidades* (35 of 69) in the cantón had registered their councils (Villavicencio Rivadeneira 1973: 149). Further, few of the communities that did sign up actually moved toward collectivizing individual peasant holdings. Consequently, to renew the drive for efficient production, the national legislature passed new measures that sought "to modernize the social relations of production in agriculture" (Almeida Vinueza 1981: 220). As the *Ley de Cooperativas* (Law of Co-operatives) puts it, "the current moment in the world impels peoples to obtain a peaceful structural transformation" in which "cooperativism is . . . the suitable system to achieve these structural changes in an orderly and democratic form, as our country desires" (the Law of Co-operatives, 1978: 3, as cited in Almeida Vinueza 1981: 220, note 111, my translation).

Enticed by financial incentives that accompanied cooperative formation, some residents in upper Agato and Ariasucu finally formed an agricultural association in 1980 named *Los Incas*. In the early years the *socios* (the association's partners) secured funding for constructing two buildings and laying in a water line. Later, in the 1990s, they received two grants worth 1,443,000 sucres (approximately U.S. $1,000) to try the commercial production of potatoes, wheat, and barley. While only four or five of Ariasucu's households joined *Los Incas*, the whole neighborhood backed the co-op at first. In their unceasing effort to get water, the community sent out *mingas* to bury pipe from a high spring down to the association's buildings and then on down to upper Ariasucu. After getting the water, though, residents turned their back on cooperative efforts.

Indeed, Ariasucu has worked actively to bar centralized councils and associations of any kind from their neighborhood. Throughout the 1980s, the sector's unofficial council struggled to keep the leaders from neighboring Agato and La Compañia from asserting jurisdiction over their area. Instead of going to the Ministry of Agriculture for official state recognition of their independence from the larger sectors, the council went to the Federation of Indigenous People and Peasants of Imbabura (FICI) in order to document the limits of other jurisdictions. After bickering for years, representatives from Ariasucu, La Compañia, and Agato finally resolved their arguments about boundaries by adopting the route of the Coca-Cola delivery truck as territorial limits. Rather than assume the official mantle of "*comuna*" (official peasant community) within a "peacefully transformed national structure," Ariasucu combined the authority of a radical peasant federation with the distribution routes of a transnational beverage corporation to create an area of relative autonomy.

Beyond demonstrating the factionalism in rural society, these political maneuvers reveal an active commitment to independent, small-hold farming. Through legislation, financial incentives, and technical support, the state has pushed cooperative farming for decades. Yet sixty years later, native peasants around Otavalo still farm at the household level. Certainly, some people have contributed parcels to associations and taken advantage of government incentives. The majority, though, keep control of their own productive resources. Rejecting state models for national rural development, Otavaleño peasants manage their fields to fit their own model of economic advancement. In an economy of textile production and wage labor, people value farming as a (relatively) stable income independent of market forces.

The history of community resistance to national cooperative farming initiatives illustrates an important point about the *ethic* of subsistence production. As Eric Wolf (1986), William Roseberry (1989), and others have noted, it is not a timeless, peasant mentality but a cultural response to ongoing disparities in power. Wolf (1955, 1957) highlighted the role of external political pressure in his descriptions of closed corporate peasant communities. According to his analysis, society must be divided, with the peasantry institutionally cut off from both political power and the opportunity to accumulate wealth, in order to push communities to focus predominantly on their subsistence base. While modern Otavaleño *parcialidades* exhibit few of the characteristics of a closed corporate community,[5] they still suffer the disadvantages of subordinate political status in a dualized society. State attempts to have peasants collectivize their farming resources amount to one more threat to Otavaleños' ability "to defend themselves with their own work." In the complex Otavaleño economy, though, government policy ranks a distant second to uncertain markets as a cause of unpredictable income and the need for economic defense.

◢ Farming as a (Minimized) Hedge ◣

The problem of "laboring-in-vain" besets any Otavaleño. Rich merchants swap stories about flying to Amsterdam with handicrafts, only to have their inventory confiscated by customs agents at their first border crossing. Local vendors can spend days at their stalls in the market without selling a thing. Every textile dealer I met had a tale of a deal gone bad, an inventory stolen, or a trip that lost them money. Others have it worse. Straining under heavy loads, poor market porters can work every Saturday market for a year and still not earn enough for a second cow for the yoke or a new poncho for a wedding. Lumped together, the wage work undertaken by Ariasucu residents reads as a catalog of *yanga trabaju* (fruitless work). Whether ruinous deal or chronic low wages, economic misfortune causes rich and poor to work to hone defensive strategies, as I learned when recording the careers of people like Santo Conejo and his wife Maria Cando.

Despite the setbacks of their young lives, Santo and Maria remain an energetic couple. Having inherited his mother's small build and his father's solid features, Santo is a handsome and agile man who learns new tasks with ease. Maria complements him. She is the same height as her husband and seems more powerful than he when she straps bundles of food and a child to her back. In conversations, her dark eyes track Santo, and she matches his joking extroversion with an observant, smiling shyness. She, like he, is an only child. Her father died when she was a young girl, and she grew up with her mother on the other side of the gully from Santo in the house they continue to live in.

The two of them have tried several schemes to become an "advanced" (materially prosperous) couple. Santo was one of the original weavers to hire young teenagers to work with him to make *fajas*

5. Indeed, few peasant communities exhibit the egalitarian, antiaccumulation characteristics of the closed corporate model, as Wolf (1986) himself has acknowledged.

(belts). At one time he had four looms in production and started to accumulate building materials for a new house. A wealthier weaver then lured his workers away and a surge in *faja* production depressed prices and his earnings. As *faja*-weaving profits dried up and his interest waned, Santo went to work for his neighbor "Chevrolet" to sell sweaters, a job that benefitted the wealthy Chevrolet more than it did Santo. Aside from his business activities, he also participated avidly in local development projects. In the late 1980s and early 1990s, he struggled into openings in several government-sponsored training courses. Inevitably, however, the programs collapsed when funding vanished and promised jobs never appeared.

As Santo shifted from one activity to the next because of boredom or bad pay, Maria adapted to the new schemes. When they had extra workers, she cooked extra food. When the workers left, Maria tried to pick up weaving, joining about a dozen other women in the sector to become the first generation of adult women to sit in looms. She soon gave it up when the demands of caring for their four kids and cooking meals kept her from producing as much as one *faja* in a day. When Santo wove ponchos with his father, Maria found herself spending more time on the other side of the gully with his parents, Antuca and Manuel, at their house to brush and assemble the final product. Unlike many other women her age, she has little hope for starting her own handicraft business because she speaks only Quichua.

In describing many of these failed ventures, Santo uses the word *yanga*. For example, in reference to a sales trip that ended in a loss for him, he would say *"yangata rircani"* (I went in vain). Speaking of his ongoing efforts to weave alone after his workers had left, he said *"yangata awajuni"* (I am weaving in vain). Similarly, he dismissed the government program that trained him to be a water inspector as *yanga trabaju* (wasted work). In these instances, *yanga* (or its adverbial form *yangata*) refers to effort spent fruitlessly—time and resources invested with no tangible result. The steady stream of *yanga trabaju* has often caused Santo and Maria's lives to shrink back to the hearths and fields of their parents.

Santo, however, dedicates himself to farming for positive as well as negative reasons. His parents have more land than many families in the sector. Between the fields ceded to Santo by his parents and the parcels held separately by Maria, they can meet almost all their food needs—a rarity in Ariasucu. In 1993, for example Santo and Maria planted four large plots, ranging in size from 1500 to 2400 square meters, with maize, beans, and *zambo*. Santo also worked with his

parents in several of their fields and shared in a harvest of *oca* and
quinua. With such land at his disposal, Santo can pawn a few of his
fields to raise money, as he did for his wedding in that year, and still
have enough to provide for his household. After the marriage celebration exhausted their finances, he and Maria lived off their own crops
through the hungry months of the late rainy season without going to
buy potatoes in the Otavalo market.

In a community where young couples now farm three or four strips
of land, some no more than three meters wide, many envy Santo and
Maria. Not only do they have access to much land, but as only children, they will inherit it all from their parents. With all their fields,
Santo and Maria cultivate a wide variety of crops, much as Santo's
grandparents did decades earlier. Not surprisingly, it was Santo who
pushed me to incorporate more information about older farming
practices in my research. Developing additional interviews with his
father and some compadres, he conceived of and executed an elaborate table showing crops and their seasonal requirements. Few of his
contemporaries would care about such things.

With little land and a growing interest in purchased commodities, most younger households streamline the agricultural schedule,
squeezing down the time spent on farm tasks and food preparation to
make room for commercial work. To simplify seasonal demands on
labor, people have cut back on the number of crops they grow. Maize,
always the dominant cultigen, has become even more popular. Although men and women must devote more time to weeding and harvesting maize than other grains, they process it quickly and prepare
it more easily for eating. *Quinua*, meanwhile, fades from the fields.
The time-consuming process of washing the bitter husk from the
grain dooms this crop to a marginal place in the diet. All totaled, respondents identified eight other crops, from wheat to *oca*, that have
been dropped or sharply cut back because people no longer think they
are worth the effort.

Along with simplifying crop plans, households also minimize cash
investments in subsistence production in order to make farming
worthwhile. The majority of households prepare the soil with cattle-
drawn plows and clod-busters (drawing 12), weed with plows and
hoes, and harvest by hand, saving money by relying on animal and
human muscle power. With these tools and techniques, growing
one's own food still means getting dirty, sore, and tired. Further,
except for the few families (about ten out of 135) with a field planted
entirely in potatoes, most used no chemical insecticides or ferti-
lizers. People went from one year to the next without spending

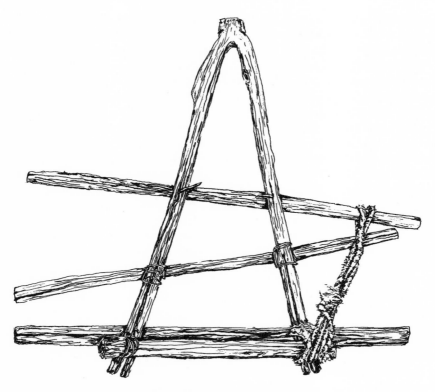

Drawing 12: Wooden Frame Used to Break up Soil Clods

anything on agricultural production except to replace a worn hoe or a forgotten sickle left behind among the stubble when the harvesters gathered up the sheaths of barley and headed home.

In the interest of saving further time, however, spending on farming has changed. In 1992, an Ariasucu family purchased a long-neglected field in the highest part of the community. Facing a week's worth of hard work of breaking up the rock-hard soil with picks, the new owners hired a tractor and harrow. In just two hours, the harrow's jagged steel disks churned the weeds and small bushes back into the gray soil, leaving a serviceable plot for the coming planting. (Renting a tractor to disk the soil had already become a common practice in the richer weaving communities near Otavalo.) Within just two years, almost one house in five had adopted the practice of using a tractor for at least some of their plowing. By spending 30,000 to 45,000 sucres per field ($15 to $22.50) a household can take care of a day's work in an hour and avoid the complications and future obligations caused by borrowing another household's cattle team.[6]

The wealthiest families have still other ways of getting crops from their fields with a minimum of their own labor. Many rely on an impoverished compadre. A rich merchant, for example, will agree to baptize the child of a destitute market porter or in some cases become godparent to an *upa* (literally someone who is a mute, a term used to refer to those who suffer cretinism or some form of mild mental retardation). These poorer compadres or godchildren usually join in with their *padrinos* (patrons) for all field tasks. At harvest time, sturdy and stooped *upas* can be seen following the household back from the field with the heaviest load of cornstalks on their backs. Absent merchants, who reside primarily in distant towns, also turn more and more to sharecropping. A young couple, not yet in possession of a house, may move into the merchant's empty home and farm their fields, splitting the yield. Even relatively well-off people, like Monica Quilla, have begun to farm others' land. When I visited in July of 1996, she told me she had peas growing on two fields of absentee landowners and would divide the crop equally with them. Through arrangements like these, richer households forsake farming, if not yet their fields.

Few with land in suburban sectors like Ariasucu have totally given up agriculture, though. Even those who think farming wastes their time can be found out in their fields. Santo told me that some men his age continue to farm, because "they are afraid." They do not want to risk angering their parents or losing part or all of their inheritance by stopping the cultivation of their fields. Santo knows this pressure too well. In 1994, provincial officials finally offered him a position he had trained for, as a caretaker for the water project. The job required moving to a community about four kilometers away. Santo wanted his father's support for accepting this job that he had long sought. One morning as they wove together in Manuel's *corredor* he tried to draw his father into the conversation about it by asking him what the legal minimum monthly wage was. Manuel said nothing. After asking another question about municipal work and still getting only stony silence, Santo dropped the subject and never pursued the job.

6. While the tractors do represent the partial commoditization of household farming, all the families who did hire tractors went on to plant, weed, and harvest by hand using the unpaid labor of the household or the family network. And, none of the food was grown as a cash crop.

In cases like this, parental sanctions can reinforce subsistence agriculture even when children are seeking ways to cut back further on
their farm work.

◢ *Yanga cosas* and the Power of Worthless Goods ◣

Santo sacrificed his best chance at a steady job in order to fulfill his
obligations to his parents and their land. While not as dramatic, others also give up time and earnings to farm. Even the well-off, who
depend on poorer compadres to cultivate their fields still make special trips home to plant, harvest, or stack cornstalks. For an activity
that takes up comparatively little time, farming exerts a great influence over schedules, the organization of gender roles, and formation
of collective identities. The demands of subsistence production exert
themselves in subtle and continual ways. Everything from the green
shoots of a new maize crop to a father's scornful look urge people to
assume their agrarian responsibilities. The most consistent remind-
ers of subsistence work—and its meager rewards—lie in the world of
domestic goods. Santo and Maria's household spaces illustrate the
social power of humble things.[7]

The couple keeps most of their possessions at Maria's mother's
house, where they sleep. Often, though, when Santo needs a special
farm tool, weaving implement, fiesta costume, or musical instrument he walks over to the other side of the gully to his parent's
house. Antuca and Manuel live in a solid adobe home built over a
half-century ago by Antuca's father. The *tulpa* (hearth) has been re-
located so many times both in the interior and the *corredor* that the
walls have been smoked black (drawing 13). Inside, ragged cobwebs
sag darkly from the treadle loom pulleys, old guitars, tethers, corn-
cobs, baskets, masks, hats, saws, and pot lids that hang suspended in
the rafters. In the gloom below, light from the door picks out parts
of a spinning wheel, ladder rungs, empty bottles, and soda crates. A
faint, eye-stinging, ammonia smell of guinea pig urine fills the air.
Entering the room sends the animals squeaking across the floor into
deeper shadows. I visit this house with Santo often. The only way I
manage to navigate the darkness is to seek out the glowing coals of
Antuca's cooking fire and inch toward it.

When I used photographs to interview people about objects like
those found in Antuca and Manuel's house, respondents often sorted

---

7. In this analysis, I draw upon the work of Douglas and Isherwood (1979) who assert
that the cultural importance of things lies in the way they make cultural categories real.
With goods, "people generate culture" as Douglas later stated more boldly (1992).

things according to gender. On the female side, people lined up axes
(used to split wood for cooking fires), pots, and stoves. Food preparation distinguishes a woman's primary work from men's; and women
present themselves in kitchens, *corredors*, and patios through the
sieves, *bateas* (wooden bowls), grindstones, and mills needed to sift,
clean, and cook raw grains. In the fields, women's efforts outpace the
men's, mainly because of their hoe-work, their time spent weeding
and mounding earth around growing maize plants (figure 4).

On the male side, people placed shovels, picks, plows, looms,

Drawing 13: *Tulpa* (open hearth)

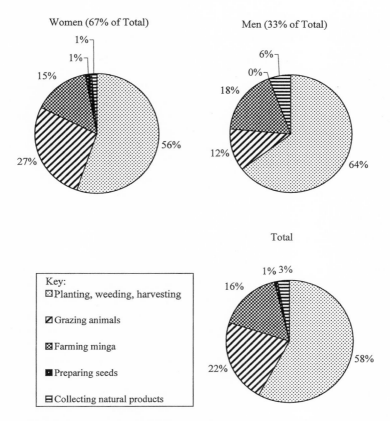

Figure 4: Percentage of agricultural time allocated among top five activities, Ariasucu, February–November, 1994. (Total agricultural observations = 306.)

warping frames, and other weaving tools. Domestically, men's work is a world of woven cloth. Respondents credited the loom especially as *jaripac valen* (suitable for men). One man put it this way when pulling the image of the loom from the stack of photos: "with this one works. We eat. It is the indigenous man's tool."[8]

As both Mary Weismantel (1988) and Catherine Allen (1988) have discussed for other Andean cases, the association of an object with

8. People volunteered these insights about gender. In the interview, I asked people to tell me what items a young couple needed to set up their own household. That respondents added whether an object served for men or women suggested the importance of the connection in their minds.

one gender does not preclude someone of the other gender from using it. In Otavalo, women can and do bear down on a plow blade and drive oxen through rows of maize seedlings. Similarly, men stand over gas stoves, stirring up toasting maize in an oiled frying pan with callused fingertips. Indeed, gas stoves, grain mills, and other newer appliances facilitate gender crossover in tasks. On occasion, a teenage boy will crack barley in a hand-cranked grain mill to help his mother. And many teenage girls have tried their hand at *faja*-weaving on treadle looms. However, in homes dependent on older technology—grind-stones, open hearths, or backstrap looms—I saw neither men cook-ing nor women weaving. These things may be low-tech, but they re-quire practiced hands and invite less involvement from the opposite gender—as the cholera deaths of men in older, *tulpa*-centered houses illustrated. The power of older goods to maintain a clearly gendered world may help explain why Manuel and Antuca's house remains so old-fashioned.

Antuca is a slight woman who is always in motion. Even in con-versation, she is intensely animate. Attending speakers with highly arched brows and deliberate nods, she strains to catch every word. Often her expression collapses into a smile amplified by deep lines around her eyes or puckers into concern upon hearing of her grand-children's misdeeds.

She has lived her life in the shadow of tricky, occasionally danger-ous men. As a young woman, she inherited the nickname of her fa-ther, a leader of the neighborhood in his day, and now few people remember her christened name. The second of four daughters, she married last. According to Santo, she might not have wedded at all. However, her younger sister had married and brought into the house a man named Ramon who was so abusive that the whole family lived in fear of him. Antuca then married Manuel, ten years her junior to secure some protection. Manuel delivered. He is a broad-shouldered man who shuffles through his daily tasks in a deliberate pigeon-toed gait. One morning Ramon returned to the house drunk, refused to tie up the oxen to plow the field, pushed around his protesting in-laws, and beat his wife. Manuel stepped in, hitting him with the back of an ax. Santo reported that after Ramon regained consciousness, he toned down his aggression.

After Santo was born, relations between Antuca and Manuel wors-ened. Although she helped assemble and clean up the ponchos and shawls that came off his loom, he rarely divided his money with her. Needing cash to buy salt, cooking fat, and other basics, she began to sell *trago* (cane liquor), *dulce* (course brown sugar), sodas, and some other necessities out of her house. With her earnings, she covered all the cash costs entailed in the daily running of the household.

Over the years, their marriage has reached equilibrium. Manuel spends his time working the fields for the household and his back-strap loom for himself (drawing 14). Antuca processes their grains on

Drawing 14: Backstrap Loom

a pockmarked old grindstone and cooks for Manuel as well as her son
and grandchildren if they are around. While she spends money from
the store on replenishing her inventory and provisioning the household, she has never put her profits toward a gas stove, grain mill, or
electric blender. Whether intentional or not, she has reinforced the
gendered complementarity—not interchangeability—of her home.
With her old wares, she has kept the men in her life at bay.

   Simple hearths, blackened cooking pots, looms, and plows more
than organize gender roles. They symbolize rural austerity. For many
Otavaleños, bad jobs coupled with subsistence farming means getting by with less. Most households rely on a limited collection of
goods they call *yanga cosas*, humble things. Indeed, when asked
about the material requirements of a home, my respondents exagger-
ated the simplicity of rural needs. Items such as *fundus* (clay water
storage jugs) and *uchurumis* (chili-pepper grindstones [drawing 15])
appeared at the top of a hypothetical list of necessities (table 2). Even
young people told me that a recently married couple needed just an
open hearth, a couple of pots, a few farm tools, a water jug, and a loom
in order to start their life together. With such equipment, they live
"shuc wajcha kawsai"—"an orphan's life," according to one informant. They would be cut off from advancement but able to get by.

Drawing 15: Chili-pepper Grindstone

Table 2. Ranking of Basic Necessities, June 1994

	Objects	
Rank	Women's Choices	Men's Choices
1	Hearth	Hearth
2	Gas stove	Utensils
3	Utensils	Gas stove (tie)
		Cauldrons (tie)
4	Cauldrons	
5	Water jugs	Water jugs
6	Grain mill	Bed
7	Aji stone	Aji stone
8	Clay jug	Loom
9	Sewing machine	Shovel, pick
10	Bed (tie)	Grain mill
	Loom (tie)	
11		Stereo/boom box

Consumer electronics, on the other hand, came near the bottom of a supposed list of key domestic objects. Santo clarified this point for me when talking about modern appliances. "To get these items [gas stove, sewing machine, and radio] it is hard. One really has to work. One has to get money." Of owning a blender, he said, "now the couple is advanced. They have other equipment in the house. They no longer eat like before; they eat like mestizos" (drawing 16). He points out a widely shared belief that indígenas must toil long and hard before gaining the material comforts of the white-mestizo world. In reality, young couples have treated such appliances as basic necessities. Ariasucu residents own more radios than *uchurumis* and more televisions than clay water jugs (table 3). The prosperity of the textile economy has filtered through to poorer families in marginal sectors like Ariasucu. Nonetheless, people persist in believing that a genuine, *Runa* (indigenous Andean) agrarian life operates through simple goods, not consumer electronics.

Comments distinguishing the "advanced life" from the "orphan's life" of humble goods reveal another meaning for the phrase *"yanga cosas."* More than "simple things," they are thought to be "worthless things." Peasants wear out their core possessions, consuming every ounce of value as they break things, fix them, and put them to new uses. *Bateas*, for example, are wide shallow wooden dishes. Women use them to sift and clean barley, to hold a batch of beans prior to cooking, to feed their chickens, or to assist with countless other

Drawing 16: Electric Blender

Table 3. Most Commonly Found Goods in Thirty-Two
Ariasucu Homes, September 1994

Rank	Object	Percentage of Sample
1	Water jugs	97
2	Hearth	94
3 (tie)	Stool, loom	91
5 (tie)	Blankets, covers	88
7	Gas stove	84
8 (tie)	Pick, table	81
10 (tie)	Spinning wheel, radio, warp frame, batea, tub, plow	78
16 (tie)	Aji stone, hoe, chest	75
19 (tie)	Grain mill, mat, shovel, bed	72
23 (tie)	Grain sifter, yoke, ax	66
26 (tie)	Sieve, food basket	63
28 (tie)	Cauldron, carrying basket	59
30	Television	56

chores. Cracked and chipped, many *bateas* have been repaired with tin strips again and again (drawing 17). While their market value disappears, their use value persists as people find ways to repair and coax more service out of them.[9]

In fact, Marx's (1976: 126) notion of "use value"—the "usefulness of a thing"—is too utilitarian a concept for the significance of these objects; it fails to capture the sense of awareness (and perhaps critique) embedded in the peasants' words. By using the term *yanga*, people define an object not just in terms of its immediate use or overuse, but to its lost economic potential. Strictly speaking, in Quichua the adjective *"mawka"* means worn out or tattered from use. By calling their goods *yanga cosas* (worthless things) instead of *mawka cosas* (worn things), indigenous people call attention to circumscribed economic power, not wear and tear. "Worthless things"— both the words and objects—keep directing attention back to exchanges that cannot take place. In this sense, *yanga cosas* are akin to *yanga trabaju:* capable of producing much, both native objects and labor often return little in the wider economy.

In the course of fieldwork, the stigma of *yanga cosas* humbled my own work. People saw little point in dwelling on the history of their basic household possessions. Many thought I wasted my time asking about them. I once interviewed an indigenous activist from a peasant community on the other side of Lake San Pablo. He regaled me with stories of confrontations with *hacienda* owners, provincial authorities, even the Pope.[10] He then asked me what I had been working on. When I showed him my drawings and tables of household possessions, he laughed. He could not believe I occupied myself with such obvious stuff. My sketchbook filled with careful studies of these objects especially amused him and others. Many could not understand why I devoted skilled effort to these banal things. When I showed the sketches, viewers would chuckle, *"chistosa . . . yanga cosas"*

9. Kopytoff (1986: 74–75) discusses how some goods never make it to the realm of commodities because people consider them utterly unworthy of exchange. They are priceless, not because of their fantastic value, but because they are "of so little worth as to have no publicly recognized exchange value." *Yanga cosas* are similarly "uniquely worthless."

10. He had been a member of a national indigenous political organization (CONAIE) in the 1980s. The Pope came to Ecuador and as part of his trip held a mass for tens of thousands of indígenas in Latacunga, Cotopaxi. After the Pope spoke of five hundred years of evangelization, my friend got up and talked of five hundred years of oppression, poverty, and struggle. He said he received three hundred letters criticizing him for what he said and another five hundred supporting him.

Drawing 17: Repaired *Batea*

("how funny . . . worthless things"). Their comments referred ambiguously to the figures in the drawings and to the drawings themselves. Through these reactions, I learned that a *yanga cosa* did not have to be beaten up and old. It could represent a lot of careful effort and yet could still be rendered worthless in the absence of shared values, knowledge, or interests.

Even the most important instrument of indigenous life—the Quichua language—suffers the taint of *yanga*-ness. Otavaleños frequently refer to their native tongue as *"yanga shimi"* rather than *runa shimi*. Like a plow or hearth, Quichua sustains the creative life within a rural sector, yet carries little force outside it. Not taught in schools (until recent efforts at bilingual education), shut out from high-waged sectors of the economy, and with little access to modern communication media, Quichua does not offer speakers an effective means of communication within the mainstream economy (cf. Mannheim 1991).

Many Otavaleños, therefore, see dependence on Quichua as a liability, despite the official ideologies of indigenous political leaders. Some married couples, especially returning migrants, have tried not to pass Quichua on to their children.[11] Believing that *runa shimi* impedes their children's chances of advancement, they speak Spanish at

11. D. Kulick (1992) records in detail the connection between negative cultural images and language shift in Papua New Guinea.

home, sometimes to just one of their children. One family went so far as to ask a neighbor to speak to their youngest son only in Spanish. The request prompted outrage among others. When Galo Ajala got wind of it, he practically shouted, "That's bad. The Indian (*el indio*) must speak *runa shimi*. To speak only Spanish is wrong." Despite Galo's and others' passionate defense of Quichua, I met an increasing number of young kids who spoke only Spanish.

All this talk of worthless things and a useless language makes it seem as if Otavaleños have taken the racist views of white-mestizo society to heart. Like the white-mestizo writer Zuniga mentioned in chapter 3, Otavaleños use the condition of their home and possessions to build an image of themselves. Also like Zuniga, that image dwells on the lowliness of rural culture. Yet for these similarities, *yanga* discourse differs from white-mestizo prejudice in one important way. Otavaleños emphasize class over race when discussing the fruitlessness of their lives.

◢ *Yanga Kawsay:* Fruitless Lives versus Clean Lives ◣

Otavaleños' understandings of the iniquities of Ecuadorian society became clearer for me during one especially grim *minga*. On that day, the engineer had asked Ariasucu *mingueros* to lay a water main along the *quebrada* that splits the community. Bordering the gully, the terrain bulged with rocks and broken boulders. As the morning wore on, tools wore out on immovable stones. Sharp corners of hoes folded over into scratched dog-ears. Pick heads loosened and twisted at the end of handles, occasionally flying off in potentially lethal curves through the workers. After four hours of work, people had managed only to scrape a shallow crooked groove into the ground.

To make matters worse, a light rain had been falling all day. Pausing from their bone-jarring work, men and women hunched under crude shawls of plastic sheets or old grain sacks to keep the water off. As they rested, they listened to the council wrangle over misspent funds. After lunch, work slowed even more. People were fed up. Here and there groups of men collected some money together and sent a delegate off to Antuca's house or some similar establishment to fetch a bottle filled with a cold filmy liquid. Over the rest of the afternoon, these *mingueros*—these gutsy entrepreneurs, delicate weavers, careful cooks, and soulful musicians—got drunk on bitter *trago*. Surveying this scene of wet, wasted bodies, quarreling leaders, and broken tools, the woman next to me said, "In the city they have water. They have a *limpiu kawsay* (a clean life). Here it is the *yanga kawsay* (humble/fruitless life)."

In this context, *yanga* takes on yet another shade of meaning.

The general notions of "labor-in-vain," "simple," and "worthless," become socially and historically specific. *Yanga* makes reference to lives that are discriminated against in the modern Ecuadorian nation-state. For all their hard work, urban experiences, and recent commercial successes, many Otavaleño lives still come down to wresting a crop from their fields and digging up the community with their own hands. This situation differs sharply from the advantages enjoyed by white-mestizo society. Many city-dwellers live a "clean life" of more active government support, contracted services, and piped water, not a muddy and "fruitless" existence.

While comments like the one by this woman allude to the hygienic racism discussed in the last chapter, native discourse does not fully adopt it. For rural Otavaleños, the structural opposition is transformed from clean life: dirty life (*limpiu kawsay: mapa kawsay*) to clean life: humble life (*limpiu kawsay: yanga kawsay*). The substitution of *yanga* for dirtiness in native racial schemes is important. It switches the emphasis from the supposed hygienic deficiencies of indígenas to the injustice of a racist economy. The words *yanga kawsay* draw attention to the dismissal of indigenous toil, the denial of worthiness of their bodies, goods, and knowledge. That is, for Quichua-speakers, the problem is not that people are unhealthy and dirty but that their labor is expended in vain. As much as they yearn to live well, they cannot succeed under the current conditions of Ecuadorian society.

In the 1990s, the image of the *yanga kawsay* best fits poor farmers who have few assets and little chance of material advancement. However, all indigenous people at risk of sudden changes of fortune, subject to discrimination, and periodically dependent on their land and family for subsistence likewise live a *yanga kawsay*. Drizzly, fruitless *mingas* periodically remind merchants of the hardships of farming life. For others, evidence of futility is more constant. Hearths, rickety treadle looms, and other patched-up possessions testify to the physical toll of peasant life.

◢ The Discursive Force of *Yanga Cosas* ◣

The point I am working up to is this: *yanga cosas* are more than either useful household implements or simple symbols of poverty. People use them in daily routines, not only for practical tasks, but also to foreground collective obligations and identities. Despite their relative economic worthlessness, the humble items of rural homes can act as interactional props that allow people to "[control] the settings in which people may show forth their potentialities and interact with others" (Wolf 1990: 586). The power vested in both old-fashioned household goods and "humble" discourse was on display the morning when Santo invited me to come by and film Manuel weaving at Antuca's and Manuel's home. By the time I arrived, two groups of drinkers patronized Antuca's *trago* business. The first included the infamous brother-in-law Ramon (no longer a resident of the house). He was drunk and his partner had passed out. In the second group, one woman held court. She was comadre Michaela and had come to celebrate Manuel's agreement to serve as the patron for Michaela's daughter's confirmation. At first, the little fiesta seemed awkward, more disruption than celebration.

Michaela was an outsider. Although raised in Ariasucu, she had spent most of the last decade living in Quito, selling handicrafts to the few tourists who visit the *Panecillo*, the statue of the Virgin in the middle of the city. Time away from home narrowed her social contacts, a problem compounded by her husband's erratic lifestyle. He moved constantly between Ariasucu and Quito. When in the city, he either tended their stall or tried to find a construction job. In Ariasucu, he hired himself out to work other people's looms and spent a lot of afternoons drinking with Manuel's brother Arturo, the new community president.

Selecting Manuel as a compadre, she was forging a link with one of Ariasucu's largest families. Manuel himself, however, seemed an odd choice for a woman who spends her life vending handicrafts. Rather than pick one of Ariasucu's successful merchants, she approached a man known for his backstrap weaving, drunkenness, and (relatively) large landholdings. He was the antithesis of modern Otavalo's savvy, textile entrepreneur. His somewhat stable agrarian way of life may have been just what attracted her, though. If so, she has company. Manuel has an unusually large number of compadres.

On the morning I visited, Santo wanted to make sure I got good footage of his father's backstrap techniques. To his annoyance, the presence of his father's new comadre distracted everyone. He had little interest in drinking with this woman, much less ratifying a new bond of *compadrazgo* with her. Dressed in his navy-blue sweatpants, a torn sweater, and with a folded T-shirt wrapped around his head, Santo came to help his father finish the blanket he was working on, not to socialize. As I took up my position with the camera in the pigpen next to his father's loom, Santo deliberately ignored Michaela and kept checking in with me. "Is it good? Is it good?" he would ask.

Michaela, however, tried to draw everyone into her party. She started with me. As I set up my camera, she yelled out *"kumpari"* (compadre) to me, purchased two bottles of Sprite from Antuca, and had me hand it out. (I am Santo's compadre and therefore potentially part of Michaela's social network.) After I finished my serving duties and retreated to a corner with my video camera, she continued to make sure that I drank each time she, Santo, or one of her companions got up to serve a round of shots. Her main interest, however, was not me but Santo. As I turned the camera back on, he had just slid a blanket segment on a pole, hung two fan-shaped brushes made from spiky seedpods on the wool fabric, and turned to consult with his father.

Michaela walked over, plucked a brush from the blanket and raked the surface of the dark blue textile. As her hand stuttered across the fabric, she called out, "We'll do this work, we have to brush this nap out very hard. Salud, *kumpari.*"

She addressed the second comment to Manuel to invite him to drink; the first to Santo, signaling she would not leave him alone. She stepped right into the middle of his work and narrated her actions, "This is the way. This is the way to brush it out . . . I did not learn this right now."

Like most people her age who grew up in Ariasucu, she probably had learned the task when she was a girl. With the blanket hanging there, she could demonstrate that she still had the skills of an indigenous woman. Santo eventually liberated the brushes from Michaela. In response, she pivoted around opposite him and pulled the blanket taut, making it easier for him. She pointed out that he needs to get the top edge and declared, "the two of us will brush this out, with godfather." She again referred to both Manuel (her daughter's soon-to-be confirmation godfather) and Santo during her statement, uniting the three of them in the same activity.

As Santo tried to brush, she told him what to do: "it still needs to be turned over," "to this side . . . from here . . . the side, the side." A second woman who had been serving shots of *trago*, passed by Michaela and returned the empty bottle to Antuca. She turned back and watched Michaela. A man who came with the two women also watched and spontaneously acted on Michaela's advice. He tried to flip the blanket over. Santo stopped him. "No, it's good, it's good," he protested.

While her own group continually affirmed Michaela's expertise, Santo did not. As the four of them physically struggle over whether to flip the corner of the blanket over, it became a medium for "constituting, i.e. establishing and negotiating, the social personae of those present" (Goodwin and Duranti 1992: 6). Holding the cloth down against the pole, Santo tried to limit people to what he considered were their appropriate roles. He acted as if Michaela was just a pestering client of his mother's *trago* shop, not a weaving expert. The contest for the blanket was part of the larger play for legitimacy in which Michaela was only partially successful at that moment.

Santo switched the focus from weaving back to an earlier topic. Michaela had been talking about her husband's unwillingness to work. Santo picked up a strand of that conversation and says, "He too wants shoes."

Michaela responded by laughing scornfully, "because he wants rice (an expensive white-mestizo dish), he wants us to walk around barefoot." (She was standing there with no shoes on). "He needs work . . ." she continued.

"Yes, that's the way it is," agreed the other man.

"We really need shoes. His work goes to *trago*. I go around so poorly," Michaela said.

Having failed to fully connect with Santo over the blanket, Michaela and he found another issue to talk about: lack of money. While Michaela complained about her husband, the others empathized, talking about men who drink too much. Eventually, they wandered back out to the outer edge of the patio. However, Santo continued to participate in the conversation and interjected the occasional "that is the way it is; that is it."

As the morning's events continued to unfold, Santo's resistance to Michaela's presence softened. Within an hour of the blanket-brushing he had become a willing accomplice in her effort to get everyone drunk, passing out two bottles of *trago* purchased by her in quick succession. Subsequent visits to this house strengthened the relationship. Three months later, when it came time for Manuel to attend confirmation classes with his new godchild, Santo accompanied him.

In making a connection with Manuel's and Santo's family, Michaela played up in both word and deed not just her Otavaleño weaving skills but also her poverty. She could have bought new *alpargatas* (espadrille sandals) with the money she spent on just the Sprite that I served, let alone all the cash that went to other drinks. However, by showing up without shoes on, brushing a blue wool blanket, and handing around sticky bottles of *trago*, she became more peasant than craft-seller and put herself in position to extend claims on others' sense of mutual obligation and support. That is, her humble actions were "not only given *in exchange* for something (e.g., request, impositions of various kinds), [they are] also a *pragmatic force* that coerces certain behaviors of actions upon people and thus index speakers' [givers', actors'] control over addressees" (Duranti 1992: 95–96, emphasis in the original). In this case, the use of *yanga cosas* was not simply an act of self-deprecation given in exchange for an agreement to be a compadre. Her actions gained authority over the others by developing her identity and relationship in the context of their joint insecurity as indigenous people living *yangata*–simply and fruitlessly.

◢ The Limits of Acceptance ◣

I have anchored my analysis of Otavaleño economic insecurity and commitment to farming with the notion of *yanga*, a rhetorical move that makes me a bit uneasy. During my fieldwork, I struggled to grasp the term's myriad meanings. At first, I thought it meant simply idleness and wasted effort. Then I got the idea of simple and humble. Eventually, the more existential meanings dawned on me. Even after I began to pay attention to the way people used the word, I could still get it wrong, sometimes badly so. My errors illustrated not only the limits of my cultural knowledge but also of my social acceptance.

For instance, after I learned enough to converse in Quichua, people frequently told me it was good that I spoke *yanga shimi*. Emboldened by the praise and my "insider's knowledge" about the word *yanga*, I tried to use the words *"yanga shimi"* myself, saying something like, *"ashagutalla yanga shimita ushani"* (I know a little "useless" language). The comment led to a painful pause and smiles frozen on faces a moment too long. It was not for me to say whose language was worthless. My talk of *yanga* only called more attention to the social and economic gaps that existed between me and my compadres and neighbors. It did not matter how many rainy *mingas* I worked or days I wore my ruined hiking boots or hours I spent meticulously sketching the grain of a useless, old *batea*. My labor and possessions could never be "worthless" in the same way as my compadres. Your interest in this book testifies to the separate value in my efforts. Using the word *yanga*, I risked undoing the solidarity I had with others in Ariasucu. It reintroduced the whiteness and "cleanliness" of my life.

The relative value that work and objects take again calls attention to the urban-based, national powers "shaping the social field action," organizing the potentialities of native peoples (Wolf 1990: 586). In the course of modernization, rural disadvantages have only become more entrenched in many Andean valleys. Thirty years of rural development directed by outside experts have resulted in misplaced sewage lines, inadequate water supplies, and misguided *mingas*, which, taken together, conspire to anchor native society within locales of perpetual poverty. Living within such zones, indigenous peoples labor hard for little return and must find ways to defend themselves with their own resources—Imbabura's maize fields, the Quichua language, dependable compadres, and their *yanga cosas*.

Peasant material culture gives up and takes on different values in this defense. As market prices spiral upward in the cities, use-values of peasant goods sometimes seem to hyperinflate in the countryside. Owners exploit them for all they are worth and then some, salvaging big things—looms, cauldrons, *bateas*, plows—by endlessly applying little things: wire, strings, lead plugs, strips of rubber, and bits of nails. Destined to collapse in some task, and probably not the one they were originally intended for, these objects have lost any exchange value. Calling them "worthless," though, owners refer not to the used (*mawka*) condition of the objects or their utility or the resourcefulness of the indigenous skills that keep them going. Rather, they call implicit attention to that which is not present: the power to circulate in the wider economy.

Casting the circumscribed realities of peasant life into sharp relief, both *yanga cosas* and their accompanying "*yanga* talk" testify daily to economic failure. The discourse of the entrepreneurial ethic— hard work, rationality, sacrifice—rings hollow in spaces filled with *yanga cosas*, while the subsistence ethic gathers new life from their presence. The tension between the market and subsistence values, however, is never resolved entirely in favor of one side or the other. The next chapter examines how people negotiate middle courses among conflicting ideals. Describing the growth of transnational, kin-based trading networks, I focus on the way the circulation of commodities and the ritualized consumption of family gatherings materialize the ideals of an increasingly dispersed society.

◢ F O U R ◣
Otavalo's Transnational Archipelago

◢ A Fraught Romance ◣

On most days, Monica and Galo's daughter Celestina brims with confidence. By the age of fourteen, she exhibited the boldness of a rising generation of handicraft dealers. She had moved out from living with her parents and siblings. Apprenticing with relatives, risking her earnings on new sales opportunities, and getting to know other dealers in distant market towns, she worked ambitiously to advance herself. Interestingly, she first devoted her talents not to commerce, but to religion. As a thirteen-year-old, she went to the provincial capital Ibarra to study to become a Roman Catholic missionary and possibly a teacher. Before completing her formal training, though, she changed her mind. She abandoned the Church for a business career, moving up to Tulcan to work for her uncle and aunt. Not long after starting out as a salesperson in their store, she began reinvesting earnings in her own inventory of sweaters. Now, three years later, she prepared to leave her uncle's and aunt's operation and to strike out on her own.

On the morning she came to visit Chesca and me in May of 1994, however, her confidence had deserted her. She came to us for advice—she was sitting on a corner of a chair at our kitchen table, unable to make eye contact, and concentrating on tying delicate knots in the threads that fringed our table cloth. As she worked her fingers across the fabric, the words tumbled out in unconnected phrases: "He is not really Mormon . . . They said we were walking together, but that is not true . . . He says he has to go to Europe." The story of her boyfriend thus slowly emerged, as well as the cause of the current crisis: she wanted to get married, but her parents opposed it. Monica and Galo insisted that seventeen (almost eighteen) was not old enough. Further, they complained that they knew nothing about the boyfriend except that he was twenty years old, came from the Otavaleño community of Peguche, and worked for a Mormon.

Making matters worse for Celestina, her boyfriend Pedro had pressed her with an ultimatum: either they get married right away or else he would go to Europe for a year, possibly two years. She did not

120

know how to interpret that. Did he really want to get married? By the time she finished talking, she was sobbing, and Chesca and I were consoling her with cups of hot chocolate. We were inclined to agree with her parents and wanted to suggest putting off any marriage plans, especially since this Pedro did not seem to be treating her fairly. However, I did not feel comfortable giving her advice. The whole thing had taken me completely by surprise and I had little idea of what one should say in these circumstances.

Talking the situation over let her regain some emotional balance. Celestina went back over to her side of the house to hash things out with her parents and Chesca and I sat there trying to figure out when this mess started. The more we talked, the more I realized that we should not have been so surprised. The signs of Celestina's parents' concern stretched back six months. When we built our room onto Monica and Galo's house the previous December, Galo went out of his way to get Celestina involved in the project. In January, he took a sudden interest in his long dormant membership in the Tulcan sweater dealers' association. Then, in March he made frequent trips to Otavalo to use a telephone to call up to Tulcan. Come April, both Monica and Galo insisted that Celestina return for her cousins' confirmation services in the town church. I originally took all these activities to be a general concern with either business affairs or family matters. In retrospect, it appears that the parents feared they were losing their daughter. Like countless other Otavaleño households, they struggled to cope with the volatile mix of teenage ambition and love and the centrifugal pressures of expatriate textile-dealing communities.

In this chapter, I review the history of long-distance trading, describe the trials and triumphs of Galo Ajala and his immediate family, and analyze the broader links between consumption and social organization of transnational textile-dealing. Resisting the radical displacement of other ethnic diasporas, Otavaleño migrant families inhabit a social world more akin to a "global archipelago." Its scattered "islands" include Imbabura's rural peasant farming communities, provincial markets, urban construction sites, and tourist pedestrian malls in Latin American, European, and North American cities. The archipelago economy integrates the complimentary resources of these settings: homegrown grains from family plots, profits from weekly market sales, wages from urban laborers, and capital from bulk export shipments. To combine, at least temporarily, some of these incomes, Otavaleño households depend on preserving unity across generations and creating lasting dyadic bonds with other households. These familial social institutions extend the reach of established traders and provide a way for young ones to get started. Further, the practices that institutionalize Ota-valeño social networks preserve the vitality of Otavalo itself as a cultural homeland.

In using the archipelago metaphor, I draw on the insights of John Murra (1972, 1985a, 1985b) and other scholars who have used it as a way to explain historic patterns of Andean dispersion and political organization. I am not arguing, however, that Otavalo exhibits some kind of timeless, Andean social organization or preserves strong historical linkages to the pre-Columbian economies of Peru. Rather, I use the analytical concepts of archipelago scholarship—reciprocity, economic complementarity, the link between ritual, place, and power—to point out the innovations and paradoxes of Otavalo's global archipelago, an entity that is itself undergoing constant change.

◢ *Mindaláes* and a Tradition of Long-Distance Trade ◣

> Among these Indians there are merchants, weavers of luxury textiles [*cumbicamayos*], potters, carpenters, and other artisans . . . These travel to the neighboring towns on account of their crafts, transactions [*contratos*], and businesses [*granjerías*], to sell their merchandise, salt, coca, clothing, and cotton, which yield them great returns.[1]

So wrote imperial Spanish *visitadores* of Otavaleños' ancestors in 1562, beginning what would become a common practice: the foreign observer who visits Otavalo and then trumpets the region's penchant for commerce. The *visitadores* found that the area had been home to both an active market as well as a class of full-time, long-distance trade specialists known as *mindaláes*. These traders enriched the area's economy and fueled the power of local elites, by dealing in gold, silver, salt, coca, and "foreign" lowland goods with high prestige value (Salomon 1986: 106). Frank Salomon's (1986) research into the northern Andean, pre-Conquest political economy reveals that while trade and markets may have been negligible in the southern Andes, they held a special status in the north. Even more specifically, trading as a vocation achieves its fullest importance in the polities that stretch from Quito northwards to the Pasto peoples of southern Colombia. The active mercantile business of Otavalo, in particular, made local merchants liable for high amounts of tribute to the Spanish crown, as imperial inspectors noted that the Otavaleños "have

---

1. This passage is Salomon's (1986: 202) translation of Gaspar de San Martín's and Nuño de Valderrama's account of Otavaleño "merchant Indians" found in their visit of 1562.

all the barter business of all Quito and its outskirts, or most of it" (quoted in Salomon 1986: 202).

Even after centuries of Spanish rule and the oppressive restructuring of the north Andean economy to provide tribute payments of labor and cloth, *mindaláes* persevered. Otavalo still contained a separate corporate group of *mindaláes* in the mid-1600s (Salomon 1986). And in Cayambe, a town lying between Otavalo and Quito, *mindaláes* show up in the records as a distinct group as late as 1782. As Salomon points out, little is known of the lives and social position of these "merchant Indians." From fragmentary records, he has put together a description that contains parallels to the careers of modern traders. First, the choice of career was linked to kinship. The sons of *mindaláes* followed in their father's footsteps. However, the status was not exclusively hereditary, as some young *mindaláes* were not related to established merchants. Second, once embarked upon, the career of a merchant Indian was a long one. Third, women, too, could have the title of *mindala*. Indeed, in modern Quichua usage near Cuenca, Ecuador, the word *mindaláes* refers to "Indian women of women of the lowest class who sell food, spices, vegetables, etc., at retail, either daily in a fixed place or walking from town to town" (Cordero Palacios 1957: 193, as cited in Salomon 1986: 102). Finally, and unlike modern traders, these exchange specialists may have oriented their work more toward politics and boosting the power of local lords rather than pursuing pure commerce (Ramírez 1995).

After Ecuadorian independence and during the early years of the republic, commerce continued as a profession in Otavalo, if not as a special social status linked to extraterritorial mobility and the *mindala* title. The weekly markets of Imbabura province bustled with traders and artisans. In 1863, Abraham Lincoln's ambassador to Ecuador, Friedrich Hassaurek (1967) reported that "At Otavalo, Cotacachi and all other such places, more business is done on Sunday than on any other day." He goes on to describe the market and its products:

> The sellers squat on the ground, sometimes under little screens of baize or sackcloth nailed to a clumsy wooden contrivance supported by a pole which is driven into the ground. Here they sell macañas, ponchos, wool, cotton, beads, rosaries, leaden crosses, strings of glass pearls, collars and bracelets of false corals and other cheap ornaments; meat, fruit, vegetables, salt, ají, barley meal and such popular dishes ready made as cariuchu, locro, choclos, mashca, toasted maize etc. (Hassaurek 1967: 175)

By the late nineteenth century, municipal authorities had switched the fairs from Sunday to Saturday, possibly for religious reasons. As

Lynn Meisch (1987: 40) points out, Otavaleños probably devoted themselves more to commerce than God on Sundays, forsaking mass for the market.

This brief sketch of Otavaleño travels and trade prior to the twentieth century raises an important issue. Given the ancient history of long-distance commerce in the region, its reemergence within the context of a global market for ethnic arts does not signal the corruption of a more "authentic" native Andean way of life. In fact, the absence of merchant Indians, long-distance exchange, and complex deals for "foreign goods" represents a diminishing of indigenous society. Some scholars have ignored native Andeans' interest in business. Michael Taussig (1980), for example, portrays the South American peasant as a kind of anticapitalist, working not to accumulate but simply to meet needs. However, to the extent that Taussig is correct when he asserts "the peasant uses cash, not capital, and sells in order to buy . . . [and] lives in a system aimed at the satisfaction of qualitatively defined needs" (Taussig 1980: 25), such a condition reflects not the natural economy, but the repression of rural peoples by *hacienda* owners and urban business interests. Such simplistic descriptions obscure the histories, careers, and aspirations of commercially minded indigenous peoples like the Otavaleños.[2]

◢ The Rebirth of Handicraft Travel ◣

Modern demand for Otavaleño textiles began expanding in the 1920s. At the time, British textile imports dominated the market for quality cloth. Prompted by urban demands for finely woven twill fabric, Otavaleño weavers began to weave imitation tweed cloth to sell to Quito consumers (Parsons 1945). The sales of this product, called *casimir or casimires* (from the English word "cashmere"), augmented the income of weavers previously dependent on sales and barter exchanges in Imbabura. Further, the new cloth provided a direct connection between Otavaleño artisans and Quito markets. Extraterritorial trade developed a profitable new segment, reintroducing Otavaleños to the formal urban economy.

In the 1940s, market forces again caused artisans to change their weavings. Domestic textile mills captured the market for high-quality textiles, and demand for handmade Otavaleño *casimires* consequently dwindled. Manufacturers thus refocused their efforts, finding new sales opportunities in the nascent market for native, ethnic arts. While more and more tourists made the trip to Otavalo, indige-

---

2. Others have critiqued Taussig's inaccurate descriptions of Andean peasants, although on slightly different grounds. See for example, Roseberry 1994: 218–22.

nous merchants did not depend on this traffic as the sole outlet for their goods. Buitrón (1947: 48–49) reports that in the 1940s some of the residents of Peguche "travel continually within and outside the country" while the residents of the nearby sector Pucará "travel from Carchi [Ecuador's northern most province] to Loja [the southern most], selling ponchos and chalinas, which they buy in the Otavalo market."

Over the next two decades, Otavaleño merchants traveled farther, stayed away longer, and established residences in remote cities. Surveying the level of economic change and acculturation in the early 1960s, Buitrón noted (1962: 319) the following:

> The radius of action of the Indians has been extended year after year. Until recently, one could count on one's fingers the Indians who had traveled outside the Cantón [county of Otavalo]. Currently, they are numerous, those who have traveled outside the Cantón, outside the Province, and outside the country.
>
> One frequently encounters the merchants from Otavalo in the airports and the hotels of Lima, Bogotá, Caracas and Panama. A few indigenous families have settled with their small textile workshops in Colombia, Venezuela, Brazil, and Uruguay.

Furthermore, Otavaleño trading practices were extending simultaneously in two directions. Not only did merchants expand into new foreign territory with each passing year, but commercial activities drew new participants from the more remote rural sectors within the Cantón. Thus, in the early 1960s, the first handicraft dealers from neighborhoods on the rural fringes of Peguche, Agato, and Pucará got their start in international travel and sales. Celestina's father, Galo, was one of the pioneers. His story bears repeating as it illustrates several themes of the textile migrant's experience, including the vulnerability of long-distance traders, the constant travel, and the steady accumulation of consumer goods and other signs of wealth.

◢ Galo Ajala and the Dealer's Career ◣

On most days, Galo smiles at the approach of strangers, flashing a wide grin of gold-repaired teeth at those who walk up the dirt road in front of his house. He climbs off the bench of his *faja* loom or leaves his wife's dark store and greets the tourist, provincial official, or whomever is passing by to ask them where they are from and where they are going. Indeed, his cheerfulness and willingness to talk to me as I walked along the cobbled road below his house was one of the fortuitous factors that led me to do research in the community.

Galo's good humor is sincere; it is also conditioned by having been a handicraft salesman in towns throughout Ecuador and Colombia since he was a boy.

His father died when he was two. His mother, Mama Rosa, provided for her four children (only two of whom survived to adulthood) by supplementing the crops of their fields with sales of wool and sheep. Galo, the youngest, attended an evangelical Protestant school for two years before dropping out to help his mother with her flock of sheep. In 1961, an older cousin of his came to his mother and convinced her and Galo that he should go to Quito and learn how to sell *artesanias* (handicrafts). They agreed and, at the age of twelve, Galo embarked upon a long career in textile dealing.[3]

Working as his cousin's assistant, Galo reinvested his earnings in his own inventory of ponchos and *chalinas*. Little by little, his wares increased. These goods still stir his imagination. When I interviewed him in my kitchen, he physically conjured the inventory out of the air. In order to clarify his achievements, he pushed his stocky body back from the table and held out his hand about a meter above the floor, catching my eye to make sure I witnessed the height of this long-gone stack of dark ponchos, striped shawls, and fine cloth. I think they have remained so important to Galo over all these years because they were the first sign of his economic advancement away from his hard, fatherless childhood. The commodities materialized his rationality, manifesting his entrepreneurial ethic to himself and others.

After four years of selling in both Quito and Cuenca, he returned to Ariasucu at the age of sixteen. He bore with him a unique emblem of his achievements: a door. His mother had long planned to tear down her old straw-roof *ujshawasi* (hut) in order to build a solid *tapiawasi* (adobe home) with a tile roof. Galo helped make it happen. He worked alongside neighbors to pack the earth walls of the new house, and then fixed the new multipaneled door in the wide threshold—a distinctive architectural detail among the simple plank doors of his neighbors (drawing 18). Not long after this triumph, though, disaster struck. Someone burrowed through the new earth walls and stole his handicraft inventory from his mother's house. He had to go back to work for his cousin until he once again had enough goods to sell on his own.

3. I know of only one other man from Ariasucu who seems to have preceded Galo in international handicraft selling. This man told me (with a laugh) that he and a friend traveled through Cali and Bogotá in the late 1950s selling green papier maché dogs. He sold these and other unusual objects for two to three years before coming home for good. He now barters soap, salt, and cooking oil for raw pelts of wool in the most isolated communities around Imbabura. In a further rejection of his old long-distance occupation, he seems to have forgotten all his Spanish or, at any rate, chooses only to speak Quichua.

Drawing 18: Panel Door

In the late 1960s, he took his career in a new direction, leaving with another maternal cousin to sell in Colombia. Residing in the Caribbean port city of Cartagena, Galo sold crafts to Asian seamen, played soccer with local Colombians, and doubled his inventory (back in the kitchen, he had to hold out both hands to show how high each stack of goods were). Misfortune struck again, this time in the form of customs inspectors who came and confiscated all his goods. Escaping back to Otavalo with some cash and a few personal items, he spent the savings from this venture on a plot of land below his mother's house. He stayed home for a while, in part, to earn money with his loom and, in part, to court Monica Quilla who lived just over the *wayku* (gully) in Agato. The two of them wed in 1973. Not long after, they moved to Cuenca with their infant daughter Clara.

In Cuenca, Galo sold sweaters while Monica split her time caring for Clara, working with Galo, and working on her own selling boiled potatoes seasoned with her special sauce to other vendors for lunch. Gradually, their inventory grew to the point where Galo had to rent space in a storeroom to guard it at night. Completing a trio of catastrophes, the storeroom burnt down. The young family packed up the cooking utensils, small chairs, and the two tables they had acquired and went back to live with their parents in Ariasucu (see drawing 19). Galo wove *chalinas* (shawls) with his father-in-law until he earned enough cash to convince Monica that they should try traveling again. In the late 1970s, they moved up to Tulcan with three young children. In yet another mishap, they lost their sweater inventory to a

Drawing 19: Chair and Stool

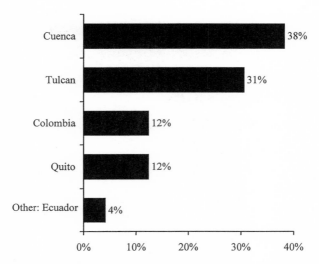

Figure 5: Top five destinations of Ariasucu handicraft dealers from thirty-three households, February–November, 1994. (Places ranked by percentage of spot observations [$n = 170$] of absences from the community. Top five account for 97 percent of total.)

robber in 1984. The loss convinced them to return to Ariasucu. Finally moving out of their parents' houses, they built their new home (the second cement-block house in the sector) on the plot Galo bought years before.

Galo's itineraries foreshadow Ariasucu's future migration patterns. By the mid-1990s, the places he visited—Cuenca, Tulcan, Colombia (Cartagena and Bogotá), and Quito—had become the top five destinations for Ariasucu's trader when places are ranked by the time merchants spend in them (figure 5). The overlap between Galo and his successors' destinations is not a coincidence. Many younger traders tap into the same extended networks of compadres and kin utilized by Galo's generation in order to get their first selling opportunity. Other sectors similarly have their own contacts and favored urban areas. In the nearby neighborhood of Trojaloma, for instance, dealers regularly travel to and stay in the Ecuadorian tourist spot of Baños, a place little visited by Ariasucu sellers. The consistency of locations testifies to the durability of Otavalo's networks and to the legacy of dyadic and fictive kin bonds, a topic taken up below.

By the 1970s, it was not just textile dealers who took advantage of family connections in order to migrate to the city. The oil economy set off a new exodus from the countryside. Cutting roads, drilling

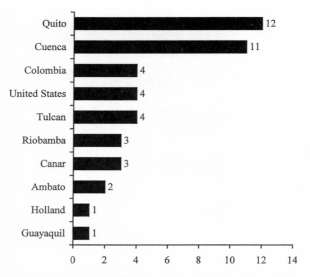

Figure 6: Location of migrant family members of thirty-three Ariasucu households, 1994.

wells, and building pipelines through the rainforest, pumping the heavy crude up and over the Andes, and refining it on the Pacific coast, the new petro-industries created thousands of jobs and substantial revenues for an expanding national government (one source estimates that 80 percent of all revenue went into government salaries [Whitaker and Greene 1990]). The oil economy spawned a construction boom in Quito, which in turn drew Otavaleño men from their fields and looms in order to mix concrete, plaster walls, and lay floors. Women came either to work as cooks or maids or vendors in Quito's busy markets and streets.

The combination of the textile trade and urban wage migration has now made dispersion a fact of life for many rural Otavaleño families. In 1994, I surveyed thirty-three married couples to see who had close family members (defined as a sibling, parent, uncle, aunt, or child) living outside the province. Only six did not have such a contact. Many had family members living in more than one place. While the most common place for a relative was Quito (twelve of the thirty-three families had someone living there), some had connections to the United States, Colombia, and Europe (figure 6).[4] Going after

4. The sample includes all thirty-two participating households in the time-allocation study plus an additional randomly selected household that originally participated in the time study but subsequently dropped out.

opportunities in any one of these places, a substantial portion of Ota-valeños exist as Celestina does. They live in one place, preserve an active social life in another, and try to bridge the social, economic, and cultural gaps thereby created with bus trips, telephone calls, occasional letters, wired money, and an increasingly eclectic set of personal belongings.

◢ Patterns of Migration and Archipelagoes ◣

The migration experience unites Otavaleños with rural societies throughout Latin America. Over the past half-century, the global expansion of capitalism, high population growth rates, and the decline of subsistence resources have pushed and pulled rural denizens to cities for jobs, schools, and economic opportunities. Early research explained migration patterns as the consequence of a stagnating agricultural sector. Both researchers and government agencies saw the influx from the countryside as a failure of rural society to meet the aspirations of its members.

Subsequent research into migrants' social networks and class identity, however, revealed their relative prosperity, not poverty, as the critical factor in movement. The people on the move often enjoyed some advantage over their peers: money, contacts, or skills (Roberts 1975, 1978). Indeed, Otavaleños offer a classic example of peasant entrepreneurs who developed connections to the city in order to advance businesses and careers already begun in the provinces. Their arrival in town is not a blind flight from rural desperation but a planned excursion with some prior contact and information and dependency on resources amassed before the move (see Roberts 1978 for a more general analysis). This structured movement means that dispersion from rural areas does not necessarily signal their decline in either economic or social importance.

For the Andean nations, city and country, in fact, exist in a dynamic relationship (Isbell 1974). Frequently, swings in economic cycles eliminate the construction work and service jobs of migrants, compelling them to fall back on subsistence agriculture for survival (de Janvry 1982, 1987; Nash 1994). Nor is adversity the only cause for the continued connection. In Ecuador, positive developments—including the agrarian reform and expanding urban job markets in the 1960s and 1970s—decreased the level of permanent migration from rural areas in the *sierra* while increasing temporary migration (Peek 1982; Waters 1997). With more economic opportunities, many peasants found work in the cities while keeping their homes on the land. Indeed, since "the value of each form of total household income is a product of its being in relation to other forms of income" (Friedman

1984: 46), the value of subsistence agricultural products may actually rise as household members traveled to earn cash. In the context of a trading economy, homegrown grains serve as a valuable form of insurance, underwriting an entrepreneur's risk-taking. Galo Ajala had to fall back upon his mother's fields at least three times in the wake of his setbacks.

Otavaleño migration, however, cannot be modeled solely in terms of the opposition and interrelationship of urban and rural places and economies. At least since the 1960s, migrants have made for dispersed destinations and multiple occupational niches, from textile sales to office caretaker to musician. The spatial diversification of resources and opportunities has an impact on Otavaleño culture beyond the effects of urbanization. In order to support Pedro's and Celestina's effort to make money in Europe, Galo called upon his partners in a sweater-selling association in Tulcan to arrange a loan and upon family contacts from his Quito days in order to augment Pedro's handicraft inventory. By integrating the resources from several different Otavaleño communities, he was able to augment the young couple's meager resources.

This practice of supporting an economy spread over distant locales through kinship networks has a long history in the Andes. Studying the records of pre-Colombian, central Andean societies, Murra (1972) argues that communities depended on exploiting discrete ecological niches dispersed by altitude: a vertical archipelago. Anticipating some aspects of current studies of diaspora and displacement, Murra (1985a, 1985b) writes that Andean archipelagoes have the following characteristics: (1) ethnic groups seek to control the maximum number of niches, (2) economic relations of the archipelago were governed by principles of reciprocity and redistribution, (3) peripheral "islands" may be shared with other ethnic groups, (4) with the creation of states, peripheral islands were located in more distant areas, and (5) these archipelagoes maintained a clear political and social center in the high, dry regions of the altiplano. Most Andean research has focused on the ecological aspects of this model (Masuda et al. 1985; Brush 1977b). Examining climatic and topological features of microenvironments, anthropologists and archaeologists have assessed the agricultural potential of different zones and analyzed the social mechanisms linking them with other zones.

Enrique Mayer (1985), however, argues that Murra's model is fundamentally political. Pointing out that agricultural production zones were man-made things, he writes that managing these zones across space and time required the integration of three nested social levels: the household, the community of groups exploiting common resources, and the ethnic group capable of mobilizing local groups. This dense, interlocking organization must contend with internal conflicts of interests. The material concerns of individuals and households, for example, can conflict with communal efforts to preserve and equitably distribute resources. Reconciling private ambition with collective obligations continually strains broader alliances.

Archipelago models of economic organization have another potential disadvantage. As people turn to members of their own group to integrate resources from dispersed zones, they isolate themselves from other ethnic groups. In his historical analysis of the northern Andes, Salomon (1986) argues that such isolation was the greatest political consequence of the Inca invasion. The imposition of an archipelago economic model on the region broke the preexisting horizontal ties among regional polities. He writes, "the 'archipelago' was inherently a radical measure, a true revolution from above. It substituted for the premises of interdependency and complex alliance, typical of the aboriginal world, flatly contrary principles of economic closure and trans-zonal self-sufficiency" (Salomon 1986: 200). Rituals and exchange within the archipelago reinforced the economic power of the center, not links with outsiders.

Now, the economic practices and political organization of modern Otavalo significantly differs from the Inca vertical archipelago. Markets and trading are the heart of the Otavalo economy, while they are just what the Inca administrators bypassed through their systems of redistribution. Cash and commodity exchange mediate the flow of goods, not reciprocal exchange. And in the global archipelago, most of the islands are complementary market niches ultimately yielding the same thing—cash—not ecological ones yielding different crops. Nonetheless, despite such differences, the archipelago model of integrated complementarity still addresses a key question: how has an indigenous Andean ethnic group expanded its handicraft industry into urban areas while anchoring its culture and social institutions in a mountain province, even after many decades of international travel and sales? [5]

5. This question borrows from Murra's (1985a: 3) original inquiry into the organization of the Inca state. As he wrote, "Given the scattered geographical distribution of Andean polities, how does one explain that for centuries and perhaps millennia the seat of power and the highest demographic density in the pre-European Andes are found at altitudes above 3400 meters?"

Despite the deviations from the Inca model, Otavalo's global, market-oriented economy exhibits institutional features identified by Murra and others with an archipelago organization. First, the niches are still diverse and complementary, including subsistence agriculture, low-risk/low-return artisan production, and high-risk tourist sales. Second, for most Otavaleños, gaining access to the more remote opportunities depends on kinship connections. Many handicraft transactions take place among compadres who have enduring moral obligations to grant favors to each other. In modern Otavalo, reciprocity still channels economic activity. Third, the networks of urban communities, trade associations, extended families, and fictive kin afford a degree of self-sufficiency. Turning to their own institutions, Otavaleños control sufficient levels of production, capital, and information to increase the productivity, profitability, and geographic range of their textile industry. This self-reliance can reinforce other external factors—from racial discrimination to the lack of proper visas—that isolate them from the wider societies in which they operate. Finally, although the political centralization of the Inca empire is lacking, ritual and economic centralization guides the movement of people and resources in Otavalo's dispersed world.

In order to grasp how this "global archipelago" functions, I will borrow from Mayer's analysis (1985) to investigate nested levels of social organization. The household remains the primary productive and integrative unit, drawing on the varied income streams afforded by farming, weaving, wages, and trading. For migrant families, synthesizing these diverse resources requires keeping members committed to the needs of Otavalo's provincial homes, especially during the period when grown children are working on their own but have not yet set up their own households. Beyond the domestic unit, people depend not so much on the general community but on limited "action sets" of family and compadres to exploit transnational niches. Adrian Mayer (1966) developed the idea of action sets to account for collective action among individuals in complex, urban societies. These sets are temporary and distinguished from other social groups by a series of transactions related to a narrow task. Brush (1977a: 141) uses the concept to describe how the potential agricultural abundance of an Andean valley is brought into individual households. Similarly, Otavaleños develop action sets to bring the "potential abundance" of the world market for ethnic crafts into their homes. In the remainder of this chapter, I concentrate on the ritual and material mechanisms that hold these family-based institutions together.

◀ Otavaleño Households in a Dispersed World ▶

In 1992, I visited Celestina at the store where she worked in Tulcan. At the time she was sixteen and lived with her aunt (her mother's sister) and uncle in a small apartment. She spent her days watching TV and waiting on the slow trickle of Colombian tourists and petty merchants who came in to buy machine-knitted, acrylic-fiber sweaters. Seeing her in this remote provincial outpost, I was struck by her poise. Whether she was wrestling large bundles of sweaters onto the sidewalk in front of the store or standing by to answer the brusque questions of hurried Colombians, she calmly took care of business.

Exhibiting her father's general goodwill, she had befriended many of the other young Otavaleños who sold on the sidewalks or in stores similar to her place of work. Socializing with them was one of the main ways she broke up the boring routines of selling. At midday, she often would push the sweaters back into her shop, march off through the congested streets to find a friend, and duck into one of those dark, one-room family restaurants that feeds both travelers and regulars throughout this border town. Warming up with bowls of hot chicken soup freckled with disintegrating bow-tie pasta and droplets of oil, Celestina and her friends gossiped about the stinginess of their bosses or shared rumors of budding romances—learning about "who was walking with whom." Despite the dankness of the city and the tedium of the work, Celestina enjoyed being with her *compañeras* (companions) and away from her strong-willed parents.

As I describe above, I learned that her apprenticeship away from home did not mean she was independent of it. Like her father thirty years earlier, Celestina's itineraries, sales opportunities, and use of savings frequently reflected the needs of her family in Ariasucu. Even as she was watching Bugs Bunny cartoons amid stacks of sweaters in Tulcan and planning how to open her own shop, she remained an important member of their household. This membership, however, could not be taken for granted. Celestina had arrived at a critical juncture in her life. Old enough to offer substantial resources to her old home, she also stood poised to make it largely on her own, apart from her parents and her siblings. Galo and Monica had to work diligently to maintain their claims on her visits, labor, or earnings.

This ambiguous position of older, unmarried children is not unique to families split by migration or to Otavaleños in general. In many peasant cultures, coping with the autonomy of young adults and formation of new households from existing ones is perhaps the most critical phase in the household development cycle (Goody 1958).

Weismantel (1989b) has described how indigenous people of Zumba-gua stretch out the formation of new, independent domestic units from established ones. Older children begin to separate themselves from their parents and younger siblings by taking up residence in an out-building removed from the main house. Upon marriage, the young couple may sleep apart but they continue to cook with the parents of either the bride or the groom. Sometime after the third generation is born, they set up a second hearth, often within the household compound of low, rectangular adobe buildings. As more children are born, the younger household gradually gains greater au-tonomy. This model of slow development still describes the practices of those Otavaleño households that farm, weave, and work mainly within the province.

The migration of adolescents to distant cities, however, pushes the development cycle in two, opposing directions. On the one hand, travel speeds the exodus of children from the household. As they be-came teenagers, both Galo and then later his daughter moved not just into a different building but to a different province. On the other hand, the frequent movement from city to city in pursuit of better markets delays a young couple's effort to build a house of their own. Galo and Monica returned repeatedly to both their parents' homes to live for periods ranging from six months to two years when they were not away selling. Celestina seems destined to follow their example.

Moving back and forth between temporary urban apartments and their parents' home, young couples may have three or four children and be close to thirty years old before they establish a home that family members recognize as being independent. A child's early exit from home and his or her delayed return to their own house, there-fore, prolongs a period of tenuous membership in a parents' house-hold: a phase of independent earnings coupled with few social attach-ments which could rival parental claims. It is precisely during this liminal time that "archipelago household" comes into its own as families diversify and augment their earnings through their children. They take advantage of a child's growing inventory, cash reserves, or market contacts in a remote locale and use them to expand weaving ventures, textile inventories, or the physical plant of the household in Otavalo.

Parents, however, cannot automatically claim their children's earnings. As research has shown in rural Ecuador and elsewhere, few household's fit Sahlins' (1972) model of a domestic unit in which all members pool their incomes and enjoy equal rights to all re-sources (Netting, Wilk, Arnould 1984; Wilk 1989a). In contrast, grown children keep their wages and profits for themselves. Younger teenage males spend their cash on Nike shoes—either imported or local knockoffs—and baseball caps embroidered with the team logos of the Charlotte Hornets or snarling tigers of Grambling State. Teenage girls buy new shiny polyester blouses and imported Italian woolen cloth for their *anakus* (wrap-around skirts). As they get older, both boys and girls change tacks and reinvest their earnings in handicrafts and other ventures to earn money. Faced with these priorities, the parents' use of their offspring's income usually comes not as a free grant but as a loan for a specific project. Galo and Monica, for example, borrowed money from all their children on different occasions for such things as acquiring a new loom, purchasing raw materials for *faja*-weaving or buying piglets to be raised and resold. Galo has also borrowed from his children's Tulcan sweater inventories in order to fill out his market stall in Otavalo's Poncho Plaza.

Economic resources thus pass among household members and across distance in concrete transactions, not generalized reciprocity. A household member will provide money for others for identifiable commodities: cones of brightly colored thread, pig feed, sacks of sugar for the family store, a dozen knitted sweaters, or a truckload of cement blocks. Even if cash is changing hands, parents or children quickly purchase the specified object and people track their money through these goods, using them to reckon who owes what to whom. I became aware of the materialized nature of the flow of resources when Chesca and I joined forces with Galo and Monica to add a room onto their home to use as our own residence in Ariasucu in 1994.

We had decided to divide the costs. Chesca and I would pay for the cement blocks, doors, windows, reinforcement bar and sacks of concrete; they would buy the tiles, beams and wooden runners for the roof. This neat arrangement threatened to unravel as soon as the work started. One day Galo came up to report that the price of wood had risen sharply and he could not afford the tile runners. The following day he declared "It is fine, it is fine, my José [his sixteen-year-old son] will buy the runners." Next, he worried that tiles had become much too expensive and that he could buy only half of what we needed. Later in the week, he beamed, reporting that he had spoken with Celestina and she agreed to loan the money for the other half. After the red tiles had been delivered to the patio, he gestured to them, reminding me, "These tiles, these tiles are from my Celestina." The fragile, curved, clay rectangles pleased him as they substantiated his daughter's loyalty and industriousness.

The purchase of these building supplies fit a broader pattern of family consumption practices. Commodities and consumer goods put a public face on intrafamily transactions. Such spending symbolically ratifies the bonds of a family split by migration and economically connects them through shared material assets. Noting a similar situation among the Kekchi Maya of Belize, Wilk (1989b) argues that the family's greatest tool in its struggle against members' competing economic agendas is the house itself. By allocating income to furnishings and building materials, the whole family can listen to the radio, walk on the concrete floor, and share in the envy of the neighbors. He writes:

> this sharing is a potent device, on the part of the parents, in the struggle to keep children attached to the household after they marry. It is a demonstrable fact that the income they donate to the household is not going to be wasted on rum for the father or clothes for the mother, but instead it will be spent on permanent improvements that the whole family can use for many years to come, and which add materially to the family's assets. (1989b: 311)

By allocating their loans to specific goods, family members have more confidence that their funds are not being squandered. Indeed, in Ariasucu, one man receives remittances in the form of cash wired to Otavalo from his thirty-five-year-old sister who works at a medical supply factory in Chicago. The cash comes with no specific instructions except that he should use it to help their mother. Not surprisingly, these funds have caused tension and distrust among mother, brother, and sister. (The mother tried to draft me into the fight, asking me to write a letter to her daughter at one point to confirm whether money was sent.) Mother and cousins alike whisper that the brother is misappropriating the cash. By promptly using the money for specific, agreed-upon purchases, even consumable items like animal feed, other families publicize spending and minimize this strife.

In contrast to the Kekchi households, though, Otavaleño expenditure is not seen in communal terms; people borrow and loan more than they share. In their own way, though, such actions, when mediated through the material world, solidify family bonds. The runners and tiles that sheltered Chesca and me for a year represented an obligation that Galo and Monica had to pay back. The roof called for a future transaction with their mobile and absent children, perpetuating a cycle of favors and exchanges. That these economic actions took a specified physical form only enhanced their social impact. For Galo, the runners spoke of "his José," and the tiles of "his Celestina."

These goods made their presence felt at home and served as bridge to them as they pursued their separate lives.

◢ Grain Mills, Water Jugs, and Migrant Household Formation ◣

Just as Otavaleños can solidify their households across great distances through commodity purchases, they also use goods to split off into new domestic units. Single men and women who live outside the province acquire everything from spinning wheels to soup cauldrons to lay the basis for their own households. In the lead-up to the confrontation over her boyfriend, Celestina alarmed her parents by spending heavily on furniture. Even as Galo and Monica warned her of the dangers of "walking with" this young man, she plotted the establishment of her own home. After a quick tour of Otavalo's carpenter shops, she spent 210,000 sucres (about $100) on a new double bed and combination dresser-wardrobe to replace her old single bed and wooden chest. Meanwhile, as if to underscore his muddled priorities, Pedro spent almost exactly the same amount (200,000 sucres), on a single pair of imported, blue-soled, white leather Reebok hightops. Rather than spend on domestic wares, he bought, at an inflated price, the same shoes that his peers wore when they came back from Europe.

In contrast to Pedro's personal extravagance, most young men on the verge of marriage spend soberly on kitchen pots and water jugs. In the late 1980s and early 1990s, Ariasucu experienced a small surge in out-migration as a new cadre of young men left to sell handicrafts in Quito, Cuenca, Cañar, and other Ecuadorian towns. Saving up their thin profits from years of tourist sales, many spent more conservatively than their peers who stayed at home did. Instead of getting a dirt bike or color TV, these migrants came back with extra large soup pots, plastic buckets, and in two cases, gas stoves. Despite being single males, they all worked to equip the feminine world of the hearth. I asked one of these migrants why he had purchased a gas stove when he was eighteen. He paused, opened his mouth to say something, stopped, shrugged, and smiled while his wife blurted out, "to catch a woman." When a young merchant's thoughts turn toward love, his money goes toward the kitchen.

The practice of outfitting the house in advance of marriage and from afar has been gaining momentum in recent years. Historically, Otavaleños have acquired the furnishings of their homes locally. Doing inventories of thirty-two houses, I learned that the majority of possessions were purchased in Otavalo (56 percent) while much of the rest of the tables, hoes, kitchen pots, and weaving equipment (29 percent) were locally made or inherited from relatives who live in Ariasucu or other indigenous communities. Put another way, of the 1,171 items that I catalogued, 85 percent of possessions came from within the province, while 15 percent had been picked up outside of it (figure 7). This low number of externally acquired goods, though, masks a new trend.

Since the late 1970s, the number of goods that have traveled back to Otavalo with their owners has grown, although not evenly. Extra-provincial purchases expanded in the early 1980s with the growth in the Quito oil economy and then declined through the middle of the decade with Ecuador's deep economic recession. These purchases climbed again with a new spurt in textile dealing, only to tail off in the 1990s as overcompetition began to cut off some trading careers (figure 8). Like Galo's and Monica's small chairs and stools, some of these goods joined the inventories of established households. In most cases, however, young people pick these nonlocal goods up just before or after they have been married.

These objects confirm Otavaleños' nomadic existence, bringing the reality of the textile archipelago into the home. Signaling local dependence on distant markets, the furniture and appliances memorialize people's entanglement with the regional and national economies. Questioning people about their goods, I found myself doing an

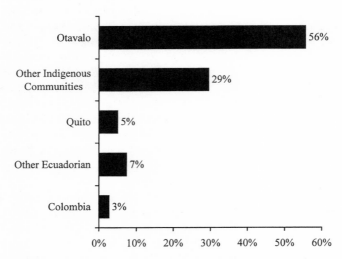

Figure 7: Place of origin of 1,171 possessions found in thirty-two Ariasucu houses, 1994.

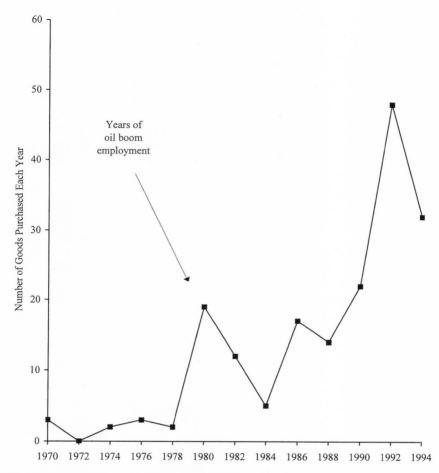

Figure 8: Growth in out-of-province purchases by thirty-two Ariasucu Households, 1970–94.

archaeology of how international economic cycles change the character of a home. The "strata" of black and white TVs, small cassette players, and two-burner gas stoves revealed the flush times of the oil economy in 1981 and 1982; a "layer" of boom boxes, "Four Tiger" blankets (a local brand), and four-burner stoves bore witness to the money that was being made selling to tourists in the early 1990s; and collections of patched-up cooking pots and repaired farm tools testify to the intermediate phases of low incomes and missing opportunities.

Juxtaposed against the humble possessions of farm life, the remotely purchased products remind Otavaleños of the reasons to travel, symbolize the potential payoffs of crafts markets, and verify this indigenous people's worldliness. Dealers even joke about a radio being "a souvenir of Bogotá" (un recuerdo de Bogotá) or the cement blocks for a house being "a souvenir of Italy." The quip, which I heard frequently when I did the inventories, inverts the standard Otavaleño roles of tourist and local. Most of these migrants made their money selling souvenir handicrafts to foreign tourists. As they insert themselves into the place of the casual traveler, the dealers think of new appliances and furniture as tokens of trips in foreign lands.

Many travelers act like tourists in other ways. They go sightseeing, take photographs or have their pictures taken as they work on the street in New York or Amsterdam. Migrants and musicians who have been to the United States or Europe insist on showing me these photographs ("Here we are in McDonald's near Time Square," "Here we are on the highway where our car broke down before the police came and took our car away"). Collecting mementos during their trips, migrants call attention to their identity as sojourners among an alien culture; people who come to make money but not to form lasting relationships or settle down (Bonacich 1973; cf. Oxfeld 1993). The image of "souvenirs" helps designate life in the "islands" of the textile archipelago as exotic—temporary interludes in a productive life based in Otavalo.

Otavaleño "souvenirs" differ from the ones that they sell to others in one key respect. While their souvenirs may remind them of Bogotá or Cuenca, they buy these goods not because they represent a foreign culture but because they fit within their own lifestyle in Otavalo. The top four out-of-town goods included blankets, grain mills, gas stoves, and radios/stereos (figure 9). Some of these items are clearly needed to live in the rented spaces in the cities where they are working. However, others, like grain mills, hoes, and water jugs often have no immediate urban use. Indeed, half of the grain mills in the homes that I inventoried have been purchased out of the province—a clear sign of the investment young couples are making in rural life and products even as they live in the cities.[6]

By buying grain mills and other implements of country life (drawing 20), migrants build up their economic incentives to return home and realize the value of their goods. Even the purchase of a TV, radio,

---

6. Unlike other Andean migrants who regularly bring produce from their fields to support themselves in the cities (Gose 1994a: 63), Otavaleños do not usually travel with their homegrown grains and instead provision their house with foods purchased in the city.

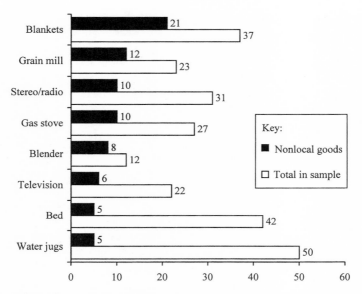

Figure 9: The eight most common nonlocal goods found in thirty-two Aria-sucu houses. (Chart compares number of objects from out-of-province with the total number of similar objects found within sample.)

and other electronic appliances can abet the productive practices of a weaving/farming household. As discussed in the next chapter, consumer electronics make long hours at the loom more palatable. By conceiving of their needs in terms of the domestic routines of Aria-sucu rather than as an unlimited demand for cash, some young merchants place a clear limit on their participation in urban handicraft markets.

In this way, the priorities of these commercial migrants differ from those of proletariat migrants elsewhere in Latin America. Josiah Heyman (1990) analyzed the household formation of Mexican migrants on the United States border and found that the consumption practices of the younger generation had the opposite effect. They turned young people away from their parents' social relations and locations and toward the city. While these cases contrast markedly in terms of both their economic and cultural specifics, together they underscore the importance of the strong links among the family development cycle, material culture, and broader social processes.[7]

7. For a more complete analysis of these issues as they relate to Otavalo, see Colloredo-Mansfeld (1998).

Drawing 20: Grain Mill

Of course, for some, economics may have nothing to do with the hoe in the corner of the city apartment. Grant McCracken (1988) has argued that singular, "out-of-context" purchases—such as the Ota-valeño man who bought a spinning wheel in Bogotá when better, cheaper ones were to be had back home—help people to recapture

"displaced meanings." He writes that people often locate their cherished values within mythical or remote times and places: a golden
past, utopic future, or distant land (McCracken 1988: 104). Goods
provide symbolic bridges to these realms, allowing people to recapture displaced ideals, such as the oft-repeated desire to "have one's
own work in one's own home," *without* having to take full respon-
sibility for them. Some do indeed cross these bridges quickly. Gas
stoves and cauldrons bought in Cuenca are used later that year to
cook a *kaldu* (broth) soup of fresh *choclo* (maize) back in Ariasucu.

For others, though, the "bridge" is wistful, preserving a link to a
romanticized life away from polluted cities, fickle construction jobs,
and indifferent tourists. I once spent an evening with a young couple
and their two children in a one-room apartment in the tourist town
of Baños. They had hung drying cobs of maize from the beams of their
small loft and kept some farm tools in the corner by their TV. For
much of the time I was with them, we talked about how they wanted
to move back to Imbabura and buy some land in the warm countryside southwest of Otavalo. For all their talking though, they had yet
to sink their tools into the fields of rich, black soil that they described for me. Indeed, they had no concrete plans to return. As with
some of the richest Otavaleño merchants, this couple's possessions
seem to both connect them with Otavalo's agrarian traditions while
making those traditions seem more fanciful than real. The ambiguous meaning of their farm tools raises questions about the future importance of the archipelago's rural center for successful, urban households, an issue taken up in chapter 6.

◢ From Households to Action Sets ◣

While households are the key units of the Otavaleño economy, the
connections among them spur its dynamic growth. Interhousehold
links often grow out of kinship, community ties, or friendship. Whatever the initial reason for these pivotal social bonds, people formal-
ize them through the rituals of *compadrazgo,* or co-parenthood.[8] At
their core, these relationships revolve around Roman Catholic church
rites that involve the sponsorship of a child's baptism, confirmation, or marriage. *Compadrazgo* can change social relations in two
ways. First, it intensifies existing family relationships when people
choose their siblings, parents, and even older children to baptize a

---

8. See Mintz and Wolf (1950) for a general description of *compadrazgo* in Latin
America. Lambert (1977), Martinez (1963), Long (1977), and Dávilo (1971) have also written usefully on the economic, personal, and social importance of compadres in an Andean
context.

child. Second, co-parenthood extends social networks as they recruit
nonrelatives, white-mestizos, or foreigners to baptize their children.
Mingling bonds of affection with periodic claims for economic assistance, compadres can both comfort each other with loyal support and
vex each other with burdensome requests for favors.

In the 1960s, anthropologists predicted that institutionalized, personal obligations would decline in social and economic importance
in Latin American peasant communities. They observed both falling participation in religious cargo festivals and rising efforts to
keep *compadrazgo* obligations from interfering with business ventures (Belote and Belote 1977). Based on this evidence, some researchers argued that as other economic opportunities rose, heavy public
investment in social obligations would decline (Wolf 1966; Smith
1977). In northern Ecuador, for instance, Walter (1981) wrote that
with the development of the Otavaleño tourist, handicraft industry,
wealthier community members' sons no longer spent money on fiesta obligations and compadre bonds. She writes, "as [the young men]
choose to explore new options in the textile sector, they abandon
not only the elaborate, expensive community festivals, but also the
elaborate, expensive family festivals associated with *compadrazgo*
initiations" (Walter 1981: 183).

In Otavalo and other parts of the Andes, however, capitalist expansion has not squeezed out *compadrazgo*. Instead, new business interests have kept dyadic ties vital, providing more resources to celebrate
these bonds and new reasons to pursue them.[9] Both the generic risks
of markets and the marginal position of Otavaleño traders combine
to perpetuate compadre bonds. Handicraft markets shift unpredict-
ably; foreign ones in unknown cities especially so. In 1995, for example, Ecuador's border war with Peru resulted in the closure of the
border with Colombia, cutting off craft supplies to Bogotá and the
flow of Colombian tourists and sweater peddlers to Tulcan. Since
the great majority of merchants operate in a mostly "informal" economy apart from banks and other sources of credit, such fluctuations
can put an end to a dealer's business. Although the shrewdest (and
usually the wealthiest) operators now can arrange grants or loans
from development agencies or financial cooperatives in times of
hardship, most Otavaleños can only protect themselves through personal ties. For the average dealer, compadres prove to be consistent

9. See Brown (1987); Long and Roberts (1978, 1984); and Smith (1979) for examples of
the value of *compadrazgo* relations in capitalist and mixed capitalist-subsistence economic contexts.

customers, flexible creditors, and reliable informants about the state of the market.

Market risk and uneven distribution of capital lead not only to "horizontal ties" between trading partners, but also "vertical" ties between patrons and clients. With the passing of time, individuals often try to extend their compadre connections beyond family especially to their wealthiest business associates who may be either indigenous or mestizo. Some ambitious traders find new powerful compadres in every town or business venture they enter into, reaching out to sweater factory-owners, transport operators and shopkeepers. The ongoing importance of dyadic business arrangements between patrons and clients underscores the growing economic differences within Otavaleño society. Dyadic bonds have long flourished in stratified societies with weak central institutions (cf. Mintz and Wolf 1950), two conditions that obtain in Otavalo's trade archipelago. Indeed, the transnational handicraft economy has exacerbated the class system within Otavaleño communities, a topic addressed in the chapter 6.

Both Galo in his time and Celestina in hers have depended on the family's extensive network of kin and fictive kin to undertake their sales trips. The construction program undertaken by Galo for our home called attention to the ongoing connections between social bonds, business aspirations, and consumption practice. Other families now add rooms onto their homes with a minimum of social effort by hiring skilled workers and day laborers to complete the job. In contrast, Galo and Monica hired a master carpenter, a *maestro;* by serving him extra food and giving him buckets of *chicha* to distribute to others who came to help, they elevated his status from technical expert to a social master of ceremonies. With the *maestro* to "officialize" both the construction and inauguration party, the work's social importance expanded to encompass the widest circle of family and neighbors (cf. Bourdieu 1977: 40).

Excluding the *maestro,* immediate family, and Chesca and me, they recruited eleven people to volunteer approximately thirty-three days of work. The helpers were local neighbors and several of Ariasucu's most prosperous dealers. Drawing from outside Ariasucu, Galo and Monica received support from one cousin who worked in Quito; from another one, named Francisco, who ran a profitable sweater exporting business out of his town home in Otavalo; and from Galo's sister and brother-in-law, who have lived on and off in Colombia. Galo called all of these participants "compadre," although in some cases, the *compadrazgo* connection was indirect—the person in question was a compadre of another relative. By the time the last tile had been set in the roof, these participants had augmented their donations of labor with other gifts, including a case of beer, eight cases of soda, about four dozen eggs, three bottles of apple wine, two live chickens, and a eucalyptus pole.

In order to host a proper inaugural party, Galo and Monica added to these gifts with ten pounds of beef, a sack of *wanlla* potatoes (specially selected large potatoes) and other delicacies. Although the celebration lasted only a day and a half and involved about thirty people—small by local standards—Galo built on the social importance of house construction by extending the presence of his illustrious work party. Cousin Francisco and his wife Zoila, for example, returned to Ariasucu early on the day of the party, driving up in their Toyota pickup truck from Otavalo. Carrying a gift of a case of Pepsi, he wore traditional *alpargatas* (white cloth sandals), white pants with a sharp crease, white shirt, and a silky-smooth, brown leather jacket. Zoila, dressed in spotless *anaku*, blouse, and shawl, followed him with a sack of eggs for Monica.

Galo's joy at their arrival dimmed when he saw his sister's son hop out of another cousin's Suzuki hatchback and realized he was here to stand in for his parents who could not come. His nephew Miguel, age fifteen, was raised mostly in Colombia and seemed to be readjusting awkwardly to rural life in Otavalo. With the exception of his long hair, he conceded little to traditional Otavaleño appearances. He wore an earring. His hair was pulled tightly back across his head into a neat braid and covered by a black, Duke baseball cap worn backwards so that the word "devils" arched neatly over his brow. He had an oversized purple shirt on, buttoned up to his neck and untucked all the way around, hanging almost to his knees. Its dark color accentuated the two silver chains hanging from his neck. Each bore a razorblade medallion. Sagging jeans and brown leather shoes completed the outfit. The style blended trends introduced by young musicians coming back from Europe as well as personal tastes that he had picked in Colombia. Galo hated it. Miguel flaunted it, reciprocating Galo's displeasure by acting like he was being held hostage at this event.

The guests took their place in the new room. Galo found his special folding chair for Francisco; Zoila arranged herself on the mats; and Monica gave soup to all the guests. Returning several times, she delivered to Zoila six more bowls, a generous, but not unusual amount. Zoila thanked Monica for the platters around her. However, having not brought a pot (as women always do in anticipation of such quantities), she could not bring the soup home with her. She ate some spoonfuls then seemed to lose interest. A few minutes later she plucked a potato out of the congealed skin forming on top of the soup and threw the white lump to a small dog. Not long after, Miguel and his cousin found an excuse to leave in the Suzuki.

I thought Galo would be upset about his cousins' aloof behavior. On the contrary, he was pleased with the way things went. When I asked him what they thought about the house, Galo beamed. He reported that Francisco said "it is very beautiful; the roof is good. These runners are very good. The round ones (cheaper, unmilled poles) are *yanga* (worthless)." Galo shrugged off his nephew's eccentricities and Zoila's boredom and declared the party a success on the basis of this compliment. Within a few months, he would have each of these guests back again for another fiesta.

Although parties are not hosted with specific business ventures in mind, enterprise inevitably draws on the goodwill generated in these events. Galo's social life, for example—his participation at other new house parties and weddings—increased markedly during a six-month period when he contemplated leaving the *faja* business and returning to handicraft selling. Meanwhile, Celestina's career came to hang on the help offered by the participants at the gatherings that her parents hosted. When provided, the assistance was not charity. Transactions among compadres are not egalitarian efforts to share the wealth, but rather socially accessed chances to further the separate (and often unequal) fortunes of the parties involved.

The scale, intensity, and geographic spread of Otavaleño social networks creates a competitive advantage that is not shared by other indigenous artisans in Ecuador. The self-sufficiency engendered by such multigenerational and transnational links harks back to the internal reliance described for earlier Andean economic archipelagos. And similarly, it contributes to Otavaleños' relative isolation within and outside of Ecuador. Certainly, some integration is happening. Long-established migrants have found acceptance in their new countries, even in Amsterdam where some Otavaleños have bought homes and married Dutch spouses (cf. Meisch 1995). Further, young traders like the rebellious Miguel act as a conduit between Otavaleño and other cultures, facilitating the mix of styles present both in Otavalo and expatriate communities. Yet, many in Otavalo's merchant class have, until now, minimized their attachment to host cities or countries. Despite traveling extensively and settling widely,

their commerce consistently reproduces the social and cultural connections back in Otavalo and the boundaries between themselves
and other groups.[10]

After almost a century of interprovincial and international trade,
textile deals are still largely a matter of patrons, clients, and compadres—and the favors that act as a currency among them. Relationships, not formal contracts, structure much of Otavalo's multi-
million-dollar transnational industry. To gain access to this business
world merchants invest their time and resources with family and fictive kin—reinforcing the significance of the gift-giving, compadre
ritual, and the locales where compadrazgo fiestas are held. Otavaleños have not abandoned institutionalized friendships; they lavishly
endorse them, cherishing them in the sounds, tastes, and sensations
of a perpetual circuit of parties.

◢ Fiestas and the Archipelago's Embodied Etiquette ◣

After that tense morning in May of 1994, Celestina resolved to marry
Pedro. Her parents came to support her decision, their resistance dis-
sipating after meeting Pedro's parents. Their future in-laws were neither aloof Mormons nor drunken farmers, as Galo had feared. They
turned out to be an older, hard-working couple who lived in a slightly
worn adobe house and made their living with looms, livestock, and
cornfields, just as Monica and Galo did. Pedro also made the decision
easier. He stopped threatening to head to another continent. Acting
more thoughtfully, he called upon his future parents-in-law, wearing
a traditional poncho, a formal dress shirt, blue jeans, and, of course,
his Reeboks.

Once Galo and Monica warmed up to their future in-laws and rec-
onciled themselves to Celestina's decision to marry, their worries
suddenly changed. How were they going to pay for the wedding? Galo
took to regularly crossing the patio between his weaving porch and
our door to come share his concerns with us. This was their first wedding, Galo pointed out. They had to lay it on—full band, plenty of

---

10. As cultural outsiders plying a specialized textile trade across international borders, Otavaleños exhibit the signs of "pariah capitalists," set out by Max Weber (1978: 13).
They lack autonomous political organization, suffer political and social disprivilege, and
retain distinctiveness in economic function. Further, in suffering official inaction, confis-
cations, and occasional theft at the hands of civic authorities in the countries where they
operate, Otavaleños must cope with the power asymmetry that is the essence of pariah
capitalism (Hamilton 1978: 4). Yet, their operations have, so far, been too small for them
to assume the structural importance that other pariah groups have within the national
economies in which they operate.

food, enough to drink—or "people will say, 'Galo does not know how to do a wedding.'"

The most important early task was to find sponsors, *padrinos*, for the event. Celestina and Pedro, in consultation with their parents, first considered approaching Monica's sister and husband who had taken care of Celestina in Tulcan. Ultimately, though, they came to Chesca and me to ask officially if we would be the *padrinos*, consecrating our three-year-old relationship with their family. Pleased to be asked, we accepted. We calculated that our responsibilities— buying gifts for the bride and groom and paying for the band—would take up most of our monthly stipend. It would be expensive, but we thought we could afford it.

Monica's requests, however, quickly showed our failings as wedding sponsors. About a month before the wedding, she and I chatted idly in the patio. Monica perched on her tiny chair, back bolt upright, was peeling a small potato by twisting it swiftly in quarter turns until the skin lay in a long ribbon on the ground. I stood nearby, tapping the stubble out of my electric razor into the pigsty outside our door. "How much do bands cost?" she asked. "I do not know," I replied, "maybe 30,000 or 45,000 sucres an hour," repeating a figure I had heard from Galo. Then, as the conversation carried on, and the pot filled with naked little potatoes, she slipped in how, these days, one had to have two days, not just one day of an *orquesta*, as the highly amplified ensembles of singer, organ player, drummer, and horn players were known. "Where will the money come from?" She asked. "I do not know," I answered with all sincerity.

These conversations grew in frequency, taking place around the patio, down by the water tap or waiting for the bus. They usually began with Monica asking, "How much does a roasted pig cost?" or "How much would it cost to pave the rest of the patio?" and wound up with the question, "Where will the money come from?" Losing our own illusions of our relative stature in this handicraft-fueled economy, we made it clear that our own funds were limited, and we would not be as generous as they (or we) might have hoped. But that did not cut back on the wish list. They just went to recruit other compadres to help with the major expenses. Assembling pledges for the band's second day and the purchase of the pig, they were able to host the kind of party that showed, that "although Galo has had all those disasters, he has had success" as his neighbor put it.

The fuss Monica and Galo made about expanding the party and improving the house reflected a simple desire to show themselves to be well off. But the meaning of the event cannot be reduced to mere "conspicuous consumption" nor to the tactical exchanges that sustain the networks of dealers discussed in the previous section. For all the prestige garnered and social ties consummated, these parties have a side that is both more visceral and more communal. The private concerns of a fiesta contribute to an enduring collective project: repairing the besieged ideals that are supposed to unite family and community.

Long-distance textile-dealing has a way of eating away at trust and respect among relatives, compadres, and/or neighbors. Celestina's confusion and her parent's fears illustrate the misunderstandings that crop up among the closest family members. During long absences, rumors often circulate about family and friends who misspend earnings or exploit junior family members or take to the bottle. For instance, when I asked one man about how his son was faring in Cañar where he went to live and work with his maternal uncle, the man had a hard time containing his anger. He felt his son had been working too hard and his brother-in-law had kept all the profits. He said bitterly: "more distant people are better. One has friendship with non-family. With family, you fight. It is better to work for others." For his part, the brother-in-law complained about being obligated to take his inexperienced nephews on as apprentices and worried that the added expense of caring for the boy would take up all his meager profits. As long as Otavaleños strive for handicraft profits by turning to family and compadres, these tensions will dog their relationships.

Amid this volatile mix of commerce and kin, fiestas afford a way to rebalance relationships. The flow of gifts and the continual servings of soup, soda, and beer reaffirms relationships in "a succession of rights and duties to consume and reciprocate" (Mauss 1990: 14). Even more than the costly gifts of soda, chickens, beer, and potatoes, the basic exchanges embedded in acts of consumption sustain goodwill within and beyond the event itself. Food at new house parties or weddings is not blindly handed out to all guests who gather within the family's patio and *corredor*. Rather, hosts monitor the status of each participant so that they can present the right amount of the appropriate dish in its proper order.

These festive meals often begin with *buda* or *buda api*, a thick soup of milled maize colored a deep reddish brown with *achiote*, delivered when guests arrive—which can occur at any time during the course of the event. Then hosts usually serve a second type of soup like *kaldu*, a clear broth of chicken and potatoes, followed later by helpings of the *midianu*, a festive meal of boiled potatoes, roasted

Drawing 21: Comadre Cooking in Outdoor Hearth

guinea pigs, and chicken.[11] The servers take care to catch up latecomers, typically feeding them *buda,* even when others are eating *kaldu,* then moving quickly onto the other dishes. Beyond sequence, hosts also vary quantity by gender and status. By carefully presenting six or eight bowls of soup to a single comadre, a woman can scale her servings to acknowledge past generosity or to elevate the current relationship to a new level of admiration or friendliness.

At a party where as many as two hundred people come and leave at irregular intervals, tracking guests strains the hosts. At Celestina and Pedro's wedding, for instance, Monica coordinated the work of five comadres working in three kitchens—one equipped with a gas stove, one temporarily set up with an open hearth in the cleaned-up pig pen (drawing 21), and the main one in the middle of the house.

11. Different hosts may have different preferences for the order of dishes, whether *buda* or *kaldu* should come first, etc. Whatever, they decide, though, they stick with for all participants.

Monica's father, Papasu, spent hour after hour trying to match the work of these kitchens to the traffic of guests. Before things got too busy and we were all pressed into service, Chesca and I videotaped part of their work. Monica, her daughter Clara, sister, mother-in-law Mama Rosa, and a compadre crowded each other in the main kitchen, which was overheated by two smoky cooking fires and three black cauldrons, bubbling with *buda* and *kaldu*. Her father hovered on the threshold between the kitchen and patio attending to the orders of the compadre who served newcomers in the crowd outside. A short transcription from the tape shows how Papasu struggled to keep abreast of the flow of guests. He was constantly calling for more bowls of soup:

> Papasu: Bowl, bowl!
> Mama Rosa: A little bowl, he says.
> Papasu: A bowl of *kaldu*, a bowl of *kaldu*, new people are coming.
> Comadre: Yes, yes.
> Papasu: Now that they are appearing, we are crying.
> Monica: Mama, please help.
> Clara: Here it is, Mama.
> Monica: There, there are the collected ones [bowls].
> Papasu: *Kaldu*, spoon [he turns to face his compadre in the patio] with a spoon, with a spoon, isn't that it, *kumpari*?
> Compadre: Yes.
> Papasu: How many, *kumpari*? [turning to the women] spoon, spoon! [back to the door] please count, *kumpari*, how many are there?
> Compadre: Three.
> Papasu: Three men, he says.
> Comadre: [looking out window] there are friends over on the *kumpari*'s side
> Papasu: [looking out door] we only know this side over here . . . [turns to comadre who is now seasoning the soup] collect some cilantro [to the women nearest him] with a spoon . . . we are bumping into each other, we'll burn ourselves.
> Monica: Here's a spoon.

So it went for ten hours on the first day and nine hours the next. Papasu, as *tayta servicio* (Master of Service) pleaded for more and more bowls of soup. The compadre in the courtyard handed each one out to the designated receiver—with spoons for men and spoonless for women, who took their share home in pots brought for the occasion. Guests promptly handed empty bowls back to servers so they could get food out to others.

In this unceasing traffic of soup and bowls flowed the life of the fiesta. The dense mass of resources assembled from all the compadres and guests blossomed into myriad, ritual acts of service. This choreography of soup bowls elevates fiestas, turning displays of wealth into the performance of ideals of reciprocal give and take. In fact, the new wealth and consumption habits of the long-distance textile dealers have made these serving rituals even more complex. Richer families have used their money not only to increase the number of compadres and *padrinos* they must honor but also to elaborate the types of food served at *compadrazgo* fiestas. Thus, tracking the status of individual guests has gotten ever more important. The most ambitious of hosts now stand vigilant to insure that all participants get helpings of the favored, new (first served in Ariasucu in 1992) prestige dish of slow-roasted *kuchi* (pig). At the most extravagant event I participated in, one woman in lower Agato served two roasted turkeys to guests at her new house party. She had the dish prepared at one of the region's most expensive hotels (a former *hacienda*) and delivered to the party in a taxi.

Compadres, fiestas, and reciprocal serving feature as central elements of indigenous societies throughout the Andes, not just in Otavalo. Allen (1988), for example, eloquently describes the place of reciprocity in the daily life and ritual practices of Sonqo, a Quechua community in the Peruvian Andes near Cuzco. "Reciprocity," she writes (1988: 93), "is like a pump at the heart of Andean life." Men and women, house and field, people and the earth bind themselves together in webs of dependence and opposition. The careful exchange of *k'intus* (small offerings of coca leaves) back and forth among neighbors gathered to harvest a field or mourners standing at a rainy graveside is a frequent and "tangible expression of their social and moral relationships" (Allen 1988: 128). As with other Andean ethnographers (see for example, Isbell 1978), she explains how the exchange of food, drink, and coca ritually construct shared values basic to interaction and activity. Such scholarship fits a broader anthropological tradition that interprets ritual as "an ideal version of the social structure. It is a model of how people suppose their relations to be organized" (Leach 1964: 286).

As in Sonqo, the flow of gifts at Otavaleño gatherings spells out the ideals underlying social relations. The problem for Otavaleños, however, is to go from expressing ideals—from producing "ideal versions" of social relations with bowls of soup—to insuring that the ideals apply in other and newer contexts. This problem is solved as much with the body as it is with explicit rules of etiquette and exchange. That is, more than a calculus of granted and received favors, "reciprocity" comes to life as a characteristic feeling produced by proper fiesta behavior. The repetitive acts of serving and eating transforms an abstract cultural ideal into a "referential experience" (Maquet 1986), a rhythm of interaction and gesture. It entails an intuitive sense of dependability, resulting from both the history of exchanges among a pair of compadres and the experiential details of ritualized, reciprocal consumption—the habits of awareness and responsiveness that inhere within the very movement of a plate of food or cup of beer. Through the patterned acts of consumption at family rituals, Otavaleños learn reciprocity as both a moral code and a discipline of the body.

At most fiestas, beverages flow in patterns of dyadic interactions. At gatherings ranging in size from our little new house party to week-long weddings, the hosts or *tayta servicios*, engage their guests to serve the drinks, including, *chicha*, soft drinks, beer, and *trago*. Typically, the host takes a bottle, finds a small glass, approaches either a man or a woman and offers him or her a drink. When it is accepted, the host hands over the bottle, receives a shot in return and then that participant serves the rest. Designating someone as a server, thus, confers a mixed blessing. On the one hand, the status distinguishes an individual from the multitude of other partygoers, bestowing some recognition. On the other hand, it subordinates the server to others' whims. The server does not drink a shot unless invited by another guest, and then he or she must do so (or be especially persuasive in refusing). As the individual with the bottle makes his or her round, that person drinks in tandem with those saying the words *"salud"* or *"ishcandi nishun"* (the two of us will drink). Furthermore, he or she must remain at the party until the whole bottle of *trago* or case of beer has been served one little cupful at a time.

The server's duty to minister to the guests, serve out the bottle, and complete specific reciprocal exchanges with particular drinkers supersedes other activities. This can lead to some awkward moments. Frequently, servers stand by mutely, waiting for a distracted drinker to break another conversation and hand back an empty shot glass. Disrupting a promise to drink together, drinkers may temporarily abandon servers to whom they have said *"salud"* because a second server (and sometimes even a third) has moved in to try and force a drink on a popular (or prolific) drinker. In these cases the original server holds his or her ground, carefully protecting a brimming shot glass, biding the time until the drinker returns to the original cycle that must be completed after the other servers are dispensed with. Serving a drink is thus always bundled in a moment of discourse that subordinates the server to the necessity of maintaining a cycle of give and take. As I learned during my time at fiestas, serving instills patience and focus in those burdened with the task—qualities intrinsic not only to doling out beverages but also to reciprocal bonds more generally.

As these rituals of service and consumption play out over several days, the action regularizes into simple mannerisms. Servers make round after round, and drinkers consume shot after shot, and the alcohol takes its toll. Before long the commands of reciprocity—*"salud," "ishcandi nishun"*—fade into a short wave of the hand, a nod, or sometimes the more explicit revolving of one hand over another to indicate that the recipient will follow the server. People learn to insist on the completion of a cycle simply by standing there, their silent body bringing about the close to the transaction. In my own fiesta experiences, I discovered that breeches of etiquette also brought forth automatic visceral reactions rather than explicit comment. One time a woman had given me a bottle of orange Fanta to serve. Having had the cup deferred toward me with the word *"salud,"* I drank it, then forgot to return a cupful to the recipient and instead poured and offered one to the next person. He flinched as if I was about to hit him. After that instance of surprise, he nodded back to the drinker I missed and I corrected myself.

The compadre fiestas, therefore, do not stop at an explicit statement about cultural values but go on to instill a physical "sense" of reciprocity. This sort of sensory enrichment reverses cultural abstractions (cf. Wagner 1986: 21). The material symbols (food and drink) and ritualized acts (serving and consuming) of "respect" and "obligation" come to stand for themselves, as the physical sensation *becomes* the meaning. A reciprocal bond with another is the moment he patiently returns to you, lightheaded, alcohol on his breath, holding a sticky shot glass in a jostling crowd, ignoring the hot, fruit-sweetened *trago* trickling over his fingers, and waiting for you to stop laughing with others to turn to him, drink the shot, and complete the cycle. This is the feeling, both a sensation and a memory, that must be rekindled on the less exuberant occasions when a favor is needed. The great accomplishment of Otavalo's unending succession of baptisms, weddings, and new house parties is the manner in which the ideal of reciprocity dissolves into the shared, unconscious feelings and etiquette of participants who have gathered from the dispersed places of Otavalo's social world.

Bourdieu has argued that this transformation of principles into conventional manners and unconscious habits of presentation protects a culture's most basic ideals:

> If all societies . . . set such store on the seemingly most insignificant details of *dress, bearing,* physical and verbal *manners,* the reason is that treating the body as a memory, they entrust to it in abbreviated and practical, i.e. mnemonic, form the fundamental principals of the arbitrary content of culture . . . Nothing seems more ineffable, more incommunicable, more inimitable, and therefore, more precious, than the values given body, made body by the transubstantiation achieved by the hidden persuasion of an implicit pedagogy. (Bourdieu 1977: 94, emphasis in the original)

Bourdieu, however, construes this "hidden persuasion" as a limited phenomenon. In his case study, only an upbringing in a traditional home seems to offer possibilities for implicit pedagogy. The fiestas of Otavalo, however, illustrate that such socialization extends beyond childhood and the architecture of a conventional house.

The activities of multiday family fiestas with their loud music, free-flowing alcohol, and carefully prepared dishes are the "total human phenomenon" that Friedman (1991: 155) writes about. They bundle together conventional rules of behavior, shared cultural meanings for the material world, and personal bodily experiences of that world. For Otavaleños, especially those who travel for extended periods, the totality of consumption elevates its importance as an arena of socialization. Consuming together reinforces values learned when growing up in Otavalo or teaches the community's etiquette and basic bodily comportment to those, like Miguel, who grew up elsewhere.

These behaviors ultimately have consequence beyond the relations of specific dealer networks. In the context of changes brought on by transnational migration, people depend on the body and its orientation to others and the built environment as a way to construct shared cultural space and identity. Oxfeld (1993: 7) for example describes the consternation of a Hakka Chinese businessman from Calcutta as he visits his son and grandchildren in Toronto:

> His grandchildren misbehave wildly in front of him, whereas the presence of a grandfather in the Calcutta Chinese community is

usually enough to put a damper on most children's rowdy horseplay. The same grandchildren pay no heed to their elders during meal-times, simply digging into the food without waiting for a signal from the most senior individual at the table.

This and other misbehavior cause him to believe his family "has abandoned some important principles of proper Chinese living" (Ox-feld 1993: 8). Similarly, in Samoan communities in southern Califor-nia, disciplining children's horseplay becomes an interaction evok-ing the rules, spaces, and material culture of a then-and-there, not a here-and-now (Duranti 1997). Samoan ideas about respect come to life in a Californian home as children obey their mother's general directive, "sit down," by taking their place next to the furniture, on the floor, lined up with their legs crossed as if they were on a wo-ven mat on a floor in Western Samoa. Duranti points out that the mother's words mediate between two worlds, separated greatly in time and space. " 'Talking space' in this way then becomes another contested ground where the battle between continuity and change can be fought' (Duranti 1997: 342). In Otavalo, change and continuity across communities, especially in connection to ideas of respect and reciprocity, likewise spring from the interplay among talk, bodies, and material culture, as much for adults as for children. In this case, though, the crucial domain is not so much "talking space" or for that matter "talking culture," but "serving culture": the rhythm of offer-ing, waiting for, anticipating, and receiving sustenance.

◢ Migration and Cultural Process ◣

Since Chesca and I left Ariasucu in 1994, we have stayed in contact with our wedding godchildren Celestina and Pedro. Although they have occasionally written, they have preferred calling on the tele-phone. Nowadays, when I lift the receiver, hear the hiss of static and the long pause that greets my "Hello," I know who is calling before they can utter the words *"Hola, Padrino"* (Hello, Godfather).

In early 1996, when they were living together in Tulcan on the Colombian border, Celestina and Pedro talked endlessly. They were bored, sitting around in the sweater shop where they worked, and pleased with themselves for figuring out how to use AT&T to make collect calls. We talked about how their baby was, how our baby was, and how business was going (usually pretty badly, first because of the border war with Peru, then because they lacked inventory). Later, af-ter Pedro went to Europe, the calls shortened. His inability to calcu-late time zones accurately usually meant very early calls; we were rather gruff at our end. For her part, Celestina had little time to talk since she not only had to take care of their toddler son, but also mind their store, find money to buy handicrafts and the time to travel down to Otavalo in order to send them to Pedro in Amsterdam. At age twenty-two, the demands of work and the dispersal of her family had squeezed her social life.

When I spoke to Pedro during his 1996 trip to Europe, the news was bad. A series of painful setbacks had jeopardized his work. "The police in Germany robbed me. They took everything," he reported. He was calling from Amsterdam where he was trying to put together some more goods to sell. "What happened?" I wanted to know. "The police took everything," he repeated.

Although I could not get anymore details, I suspect Pedro had met the fate of other Euro-traveling Otavaleños who had all their goods confiscated because they lacked proper papers. Compounding Pedro's problems was a falling out he had with Celestina's uncle, with whom he had bought a used car in Holland so they could travel together. According to Pedro, the uncle had gotten lazy. He was not willing to sell very often or move around, so Pedro said he was going to travel on his own. Thus, like Galo thirty years before him, Pedro faced having to build up his inventory and start from scratch.

In the thirty years separating Galo's confrontation with Colombian authorities in a tropical seaport and Pedro's run-in with the law on a cold fall day in the Rhine River valley, however, Otavaleños have established themselves more securely abroad. Handicraft inventories are now measured by the ton on air shipment Bills of Lading, not by calloused hands held three feet off the kitchen floor. So many young men have moved to Tulcan, Bogotá or Amsterdam that, when they want to play soccer, they can form their own teams rather than join in with local men. Nowadays, the expatriate community of Otavaleños in Amsterdam includes enough traders that people can choose their traveling companions when they get there. Further, some of the pioneers of the European market have settled in Holland, becoming *mayoristas*, large merchants who import in bulk from Ecuador and sell wholesale to small operators in Europe such as Pedro. Starting over after a disaster no longer means having to come home to farm and weave.

And yet, salvaging Pedro's trip still depends on the resourcefulness of Celestina back in Tulcan and Otavalo. Because the *mayoristas* charge such high prices, Pedro needs her to ship goods directly to him if he is to realize a proper profit. She in turn depends on her parents to help her save money on food and rent in the off-season when sales are low up on the border and it is no longer profitable to stay there. After three years of marriage, she has yet to move her new bed and wardrobe out of their home to an apartment in Tulcan; she remains a part of the life and economy of her parent's rural household.

Due to Pedro's problems, she again must approach her compadres for favors, to extend loans and to scrape together whatever handicrafts they can afford to give her on favorable terms. These requests come with small gifts, extended social calls, and lengthy conversations that make business seem like a family matter. All of us compadres have honored her and Pedro's pleas in one way or another. So far, the combination of their Tulcan sweater operation and European trip has plunged them into U.S. $8,000 worth of debt. No matter how well the rest of Pedro's effort goes, they will be deeply obligated for years to come. This predicament did not seem to faze anyone. In early May of 1997, I received a letter from Galo saying they were trying to get organized so that Galo himself could once again begin selling abroad.

Celestina, Pedro, Monica, and Galo illustrate the combination of debt, misfortune, and optimism that the transnational textile industry has brought to the Imbabura countryside. While the history of *mindaláes* and *casimires* and the specific cuisine of family rituals may make Otavaleños unique, the general experience of becoming mobile economic actors on the fringe of the world economy unites them with rural peoples from other regions of Ecuador and the Andes.[12] Describing the changing realities of peasant societies throughout Latin America, Kearney (1996: 8) notes that "the now emerging postpeasant subject often has a transnational identity."

The metaphor of a global archipelago helps illuminate the key economic features of this one group's migration practices: the complementarity of resources from different market and subsistence niches, the isolation of Otavaleños from their host countries, the importance of reciprocal relations, the moral and social work of ritual, and above all, the centrality of Otavalo as the place of social authority mediating access to opportunities in the expatriate "islands"

---

12. Miles (1997) describes the movement of men from Cuenca and its rural periphery to the United States. Providing a vivid visual portrait, Martinez and Gelles's film *Transnational Fiesta* documents the lives of men and women who have migrated from Cabana Conde in the Colca Valley of southeastern Peru to Washington, DC, and the fiesta that has, at least momentarily, united these worlds.

of the archipelago. In appropriating Murra's metaphor, however, I want to avoid rigidly fixing Otavaleño social organization to one specific model. Rather than define an organizational type, I am concerned with processes of archipelago formation—and dissolution. What Salomon (1985) argues for pre-Hispanic archipelago organization applies with equal validity to today's transnational society. The complementarity, reciprocity, and centralization of Otavalo's social economy should not be understood as a permanent essence of indigenous culture, "but a collective project, continually renewed through processes of adjustment, mobilization, innovation, and conflict" (Salomon 1985: 521).

For Otavaleños, inextricable involvement in national and international markets means that the organization of the archipelago intensifies or weakens with broader economic cycles. Oil booms, rising demand for handicrafts, or the economic stagnation brought on by border conflicts between Ecuador and Peru have all impacted the flow of migrants among Otavalo's dispersed communities. Signs of a new, more fragmented phase of social organization have already appeared. The economic developments of the 1980s and 1990s have augmented the forces of capital accumulation and class formation within indigenous society. As the next two chapters detail, growing social stratification has brought about new patterns of production, commuting, and consumption.

Returning from the river with tubs of clean laundry. Mount Imbabura rises into the clouds in the background.

Busting clods in preparation for planting maize.

Inspecting the field prior to planting maize and beans. (Photograph by Lucy Varcoe)

Working with *maestro* (master carpenter, on right) to set cross beams into the rafters.

Threading the final pass of the weft for a blanket woven on a backstrap loom.

Faja workshop: paid weaver staring through the rubber strips that hold the warp guiding frames.

Faja workshop: breaking for mid-morning *café*.

Serving culture: comadres working together to divide up and pass out toasted grain at a confirmation party.

Bride and groom break from dancing on the first day of their wedding celebration.

Enjoying bowls of *buda api* at a baptism. (Photograph by Chesca Colloredo-Mansfeld)

Minga: Residents of several communities have gathered to clear ground for water pumps.

Minga: Ariasucu residents dig ditch for potable water pipeline.

The author and compadres review recent footage of a church service. (Photograph by Chesca Colloredo-Mansfeld)

Introducing the recently crowned *Sara Ñusta* (Maize Princess) at the festival of Yamor.

Showing off a newly purchased car.

Otavalo Market: Slow day in the Poncho Plaza.

Otavalo Market: Young women and the possibilities for personal expression in hairstyles. (Photograph by Lucy Varcoe)

◢ FIVE ◣
The Artisan as Consumer: Commercial Faja-Weaving

◢ The "Thin Mormon" and Other Contradictions ◣
Migrants return home to Otavalo in many ways. Some merchants visit briefly to renew friendships and refresh memories before carrying on life elsewhere. Others give up jobs or trading careers, come home, and settle for good on their inherited land. Still others find themselves looking for work in the Imbabura countryside after losing urban jobs. Depending on the weaving or selling opportunities that turn up, they may stay for a few months or a few years. Eventually boredom or the chances for work elsewhere draw many back to the city. However long they stay, though, return migrants sharpen the contrasts of indigenous life. They introduce new goods and routines and, what is perhaps even more disruptive, they put old ideas, production practices, and dyadic relationships to work in new ways.

Beginning in the early 1980s, migrants returned to Ariasucu and transformed *faja* (belt) weaving practices. To do so, they crossbred the discipline of wage labor with the familial sociality of peasant artisan production. Their efforts launched them into morally ambiguous terrain. With their transformed artisan practices, *faja*-weavers illustrated the cultural eclecticism found in workshops throughout Otavalo and among native groups elsewhere in the Americas. As with handicraft dealers, weavers' use of consumer goods helped to devise new gender and social roles within these operations. Proprietors both mapped out and legitimized relations of production using the space and commodities of a rural hearth. Their efforts paid off in profitable enterprises. At the same time, *faja*-weaving's mixed cultural forms revealed the vulnerability of indigenous institutions. These tensions become most apparent in the large operations of the successful weavers, like that of *el Mormon*.

In the summer of 1991, I saw little of Galo's and Monica's two sons during the week. Each morning, José and Luis left the house before 7:00 A.M. and joined about seven other boys at the house of *"el Mormon,"* the sector's largest *faja*-weaver. By the end of the summer, I

163

had spent many afternoons at other multiloom operations in Ariasucu and asked them if I could also come and visit them at work in
their looms. Although they said it would be fine, I never made it.
When I crossed over the gully into the neighborhood where they
supposedly worked, I became confused. I could see only four or five
unpainted *tapial* houses (houses with packed adobe walls). Even the
largest, a windowless, two-story house with plastic sheeting hanging
from its eaves, seemed too small and humble for an operation of *el*
Mormon's size and reputation. I assumed the house must be located
just over the border among the larger homes nearer to lower Agato
and did not venture further.

Only the following year did I find out that the two-story house did
belong to *el Mormon*—Enrique Teran and his wife Mercedes Males.
Had I gone into the home, the house's interior would have fit my expectations of material prosperity. While the couple had not fixed up
the house's plain exterior, they had splurged on furnishings. When I
did an inventory in 1994, I found they owned a refrigerator, two gas
stoves, three TVs, a VCR, and three stereos. The contrast between
possessions and architecture was only one of many incongruities in
the lives of Enrique and Mercedes.

Although others now cite Enrique as Mercedes as people who "really know *fajas*," the couple actually came to *faja*-making relatively
late. While others were weaving, Enrique worked various jobs in
Quito, and Mercedes earned a living as a cook. They both liked aspects of city life. Mercedes enjoyed having an income and learning
recipes in the kitchen of a North American woman for whom she
briefly worked. For his part, Enrique earned steady wages at good
jobs during the economic expansion of the oil boom. Both their son
Rodrigo and their daughter Lucita were born in Quito. Expanding
their Quiteño social network, Enrique chose a well-to-do mestizo
machine-shop owner as a godparent for Rodrigo. The selection partly
reflected Enrique's belief that his children might grow up in the city.

As the 1980s wore on, though, a severe recession hit the labor market, eliminating good manual jobs. Having lost Enrique's wages, the
couple gave up the city and returned home. Enrique learned to make
fajas from his sister's husband, Mario Quispe, and started his own
operation in 1986. Concentrating on the more elaborate designs of
heart, diamond, and sun patterns that utilized six- and nine-peddle
looms, Enrique produced good quality belts which could be sold at
better prices. His success, however, has not been because he introduced any new design or technique. Rather, he and his wife have been

the best at recruiting and keeping workers like Galo's sons. When operating at full capacity, Enrique, Mercedes, and nine workers produce over one hundred *fajas* a day, compared with the three or four per week a single weaver with a backstrap loom used to make.

Steady production has generated consistent profits. With the higher incomes, they have not only bought a house full of consumer electronics, but also a small, yellow Datsun pickup truck. The fourth vehicle owned by an Ariasucu resident, it was the first purchased with weaving, rather than trading, earnings. They also have paid to continue their son's education. After Rodrigo graduated from the Catholic parochial elementary school in Agato, he enrolled in the *colegio* (high school) down in Otavalo—the only child from Ariasucu to do so at the time. The additional schooling not only required money for fees, but also spending on school uniforms, supplies, and daily bus trips back and forth to Otavalo. Enrique willingly shelled out the cash. Of all the possessions in his home, he was proudest of the typewriter that Rodrigo used for his homework.

At thirty-seven years old, Enrique has acquired many trappings of economic success. His good fortune, however, has amplified rather than transcended the contradictions of Andean life. His career unfolds through the compromises he must make between the opportunities of wealth with his obligations to family and community. Over the seven-year span of the potable water project, for example, Enrique has been the most consistent participant. Other wealthy households have chosen to pay fines in order to accumulate the daily point given out for *minga* participation rather than turn out for manual labor. These entrepreneurs have used cash to acquire the total of fifty points needed to qualify for water. Enrique, on the other hand, amassed seventy-two points, each one by dint of his own attendance. His community involvement has grown with his earnings.

His compadres offered another example of commitment to others. Some use their conversion to Protestantism to sever baptismal ties with those of other faiths (Rohr 1990; cf. Annis 1987). Enrique, on the other hand, extended his connections with his Roman Catholic neighbors and relatives, accumulating nine godchildren, many more than the three or four that other successful weavers had.

Finally, in a community where many men can get swept up in the obligations of social life, from fiestas to athletics, Enrique's sense of duty was strongest when it came to his own children. During Carnival in 1994, Rodrigo went swimming in Lake San Pablo and suffered some kind of seizure. Rather than spend his time and money over in

Agato hanging out with his friends, the wealthy artisans and dealers of *Club Deportivo Argentina* (Ariasucu's soccer club), he stayed home and to help Mercedes care for the fourteen-year-old boy.

His values, money, and affiliations have secured Enrique a unique reputation. Neighbors tend to identify him by his religion and his weight. People often spoke of him as *"el Mormon."* His strong association with the Mormons, though, seems out of place. While Enrique converted to Mormonism in the 1980s, he was not the first from Ariasucu to do so. Further, he has long since stopped accompanying Mercedes to the church's services. However, community preoccupation with church affiliation has less to do with faith than money. Many of the wealthier people in and around Otavalo had abandoned Roman Catholicism for a Protestant faith[1] and some of the richest have picked Mormonism. For his neighbors, Enrique Teran's conversion to a foreign religion confirms his growing material fortune, regardless of his actual religious practices.

Second, his neighbors, family, and would-be compadres described him as *el flaco* (the thin one) or remarked that he is not a fat man. As detailed in chapter 6, becoming fat in Ariasucu signifies growing riches. Further, the conflation of body type and class has specific ethnic and racial meanings. The problems indigenous people face—bad jobs, neglect by the state, and the struggle to make a living on tired subsistence plots—produce lean, undernourished bodies. Being Indian means being thin. Some take Enrique's gaunt cheeks and tight belt as a sign of *runa* (native Andean) integrity. As a thin Mormon, Enrique Teran thus embodies a paradox of modern Ecuador: the wealthy indígena.

◢ Global Forces and Hybrid Craft Cultures ◣

The blend of cottage textile industry with urban or even transnational careers has become commonplace in much of Latin America, where economic development ironically encourages rather than eliminates handicraft economies. Mexico, for example, shares its neoliberal economic reforms and "accelerated industrial reconversion with an intense support of artisanal production—the greatest on the continent and with a high number of producers: 6 million" (García Canclini 1995a: 154). Handicrafts' esteemed place in both popular culture and national economies (it accounts for 28 percent of Mexico's economically active population [García Canclini 1995a: 154]) subverts simple models of economic or cultural progress. Cloth

---

1. See Annis (1987) for a similar phenomenon in Guatemala.

manufacture, silversmithing, and folklore painting are among the many cash enterprises which people have "grafted" (Smith 1979) onto household and kinship relations.[2] Past artisan scholarship has, in fact, anticipated current writings about fluid subjectivities, documenting the way a craftsperson may begin as an indigenous peasant, become a rural laborer, move to urban odd jobs, then become a street merchant, before reconstituting him- or herself as a "traditional" weaver (cf. Kearney 1996).

Both Kearney and García Canclini argue that the current circulation of artisans and folklore tears away the barriers between modern and traditional. In the city, indigenous crafts and vanguard art catalogs rest on the same coffee table. Meanwhile in rural areas, "folklore today does not have the closed and stable character of an archaic universe, since it is developed in the variable relations that traditions weave with urban life, migration, tourism, secularization, and the symbolic options offered both by the electronic media and by new religious movements" (García Canclini 1995: 155). More succinctly, the world market for crafts has placed "weaving in the fast lane" (Stephen 1991a). New commodities, cash, "rationalized" relations of production, and consumption practices speed up and alter production techniques and designs. The synthesis alters gender, ethnic, and class identities (see, for example, the contributors to Nash 1993).

While research has captured the complexity of a hybrid present, it implicitly overstates the homogeneity of the past. Craft industries in the Andes have probably not had "the closed and stable character of an archaic universe" for six hundred years. Economically vital and politically charged, textile production, in particular, incorporated new technologies, materials, and purposes in advance of other occupations and cultural realms. Especially in Otavalo, weavers stood in the front lines of engagement with other societies. I mention below only a few of the major shifts that they have experienced: the expansion of the Inca empire, the Spanish invasion, and the advance of nineteenth-century British capitalism.

Before the Inca invaded in the 1400s, the inhabitants of the valley, an ethnic group known as the Caranqui, already included people who specialized as weavers and traders (Parsons 1945; Murra 1946).

2. The literature on simple commodity production is extensive. Authors have focused on all aspects from gender issues and household structure (Stephen 1991a) to the relationships between middlemen and producers (Littlefield 1979) to the connections between cash enterprises, paid labor, and household development cycles (Friedman 1978). The volumes edited by Norman Long and Bryan Roberts (1978, 1984) like Scott Cook's and L. Binford's (1990) work, offer sensitive regional analysis of small-scale enterprises.

Craftspeople worked with backstrap looms and cotton imported from warmer regions at lower altitudes. Most likely, their wares included both subsistence goods and costly objects that enhanced the prestige of local political leaders (Salomon 1986). With the Incas' bloody conquest, producers in the region used their old weaving craft and a new fiber (wool from llamas and alpacas) to secure relative autonomy through tribute payments (Salomon 1981: 435).

Shortly after the Inca military victory, Spanish *conquistadors* replaced the central Andean empire as the paramount political authority in the region. Again, the residents had to adapt their industry. The Spanish introduced sheep, new looms, and an oppressive institutional mechanism—the *obraje* factories—to extract wealth from the local textile skills (Rueda Novoa 1988). Otavaleños, though, appropriated the conquistadors' materials and technology to fend for themselves. With sheep's wool and treadle looms, they produced ponchos, shawls, and cloth used to make pants and sold them for profit during the eighteenth and nineteenth centuries (Chavez 1982: 36).

Late in the nineteenth century, British cash and products arrived as the instruments of a new type of *conquistador:* the global capitalist. British investments in Ecuador at the turn of the century were significant. By 1914, Britain held 100 percent of Ecuador's foreign external debt and represented 72 percent of foreign direct investment in the Andean nation (Bulmer-Thomas 1994). As with other conquests, this one, too, occurred through the complicity of local agents. Urban Ecuadorians, like their counterparts in Lima, Santiago, and elsewhere in cosmopolitan Latin America, had succumbed to the "allure of the foreign" (Orlove and Bauer 1997). Their demand for English cloth meant that nearly 30 percent of Ecuador's imports came in the form of British textiles. These goods limited the growth of indigenous cottage industry as English products controlled the urban markets (Salomon 1981: 441). However, they also opened an opportunity.

In 1917, F. A. Uribe, a native of Quito, sought out a weaver named José Cajas who lived in the native community of Peguche near Otavalo. Uribe had been impressed by the quality of a poncho made by Cajas and commissioned him to produce tweed fabric modeled on the design of expensive English imports (Parsons 1945). The cloth, called *casimires,* sold well. Cajas expanded production on a borrowed upright treadle loom, secured steady orders, and ultimately passed business on to other family members and neighbors. Weavers from other sectors similarly found their own entry into urban markets around this time (Korovkin 1998). The market grew and remained profitable for several decades until new competition, this time from national industries, undercut Otavaleño weavers in the 1940s. By that time, entrepreneurs had begun to adapt their work for the nascent tourist market.

◢ The Rise of Commercial *Faja*-Making ◣

Faja-weaving has only tangentially engaged the recent growth of the textile market. Historically, *fajas* did not earn much money. The final buyers of the product were (and still are) indigenous women, a segment without much disposable income. Further, the weaving techniques had changed little over the centuries. Along with ponchos, they remained one of the few products consistently woven on a backstrap loom until the 1970s. Those who specialized in this craft were the poorest artisans around Otavalo (Meier 1978, 1985; Naranjo 1989). Not yet commoditized, *fajas* made in the 1970s exhibited more individuality than other woven goods. Some men wove their wives names into the belt, others tailored the length or width to a spouse or daughter's preferences. These sashes endured as one of the last subsistence crafts in the area, minimally touched by the growing tourist trade.

In 1978, Mario Quispe reinvented the *faja* business in Ariasucu. He was eighteen and spending part of his time selling sweaters in Tulcan on the Colombian border. Otherwise he stayed in Ariasucu, where he wove *chalinas* (shawls) and ponchos on a treadle loom and *fajas* with a backstrap. Making a decision that many future *faja*-weavers were to emulate, he gave up the risky venture of sales for the more secure if less profitable weaving vocation. Despite *fajas'* lowly past, he chose to concentrate on them precisely because of all products he knew, the *faja* offered the greatest opportunity for growth. Prices of ponchos and chalinas had bottomed out due to competition from electric looms. "One could not make money with them," Mario said. Indeed, by 1994, few weavers still specialized in the product—the poncho—that had previously been the mainstay of the community's economy and craft reputation (figure 10).

Introducing a crucial innovation, Mario redesigned his *fajas* so that he could weave them on a treadle loom to speed up production. He soon produced as many *fajas* in a single morning (three to four) as he had in a week. As business grew, he taught his brother and the two of them eventually hired some teenage boys to weave on additional looms. Within a few years, however, their business stagnated. Mario

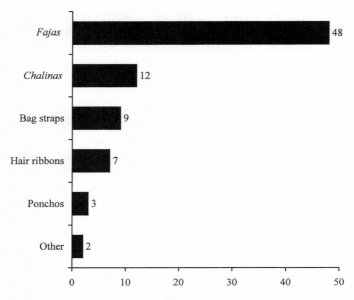

Figure 10: Weaving specialties, Ariasucu, January, 1994.

had a hard time retaining paid weavers. Frequently, workers left to try their hand in the tourist industry, work for wages in the city, or to start their own shops.[3] To keep workers around, owners had to compete with the pay scale of urban construction jobs and thus pay relatively high wages.[4]

Indeed, over the twenty-year history of the business, the high cost and scarcity of labor has kept the *faja* industry from transforming into more expanded commodity production (cf. Smith 1984). To be sure, some proprietors like Enrique and Mercedes enjoy the advantage of a consistent and relatively high cash flow. Such financial strength helps to hold workers and lets a few households accrue profits.

3. See Carol Smith's (1984) article for a thorough analysis of worker mobility and the limits to accumulation in Guatemalan textile production. Her case contains important similarities to the one discussed here.

4. The 250 to 500 sucres spent per piece for labor in 1994 could amount to one third of the overall cost of production and was more than double average profit. In one household, a proprietor not only failed to realize a profit after paying his workers but also had to cover the cost of their wages with the earnings he made from the belts that came off his own loom, resulting in a de facto wage for his own work that was half the prevailing rate.

However, no one in the *faja* business has earned enough cash to re-invest in power looms or other substantial capital equipment.

Changes in the world economy, however, resolved Mario's problem with worker retention in the mid-1980s. Throughout the 1970s, Ecuador's economy expanded on revenues earned from crude oil pumped out of Amazonian reserves. Oil profits led to the construction boom in Quito, which in turn attracted many ambitious and hard-working men and women such as Enrique and Mercedes to the capital city. By 1982, however, the oil boom collapsed. World prices fell, hitting Ecuador's heavy crude especially hard. More critically, the world financial system cut off credit to Latin American capital markets. These macroeconomic shocks convulsed Ecuador's labor markets. Work for Otavaleño migrants became, in the words of one *"un poco más o menos"* (a little more or less, that is, unreliable and low paid). Many migrants returned home and turned to the fledgling *faja* industry for a chance to earn money. As they became involved, the number of looms in Ariasucu multiplied rapidly (figure 11).

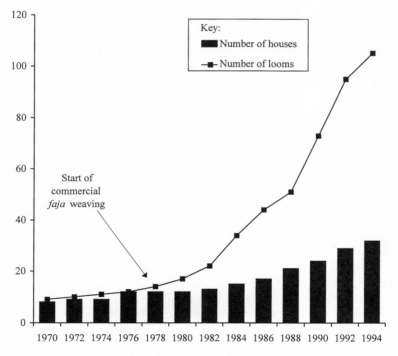

Figure 11: Growth in loom ownership, Ariasucu, 1970–94.

For Mario Quispe, these returning migrants were a boon. Through kinship connections, he successfully recruited several of them into his workshop. Burned by the capriciousness of waged employment, these new workers entered the *faja* business because it seemed to offer some control over their economic fate. As more than one weaver told me, *fajas* offered a chance "to defend oneself with one's own work." This desire to resist the uncertainties of fleeting jobs and new markets led to conservative choices in products. For example, Ariasucu's weavers avoided making straps for tourist bags until the 1990s. The decision cost them early entrance into the fast-growing bag segment of the market and cut most *faja*-weavers off from the profitable tourist craft sales altogether.

As local weavers went on to start up their basic *faja* operations, they pulled the trade from the grip of a few proprietors in one extended family and made it a communitywide venture. Rather than fight the twin problems of worker attrition and increased competition, Mario and others paradoxically helped weavers get started by loaning them looms, providing technical support, and giving them marketing tips. This self-defeating assistance to one's rivals testifies to the moral awkwardness of these ventures. The exploitative wage labor practices of piecework labor potentially—but not definitively—ran afoul of reciprocal obligations among family and compadres. In these murky social circumstances, transfers of profits to proprietors and commercial skills to workers were culturally redefined. Workers and owners talked as if profits and skills were part of the exchanges that befit longer-term relationships.

Thus, for example, when explaining the history of his business to me, one man prided himself on demonstrating to his compadres a profitable, diamond-shaped design. Further, he claimed that he visited them in their own homes to teach them on their own looms. When I went to verify this with his former workers, they scoffed at his remarks and assured me that they had worked in his home as his laborer. Conversely, the parents of workers in prospering shops sometimes saw their child's labor as a favor which owners ought to pay back. Indeed, one man took to calling Enrique "compadre" after his sons went to work in Enrique's shop. The adoption of this fictive kinship term signaled this man's belief that he now had a long-term reciprocal relationship with Enrique. The false claims about teaching and ad-hoc use of the compadre title indicated that market forces and wage rates alone did not constrain proprietors' push for profits. The others still held entrepreneurs socially accountable for their business behavior and were willing to extend the affairs of *faja* operations into other social arenas in an effort to redress what they perceived as imbalances in the structure of exchange. The simmering conflict discussed in the next section illustrates the potential for strife.

◢ The Contentious Relationship of "Chevrolet" and "Bread"[5] ◣

As the profits of *faja*-making became apparent, the craft attracted the attention of a few Ariasucu handicraft merchants, men with little weaving experience. Several of the most successful dealers bought looms and set up weaving operations in Ariasucu—men like Bernardo Santillan and Miguel Cando (whom I will refer to by his nickname, "Chevrolet," following the practice of the rest of the community who seem to have long forgotten his "real" name). Unlike Mario, Enrique, and other male proprietors, these dealers spent weeks at a time away from their weavers, leaving their spouses or children in charge. Preoccupied with other jobs, they never learned the intricacies of *faja*-making. For instance, the ability to order the 190 threads that form both the structure and design of the *faja*'s supplemental warp weave eluded the craft businessmen. To improve the quality and output of their operations, absent proprietors called upon their skilled, poorer compadres to help out.

These arrangements complicated the social relations not only of *faja* production but also of community life more generally. With compadres depending on each other at baptismal fiestas, during new house construction, in marketplaces, for community council matters, and now on weaving porches, misunderstandings that have their origin in the *faja* business have a way of cropping up elsewhere. The contentious relationship of Compadres Chevrolet and Bread illustrate the porous boundaries between economic, social, and political affairs in the Imbabura countryside.

In early February of 1994, I dropped by Chevrolet's house to say hello. When I arrived, I found him pacing around his *corredor*, stripped to the waist, gnawing on a potato. His thin, graying braid shone with sweat. Chaff and leaves clung to his rounded belly, which hung over his white pants. "Hey friend! I just arrived," he yelled to me as I stepped into his patio. He gestured toward five or six sheaves of *quinua* stacked along a wall and explained he just had a *minga* to bring in his crop. Having sold his *fajas* earlier in the week and

5. Nicknames are fictitious, approximating the general meanings of true nicknames.

harvested the last of his fields the past crop season, Chevrolet was in a jolly mood. As I left, he also set off to round up players for a volley-ball game.

I went to visit Santo inside his weaving shed. Moments later Chevrolet himself strolled down the path. He had come to recruit more volleyball players. "Compadre Bread," he called out, using Santo's nickname. "Bread" is a flippant moniker referring to Santo's supposedly expensive tastes as a kid. His nickname stands in ironic contrasts to Chevrolet's imported brand name. "Chevrolet" suggests a true modern luxury, not just a tasty item that was cherished because of its scarcity in a poor rural parish. He earned the automobile name later in life when he joked with other Ariasucu expatriates living in Cuenca that he was "as tough as a Chevrolet car." Echoing of profitable sales trips and worldly experiences, the name fit the man's individual advancement and ambition.

Santo cringed at the sound of Chevrolet's voice. He sent Maria out to get rid of him. After Chevrolet left, Santo told me that Chevrolet had taken eighty *fajas* from Santo to go sell with his own limited inventory late last week. Chevrolet needed to diversify his selection and he promised to save Santo the cost of a sales trip. While he managed to sell them all, Chevrolet also accepted pitifully low prices for Santo's products. Chevrolet then lent some of the proceeds to a third man, returning only a fraction of the money that Santo expected to make.

Santo then switched subjects to other things he had done that week. He surprised me by saying that the day after learning about the *faja* debacle he went down to Chevrolet's house to provide the older man with crucial assistance in preparing materials for his next group of *fajas*. Despite Santo's anger over the mishandled sale, he had spent the afternoon guiding hundreds of meters of thread onto Chevrolet's old warping frame–without getting paid a single sucre. The two of them worked together, watched TV, shared an afternoon meal of soup, and talked about the baptism of Santo's son the coming Saturday. Later in the week, Santo went back down to Chevrolet's and borrowed a table and chairs for the baptismal fiesta.

The loan of furniture, however, did not lessen Santo's ire over the sale. Two months later, he transformed this private financial dispute into a minor community crisis. Santo had owed the council 40,000 sucres, about the same amount he reckoned he lost in Chevrolet's sale. In the course of a rainy potable water *minga,* Santo explained to the council president that Chevrolet would pay Santo's debt with the money owed for the *fajas*. The council then announced Compadre Bread's arrangement to all the workers gathered on Ariasucu's volley-ball court at the end of the day. A flustered Chevrolet raced over to the council, grabbed the loudspeaker, and declared that Santo had his facts wrong. At this point, one of the drunkest workers and long-time enemy of Chevrolet staggered over. He badgered Chevrolet, shouting incoherently over the loudspeaker, insisting that he pay the council. Chevrolet put the loudspeaker down and prepared to fight the man. The council members jumped in to break them up. Meanwhile, Santo had left. His back hunched against the drizzle and commotion, he and a compadre strolled away through a maize field toward his home to fight the damp with a "little cup" of *trago*.

To keep a multiloom *faja* operation going, proprietors pull to-gether skills, materials, and labor from whomever and wherever they have a claim. The effort can misfire. Resentment can creep into com-padre relations and manifests itself in exchanges that have little to do with belt-weaving. Nonetheless, those who have managed the cross-cutting social and economic arrangements have been rewarded by ac-cumulating consumer goods and productive stock at a faster rate than many other households. In 1994, I asked a sample of thirty-two house-holds about the goods they owned. The median replacement value of the weavers' possessions (U.S. $1,189) turned out to be more than twice that of a random sample of nonspecialists (U.S. $555).

By 1994, *faja* manufacture became a dominant commercial ac-tivity, squeezing out other occupations in households that came to specialize in *fajas*. Almost half of Ariasucu's households (47 percent) had gotten into the business. Forty-eight homes had among them 109 looms dedicated to *faja* production. Another seventeen houses had tried making *fajas* and occasionally returned to their looms depend-ing on the market's profitability. From its origins as a minor subsis-tence craft, *faja*-making became a potent force of economic change, inserting the practices of wage labor into the community's domestic economies.

Built on preexisting institutions and relationships, however, *faja* workshops are never simply economic enterprises. Because of the "multiplex" (Gluckman 1962) relations of those who work there, a *faja* shop often becomes a vehicle for furthering relationships and business that has little to do with indigenous women's belts. Con-versely, any realm of social relations in Ariasucu these days can become extension of the *faja* trade—family fiestas, political meet-ings, or volleyball games. As they juggled their roles and obligations, proprietors have had to find the practical and symbolic means to hold their operations together against conflicting interests. The answer for many lay in the material world.

◢ Agency, Gender, and Material Culture ◣

For both large and small weaving operations, managing work has meant devising the proper settings. As Robert Desjarlais (1996: 894) writes, agency is "context dependent, if we take context to mean both a specific "place" and the social, political, economic, and cultural dynamics that give rise to that place." Adapting to Otavalo's economic and moral dynamics, proprietors physically reshape their homes as places that balance a new enterprise among the multiple occupations, social roles, and interests of household members and employees. Goods and appliances assume a key organizational role. They become vehicles for "identifying, defining, and manipulating [the] social concepts and maps" which guide the household (Wilk 1989b: 312).

Using objects as both practical and social instruments, small operators reconstitute themselves and their homes in small and gradual ways. In their early years, these *kusawarmi* (husband/wife) shops must defend commercial weaving's place against the demands of farming, raising children, preparing food, and the tedium of the work. If workshops grow, proprietors must meet new challenges, such as maintaining the loyalty of their paid weavers. No matter what the scale, the TVs and gas stoves brought into the home do not replace existing possessions so much as add to them. They expand the cultural repertoires of occupants without precluding past routines.

In the early 1980s, when weavers first set up their shops, they worked as their *casimires-* and poncho-weaving grandparents did. Women prepared threads and cleaned up finished *fajas.* Men wrapped the warp, wove the products and went to sell them (figure 12). As the industry grew more competitive, however, proprietors had to find a new balance among agriculture, food preparation, socializing, and other daily activities. This meant a redefinition of traditional roles for men and women.

Culturally and economically, the most significant change is the movement of women to looms (figure 12). To be sure, men continue to do three times as much weaving. However, the 22 percent of *faja*-manufacturing time that women actually spend weaving (accounting for 9 percent of all weaving) reflects real growth from 1991, when I saw no adult women weaving and only a few teenage girls working as paid weavers. Since 1994, at least fifteen adult women now weave

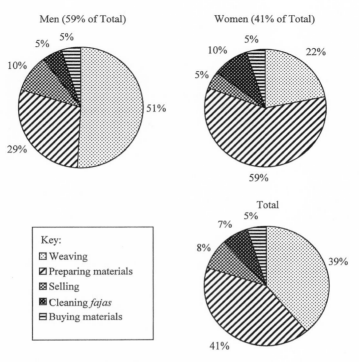

Figure 12: Percentage of *faja* manufacturing time allocated among productive activities, Ariasucu, February–November, 1994. (Total *faja* manufacturing observations = 560.)

Table 4. Composition of *Faja*-Weaving Workforce, January 1994

| Proprietors | | Wage Labor | |
Male	Female	Proprietor's Offspring	Non-household
45	15	20	53

(table 4). When I inquire about the change, both men and women usually say it is "for the money." Cook and Binford (1990) note a similar crossover of women to treadle looms in some communities near Oaxaca. They write "the allocation of available labor power to loom work is the best means available to many households to cope with the 'simple reproduction squeeze' (Bernstein 1979: 427) or to realize their aspirations for petty capital accumulation" (Cook and Binford 1990: 96–97). In Otavalo, as in Oaxaca, women must raise their commercial profile because weaving's economic rewards are in decline.

The more time women spend on the looms, the less time they have for other chores, especially food preparation. Thus, an important component of *faja* specialization in *kusawarmi* (husband/wife) operations is the modernization of the kitchen. People replace hearths, grindstones, and *ají* stones (millstones used to make hot sauce) with gas stoves, grain mills, and blenders. Back in 1994, for example, after one weaver lost his workforce of three teenagers, he and his wife agreed that she should try to weave. Although she quickly learned a basic pattern, she rarely made more than five *fajas* a week. Cooking and children interfered. After a month of frustratingly low productivity, her husband asked me for a loan so that he could buy a gas stove (drawing 22). Indeed, precisely because of the time it makes available for commercial tasks, most people in Ariasucu ranked gas stoves as one of the most important household objects (see table 2 in chapter 3).[6]

Consumer goods also redefine male roles, paradoxically, by "redomesticating" men. At least since the 1960s, men have left indigenous communities to look for jobs in national labor markets. In addition to earning money, young men go because they are bored of the countryside and want to experience life in the city. Even when they can earn adequately from their looms, returning migrants chafe at the slowness of local life and the boredom of long weaving days. Many tell me of the need for entertainment, for TVs, stereos, and boom boxes (drawing 23). As one man puts it, *"televisioncunaca valen; tshishita kushichihun"* (Televisions are worthwhile; they make the afternoon happy). Not surprisingly, looms and televisions have become the most frequently utilized objects in the community (figure 13). Taken together, the two objects help keep men at home— *faja*-weavers now spend 49 percent of their time in and around the house, 50 percent more than other men in Ariasucu—and a few older traditions alive.

In the years since he has returned from Quito, for example, one former construction worker has learned to entertain himself by both watching *MacGyver* and converting his loom among different products. Thus, every now and then, as he follows MacGyver's exploits

6. Rural Otavaleños do not, however, see the stove as replacing the open hearth, which because of its value in preparing homegrown grains, especially for social occasions, is still considered the most important feature of a home.

Drawing 22: Gas Stove

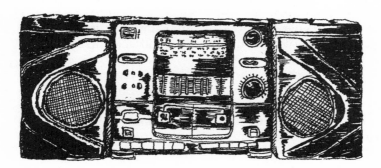

Drawing 23: Boom Box

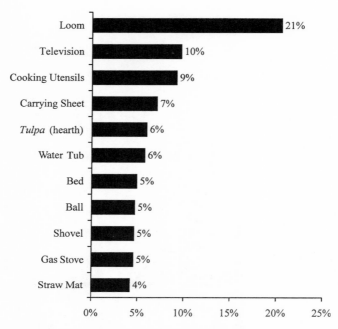

Figure 13: Most commonly used objects within thirty-two Ariasucu house-holds, February–November, 1994. (Rankings based on percentage of 1,418 observations in which an object was instrumental to the action.)

on his black-and-white TV, he weaves handspun wool into a broad, white cloth, which his mother will use to make full-length *anakus*. These sleeveless tunics, worn pinned at the shoulders, were given up by most Otavaleño women decades earlier. The number of weavers in Ariasucu who know how to make them has dwindled to just two. By keeping this man at his loom, therefore, MacGyver has ironically done what probably no national folklore project probably could have. He has helped to preserve an outfit with a 600-year history and a small but loyal group of modern wearers.

With their fully equipped homes, husbands, wives, and older children can periodically concentrate all their effort on *fajas*, cranking out the belts for the better part of a morning. One of my lingering images of a *kusawarmi* operation, in fact, is a home filled with loud music from a newly purchased stereo in which the husband wove in the middle of the *corredor*, the twelve-year-old son wove next to him, and the wife worked in the far corner. Between her loom and her husband's ran a long hammock suspending their infant daughter who rocked with the rhythmic swaying of the parents' looms.

From Instrumentality to Ideology

The importance of the material world, however, does not stop at its practical functions like reducing food preparation time. As detailed in the earlier discussion of family fiestas, acts of consumption are fundamentally ideological. They can legitimize structures of authority, principles of economic relationships, and visions of the future.[7] As an ideological code, material culture does suffer certain disadvantages. For example, it lacks spoken language's flexibility and range and fails to offer the depth and complexity of writing. Nevertheless, the communicative limitations of the physical world are also its strengths.

Taken as a natural part of the setting, goods communicate unobtrusively. Messages sent by possessions and commodities arrive unconsciously and do not undergo close scrutiny. McCracken (1988) argues that because of this subtlety, goods can partake in cultural innovations while at the same time disarm them, diminishing the chance of real change. The object code, he writes, "is capable of encompassing even its own departures" (McCracken 1988: 134). This duality inheres in the material life of a *faja* workshop where people utilize space, possessions, cuisine, and linguistic registers to invent new work relations. At the same time, consumption helps recreate the values of mutual assistance within these new economic roles. To illustrate the flow of activity, I return to the home of Enrique and Mercedes.

On a slow morning in November of 1994, Mercedes let me videotape the weavers at their place. On this day, the six workers, four young teenagers and two in their twenties, had arrived at their looms by 7:00 A.M. Not long afterwards, the weavers rocked in their seats to the salsa, disco, or Latin rap blasting from Sony speakers hanging on the wall. (Like TVs, stereos make a shop happy; workers have been known to switch employers for better music.) The looms, too, pulsed with sound. Pedals slapped the floor and shuttles knocked the beat on the looms' swinging frames. The multiple components of uprights, cross bars, hanging wire guides, and benches cut up the *corredor* into a dense collection of rectangles. Walking through the space gave the

---

7. For a valuable archaeological discussion of the ways in which the physical world materializes ideology, see DeMarrais et al. 1996.

impression of being inside a solitary, musically regulated, human-powered wood and wire mechanism.

Mornings before their break were the weavers' most productive time. Concentrating at their task, they generally produced one *faja* an hour. On this day, all the weavers worked steadily until 10:00 A.M. when Mercedes brought out their morning meal: a big enamel bowl heaped with a salty mixture of toasted maize, lentils and rice, and crowned by a ring of spoons. She set it in the pathway in the middle of the looms and the boys pulled up stools and water jugs, plucked out the spoons, and ate.

The food and its presentation had symbolic value. The dense mix of grains and lentils was the type of food often prepared as a *kukabi*, a meal eaten by a family out working in their fields or at a *minga*. In other shops workers spent their midmorning break suspended in their loom sipping a steaming cup of *café* (sweetened herbal tea) and eating bread rolls. Here, Mercedes brought her weavers together. Serving all her workers from a single large bowl suggested that this commercial work was familial and collective, a joint effort undertaken by people with a lasting connection.

As they finished up, the younger weavers wrestled, while the older ones returned to their looms promptly. When the boys finally got back to work, they held their shuttle at any distraction: to laugh at another worker dropping his shuttle, to examine me as I swiveled my camera, or to search for a kitten hiding among the looms: "Hey, hey," called a worker upon seeing the kitten, "this is the way it left."

"Hurry, hurry and weave, the cat is already (gone) . . . weave fast, weave fast," interrupted Mercedes from inside when the looms went silent. She used an abrupt command form for "weave" (*away* instead of the polite *awapay*), a register suitable for errant children. She repeated to them, "sit down, weave!" until she heard the looms working again. Younger weavers rarely feel the older worker's pressure to maximize their daily income. Mercedes, therefore, had to keep after them the same way their mothers back home would nag them to finish their chores.

She maintained her watch while sitting inside on a small stool, peeling potatoes. Indeed, as *faja* operations got larger, women's work often reverted back from looms to stoves. More time was needed to feed a growing workforce. Mercedes' case was special, though. After his seizure, Rodrigo never fully recovered his health and instead got worse. Impatient with the slow response of Otavalo's doctor's, Enrique took Rodrigo to the children's hospital in Quito. As Enrique remained in Quito with their son, Mercedes stayed at home with their daughter and to cook for their weavers. During the course of her son's and husband's long absences, she had learned to cover his tasks.

A worker came inside from the *corredor* to set up cones of thread used for the weft and began spinning bobbins. The thin white acrylic filaments hissed through the wire loops tacked into the ceiling above the cones and spun into thick white cocoons on the sticks that ride in the middle of the shuttle. He wrapped up about a half-dozen, then put the cones away.

Before the worker left, Mercedes remembered she needed her own shuttle bobbins. She hopped up from her stool and asked for three of boy's newly spun ones. Taking them, she then thanked him formally, raising the tone of her voice and enunciating *"Dyuslpagui, Dyuslpagui,"* ("thank you, thank you") several times in undulating rhythms.[8] Mercedes had switched linguistic codes. The politeness, however, did not connote impersonal gratitude. Standing in the midst of her kitchen and thanking someone so enthusiastically, Mercedes seemed like a comadre thanking a compadre who would come in and help out on a special occasion.

After the worker left, Mercedes went to the stove, stirred a large cauldron of soup, then returned to peel more potatoes. Other workers came and went. Some worked the spinning wheels, while others came in to chat or change the cassette or CD in the stereo.

Shortly before 1:00 P.M., the workers broke again to eat lunch. They sat around inside, joking and watching some Hollywood movie in which a lot of blond-haired people in bell-bottoms coped with an errant chimpanzee. They turned to me as a key informant, asking me for plot explanations that I could not provide. After finishing second helpings of chicken soup with chunks of potatoes and thick, blistered maize kernels, they returned to their looms. The bored ones left early, around three o'clock; the older ones who need the money stayed until 4:30 or 5:00 P.M. Most made their way to the volleyball court. When the oldest worker (twenty-seven years old) caught up to the others, he joined in a three-man team which included his previous employer and a neighbor and went on to bet a day's earnings on the outcome of the match.

In domestic workshops such as this one, both economic roles and social identities emerge through linguistic, culinary, spatial, and material channels of communication. Thus, for instance, despite most proprietors' and workers' fluency in Spanish, people speak Quichua. The use of *runa shimi* (the [Andean] people's tongue) marks

---

8. See Allen and Garner 1995 for translated examples of the polite, formal Quechua.

commercial weaving as an indigenous activity. The language signals workers' and owners' common ethnicity, uniting them in a shared moral universe. Switching between formal and informal registers suggest other nuances in workshop relationships. Owners often speak to workers casually as if they were junior members of the household. However, in all workshops, I heard occasional formal requests or expressions of gratitude; proprietors tacitly acknowledged the autonomous aspects of piecework—the fact that the worker is not simply a child but an artisan trying to earn money.

Meals similarly send dual messages. Owners emphasize bonds with workers through eating together. Even those who do not offer a *minga*-style collective midmorning break will share the lunch as one big family. However, owners are also careful to stick to urban meal times when they have workers. As one proprietor explained to me "We indigenous people eat early in the country. But if we have workers, we eat in the middle of the day." Replacing the flexible, agriculturally sensitive indigenous meal pattern with a rigid Western schedule, proprietors emphasize discipline and the commercial purpose of the workday (cf. Weismantel 1997).

Like time, space has its strategic uses. Along with Enrique and Mercedes, all the proprietors grant workers considerable freedom within their home. Workers not only come and go freely to prepare more materials for their use but also literally to make themselves at home. Owners who have a TV let their weavers watch it; those with boom boxes let workers call the tune. Often when I visit houses, I find the whole household and all the workers sitting together on a bed, having lunch, and watching TV.

This use of the home is remarkable. In Otavalo, people carefully respect a house's space. Nonhousehold members do not venture into the patio outside the house without being greeted formally by a household member with the words *"shamupaylla, shamupaylla"* ("come in, come in"). So deep is the respect for the hearth, that some parents rarely enter their children's homes and will even eat a bowl of soup outside while the rest of the family eats inside. To allow young paid weavers the run of the house when close family members keep a formal distance signals the workers' special status. Along with paid employment comes a quasi-household membership.

In short, the action of a *faja* workshop emerges not only from specific historical and economic contexts but from physical ones as well. The significance of patio, porch, and kitchen invest new weaving operations with coherence and meaning. Giddens (1981) argues that such settings are an essential part of any social structure. He writes, "the locales of collectivities are integrally involved with the structural constitution of social systems, since common awareness of properties of the setting of interaction is a vital element involved in the sustaining of meaningful communication between the actors" (1981: 39). In Otavalo, weavers use this common awareness to stretch the meanings of past relations into current productive activities and use current activities to project future commitments.[9]

◢ The Future of *Fajas* ◣

As a hybrid of commercial work routines, dyadic relations, consumer electronics, and peasant households, *faja* workshops meld together Otavalo's diverse social and economic realities. After fifteen years, these operations now alter some of the institutions that gave rise to them. In particular, commercial habits have streamlined the social roles of the peasant household, stripping them of obligations to fields, kitchens, and other sites of agrarian production. I have already mentioned how the appliance-filled home "frees" women to work commercially. Children, too, have become liberated in some respects. Now that Ariasucu has an internal labor market for young weavers, both boys and girls take up employment in other homes, often when they are ten or eleven. Domestic development cycles speed up, with parents losing their offspring's labor at a younger age.

Other changes, such as the emergence of an entrenched class of large shop operators, seem unlikely. *Faja*-weaving has lost much economic steam. In 1994, weavers sold their products for nearly the same prices they received in 1991, despite the doubling of the price of thread since then. Inflation was only part of the problem. The steady increase in the number of producers in Ariasucu and other communities glutted the market. *Faja* sellers traveled farther to smaller towns and settled for lower prices. One weaver who worked with his two sons barely cleared U.S. $10 in profit on 100 *fajas* (about six weeks' worth of products) in 1994, less than one fifth of what he had earned on other occasions. Under these intensely competitive conditions, more and more weavers withdrew looms from production. A few of the poorest gave up operating independently and adapted their skills in order to weave simple straps for handbags. They received their materials from urban merchants and got paid only for the labor they expend making the straps (cf. Littlefield 1979; Chevalier 1983). For these workers, textile production differed little

---

9. Henrietta Moore (1986) provides related examples of the discursive use of space and the material world from her work in east Africa.

from other forms of wage labor. Sometimes, when I went to visit piecework weavers, household members told me that they had gone to Quito to look for construction jobs as a "break" from the loom.

With the decline in *faja* weaving's economic potential, the practical benefits of the workshop's social life become clearer. Weavers turn to the dyadic networks implicated within weaving operations in order to make a living in other ways. Although Mario, Enrique, and others continue to churn out the belts, they keep their eyes open for craft-dealing opportunities. Some enter into sweater wholesaling with their compadres while others form retailing partnerships with former employees. Even Chevrolet and Bread patched up their differences and went into business together. With Chevrolet's capital, they bought hundreds of machine-knit sweaters and took them to the Peruvian border. On their first outing, they sold them for a respectable profit during Father's Day.

Enrique's and Mercedes' story does not end so happily. Two and one-half months after first being stricken, their son Rodrigo died. During the last month of his life, Enrique tried everything within his means to have the boy cured. He gave up on the biomedical establishment when extended hospitalization in Quito could not even come up with a proper diagnosis, let alone an effective remedy. Returning to Imbabura, they visited a string of *curanderos* (indigenous healers) in Otavalo and various native communities. They, too, could not help. The child slowly wasted away and finally died in his bed in a corner upstairs above the kitchen with his parents by his side, away from the looms and the TVs.

On the day of his death, Mercedes washed his corpse with water and flower petals. Enrique dressed him, completing the funerary outfit by easing his son's favorite baseball cap over his braided black hair. They then held a Mormon service for him in their home. Two days later, he was taken down to town to be buried. Enrique chartered four *Imbaburapac* buses to take along other mourners from the sector. Each one filled up, with extra riders standing in the aisles. The collective grief surprised some of the participants who would comment on the large turnout even months after the fact. As they passed through town, Enrique had the procession stop at the Catholic church. His brothers and compadres carried Rodrigo's coffin inside and up to the altar for last rites. They then returned to the buses and went on to the main (Roman Catholic) cemetery.

In prosperity and tragedy, Mercedes and Enrique extend Otavalo's long tradition of cultural mixing. Such blending occurs across all contexts of social life, from religion to medicine. Here I have concentrated on but one, artisan production, and have tried to show how it fits a historic pattern of engagement, cultural diversification, and retrenchment. For centuries, people living in Imbabura have developed their livelihood by working with the new demands and materials of such varied entities as the Inca Empire, Spanish colonialism, British capitalism, and the global trade in ethnic arts. While the current blending of cultural traditions may represent new sources of influence, these are differences of degree rather than kind. Cultural crossbreeding through craft production is not a new practice; it has both underwritten the energetic development of Otavalo society and been a part of its cyclical reversals. The eclecticism of *faja* workshops, the weavers and their TVs, is but its latest manifestation.

◢ SIX ◣
The Native Leisure Class

In chapters 2 and 3, I set out some of the conflicting values that shape Otavalo's social world: racial ideologies, an entrepreneurial ethic, and a subsistence ethic. More than cognitive models, such ideals have a physical presence and are made real through overlapping, ever-changing material cultures. Chapters 4 and 5 examined the institutionalization of two distinctive Otavaleño enterprises: the social networks of migrant craft dealers and the artisan operations of proprietors and piecework labor. In each case, entrepreneurs depend on shared understandings of settings and consumption practices to work out the social and moral problems that arise when using kin and compadre relations in business ventures. Now I consider the cultural world that indigenous wealth is making: the regional rise of a native "leisure class." The story continues with a return to the matter of buses.

◢ Otavalo's New Bus Company ◣

After the strike drove the white-mestizo-owned bus company from Agato and surrounding communities in 1986 (see chapter 2), community leaders tried to recruit other transportation co-ops to take over the routes. They had little success. By 1989, they gave up on outsiders and started their own cooperative, called *Cooperativa Imbaburapac Churimi Canchic* ("We Are Imbabura's Sons Co-operative"). The co-op's *socios* (associates), a group of well-to-do weavers, merchants, and community council members, bought their first bus with money donated by the Dutch development agency and acquired the second with cash raised among themselves. Since its beginnings, the co-op has expanded its routes to the rougher, upper rural roads on Imbabura and out to Cayambe in the province of Pichincha. Internal rivalries and small controversies beset daily operations. Some partners complain that the directors of the co-op withhold the money from other members. Rumors circulate about mishandled donations from NGOs and some riders believe the co-op raises prices too fast. Despite these grievances, the *Imbaburapac* buses have humanized bus service, making it a valuable extension of community life.

188

The drivers and conductors—most of whom are white-mestizos—take their mandate to serve the community seriously. In the mornings, they operate as de facto school buses by ferrying the wealthier kids to the better schools in Otavalo. As school children push aboard, yelling at each other and scrambling for seats, drivers keep an eye on nearby footpaths. They often hold the bus for the tardy boy or girl tugging on their red or blue school sweater, racing down the hill to catch up with their classmates. Throughout the day, drivers show similar patience for other riders. I have ridden a bus that has stopped and backed up for a woman running after it to catch a ride and another one that detoured off route so that a man carrying the timbers from his deceased father's house would not have to walk as far with his heavy load. The old company refused to pick up drunken passengers from baptisms or other family fiestas. In contrast, the new drivers have been flagged down by party-goers, saddled with an inebriated body, and given instructions on where to deliver the person and from whom to collect the fare.

More than simply transporting the community, the rickety, red *Imbaburapac* buses help constitute it. They bring people together and acquaint them with a shared "jurisdiction" of thickening rural settlements, expanding suburbs, and a crowded market town. Rare is the person who climbs aboard on a market day and does not see a compadre they can meet with the request, *"Pushawaychiy, kumpari"* ("Take me with you, compadre"). The trip to town may be the only time to catch up with friends or kin one rarely sees. Perhaps more important than uniting companions, a bus journey also endows strangers with a common experience. Mormons and Roman Catholics share black vinyl seats; Euro-traveling musicians and Quiteño market porters stand side by side as buses pull out from Otavalo and return people to their homes. While the vehicle grinds out its slow rounds, the disparate occupants can witness *mingueros* at work in a trench, observe the revelry of teenagers going to a dealer's welcome-home party, and smile at a fellow passenger trying to stuff two flapping chickens back into a bag. A trip in the bus allows people to imagine shared fellowship in the busy life of Imbabura's best-known *cantón*.

In his much-cited work, Benedict Anderson (1991: 6) emphasizes the power of imagination in the creation a community: "Communities are to be distinguished, not by their falsity/genuineness, but by the style in which they are imagined." He argues that communal bonds and territorial loyalties depend less on elaborate rituals and more on the regular experiences that give a sense of inhabiting shared space and time. In the emergence of Latin American nations from the old Spanish colonial territories, for instance, such practical matters as the administrative journeys of state officials help create new homelands. The administrators' travel through a string of dreary provincial outposts transformed them from an abstract political jurisdiction into a meaningful territory, a future motherland. Similarly, the consumption of local gazettes synchronized schedules and united people who lived within reach of a periodical's circulation. Newspapers pulled together "on the same page, *this* marriage, with *that* ship, *this* price with *that* bishop" because of coincidences in the arbitrary schedules of people and products in Latin America's expanding market system. "In this way, the newspaper of Caracas [or Quito, or Guayaquil] quite naturally and even apolitically created an imagined community among a specific assemblage of fellow readers to whom *these* ships, brides, bishops, and prices belonged" (Anderson 1991: 62, emphasis in original).

Around Otavalo, bus rides combine the power of both travel and newspapers in the creation of a community's imagination. Each day, hundreds of people partake vicariously in important and minor events meaningfully connected only by the route and timing of a bus trip. Further, the co-op even connects people when they are not traveling. Buses constantly remind everyone of their presence with piercing horns, squealing brakes, and the pulses of passengers moving to or from the bus throughout the day. Men in their looms or women tethering pigs will stop what they are doing when they hear a familiar bus horn on an unfamiliar route and speculate on the causes for the change (a funeral or a wedding, for instance, might pull a bus into a different sector on a special charter). Since virtually all Otavaleños on Imbabura's southern slope will board a bus at some point to earn a living or provision a household, residents are ever sensitive to the buses cycles. Sounding a horn to the mountain's daily rhythms, exposing passengers to others' activities, and gathering people to share (or create) gossip, *Imbaburapac's* buses have helped make regional culture and society.

However, while the practicalities of travel unite Otavaleños, the differential rewards of those trips again divide them. Some communities have prospered through constant commuting where others have stagnated. In 1992, these inequalities elevated the stakes of what ostensibly should have been a minor restructuring of bus services. By that year, the buses had become so crowded that riders from the communities nearest Otavalo—Peguche and Quinchuqui—never got seats and often stood by to watch overcrowded buses pass without stopping. They demanded their own, dedicated service. The leaders of the co-op refused. The Quinchuqui council then recruited

the same co-op that they had fought so bitterly against six years earlier.[1] When people in Agato, Ariasucu, and La Compañia heard about
the change, many became angry; some went to Quinchuqui to protest. Participants reported that several days of fighting followed. The
greatest casualty was the Quinchuqui water system. According to
the president of upper Quinchuqui, people from Agato and Ariasucu
invaded their community in the middle of the night and tore up the
water pipes, precipitating months of repair work.

The protest's extremity surprised me. Ariasucu and certain neighborhoods of Agato suffered at least fifteen years of dryness while
Quinchuqui enjoyed the fruits of their joint water *mingas*. Yet,
people did not sabotage the water system over that injustice. Rather,
they attacked Quinchuqui over a change in bus routes. The president
of Quinchuqui explained the action by saying that those from upper
Agato, *"no son racionales"* (they are not rational). His criticism of
his neighbors echoed the white-mestizo negative stereotypes of all
indígenas as "irrational, lazy, and backward." Adopting the language
of racism, he made it clear that more separated his sector from his
southern neighbors than some maize fields or opinions about bus
routes. He believed that his community had become more "advanced," more "rational" than others on Imbabura.

The comments of residents in upper Agato and Ariasucu similarly rang with racially related criticisms of Quinchuqui. People
criticized the president and those of his ilk for becoming more like
white-mestizos. The restructuring of bus routes confirmed many
rural residents' suspicions: the wealthiest sectors were losing both
their culture and respect for fellow indígenas. Their move to a new
bus company was, thus, not simply a matter of securing more seats
at a better price. By inviting the old bus co-op back, Quinchuqui
was breaking up a regional community and turning their backs on
the poor.

⊿ Class in Andean Society ⊾

Researchers have burrowed deeply into the topics of class and cultural identity in the Andes. Historians record the spread of capitalism and the reproduction of a Quechua peasantry within proletariat class structure in the nineteenth and early twentieth centuries
(Mallon 1983). Others focus on how the mechanics of a commodity

---

1. Going back to their old nemesis was not a surprise. In fact, many had gone to
the company immediately after the strike and pleaded with them to return. Only after
the company itself turned down the councils did the communities eventually form their
own co-op.

economy create the social spaces of rural Andean life. The analysis of coffee production in Venezuela (Roseberry 1983), provisioning a household in Ecuador (Weismantel 1988), seasonal migrations (Collins 1988), and the management of irrigation systems in Peru (Gelles 1995) reveal how class configures basic cultural categories. Concepts of space, time, cuisine, and the self relate to the specific Andean histories of extractive colonial and capitalist economies.

The corollary to arguments linking Quichua culture with class is the claim that economic mobility—either individual or collective—means changing cultures (van den Berghe and Primov 1977). Scholars have followed folk models in this regard. Throughout highland Ecuador, both indígenas and white-mestizos believe that giving up farming, gaining a higher material standard of living, moving to a city, and becoming fluent in Spanish all fit a pattern of becoming "more white." Picking up on these sentiments, anthropologists describe commodity culture in native communities as the "trappings of whiteness" (Weismantel 1988: 83). Culture and class fuse together. The peasant/proletariat and their subsistence goods are Quichua while the petty bourgeois with their consumer goods are white-mestizo.

Internal class differences within native society receive narrower treatment. Some address class in terms of economic and social status. Billie Jean Isbell (1978), for example, divides the Quechua-speaking community of Chuschi, Peru, using the local categories: *apukuna* (rich ones), *wakchakuna* (poor ones, "orphans"), and *tiyayapakuq* (landless, "those who roost on land belonging to others"). She explains the differences among these groups in terms of access to agricultural and kinship resources. Others address the indigenous structures that reproduce inequality. Reciprocal labor mechanisms, in particular, can be used by wealthier peasants to monopolize a community's labor resources (Orlove 1977; Mitchell 1991). Still others write about how ethnic and racial stereotypes, historically used to subordinate the native peasantry, get deployed by peasants themselves to accentuate socioeconomic gaps within peasant society (Gelles 1992).

For all their strengths, these analyses miss the different class *cultures* within native society. Anthropologists have traced the cultural divide between native peasants and white-mestizo tradespeople and the economic gaps between rich indígena and poor. Yet, few address the cultural dimensions of the latter division. The lacuna partly has an empirical basis. Quichua speakers who accumulate wealth frequently *do* abandon their culture for the opportunity to advance in national society. Yet a (relatively) wealthy strata persists in Quichua society with tastes, styles, and symbols that potentially distinguish it from other segments of both white-mestizo and Quichua society. Dismissing these tastes as "white" pretension allies the ethnographer with older, more conservative elements of native society, who likewise see changes in jobs and material culture as movement away from true native culture. However, such a bias obscures important diversity within Quichua culture and can lead to an idealized, romantic view of a Quichua culture (if not society) that is uniformly egalitarian (cf. Starn 1994). Further, sensitivity to class differences offers clues to the dynamics of Andean culture change in a time of growing commodity wealth and declining subsistence resources.

In Otavalo, the ethnographer cannot avoid the problem of class-based cultural distinctions within Quichua society.[2] Bus routes, clothing choices, house styles, fiesta meals, and even body weight all speak of growing gaps in social position and cultural sensibilities. The material realities of class affect all domains of Otavalo life. Economically, the earnings made from handicraft sales speed the geographic restructuring of Imbabura settlements. Socially, class position stabilizes itself through dyadic bonds and kinship networks. Culturally, the prosperous develop their identity and connections with other advantaged people through consumption—by acquiring a taste for appropriate things.

As a stratum of well-to-do indígenas institutionalizes itself, antagonisms mount. The fight over bus routes offers one telling instance of this tension. Poorer people express their anger by decrying the "whitening" of the elite. In reality, however, the wealthy have broken sharply from the practice of using their money to pass into white-mestizo society. Instead, Otavaleños amplify their old habits of holding fast to visible signs of their ethnicity while finding new ways to accumulate and display wealth. In the process, they radically diversify cultural expressions and develop new means for imagining themselves as native Andean.

◢ Capital Accumulation—Economic, Social, and Cultural ◣

Throughout the twentieth century, native Otavaleños have invested earnings in productive assets. Before the modern expansion of the handicraft economy, successful poncho weavers and dealers spent

2. Leo Chavez (1982) addresses at length the growing cultural divide between town and country Quichua culture in Otavalo. While mentioning wealth disparities, his analysis concentrates less on class relations and more on the self-image and ethos of commercial weavers. His ethnography provides a clear, useful description of urban Otavaleño society in the 1970s. His characterizations of the countryside, however, reproduce general stereotypes of poor peasants without examining the racial or ethnic stereotypes that may shape his informants discourse.

their money on land. Ninety years ago, one observer noted "[e]very-
day they are buying more and more land." He believed Indians would
become economically self-sufficient and wondered "who will work
the fields [of the *haciendas*]?"[3] Decades later Buitrón and Buitrón
(1945) similarly describe how two different groups of indígenas got
into a bidding war over an *hacienda*. The first group offered 130,000
sucres—about the fair market value. They lost the land to a second
group of 100 indígenas who had pooled 200,000 sucres—a substantial premium amassed in order to secure land they considered to be
in their territory.

From about the 1950s, investment strategies of many artisans
shifted from land to textile inventories and manufacturing equipment. When discussing the growth of capital and material stock, informants stress the slow pace of accumulation sustained by personal
savings, not bank loans. In Ariasucu, for example, commercial *faja*-
weavers made it clear to me that their operations expanded one loom
at a time. Of the nineteen proprietors that had three or more treadle
looms for *fajas*, only one reported buying multiple looms in one year.
All other *faja* entrepreneurs followed the example of earlier Quichua business people for whom, "the limitations of capital . . . has
necessitated the gradual growth of commercial activities" (Chavez
1982: 133).

Elsewhere researchers have characterized this process as "petty
capital accumulation," small in scale and limited in its political and
economic consequences (cf. Cook 1984; Cook and Binford 1990). After decades of such savings and investments, however, Otavaleño
capital is no longer so petty. My wife Chesca spent some of her time
working for a North American woman who had started a clothing company employing over 100 workers outside of Otavalo. This
woman had been coming to Otavalo for years and had close friends
among the wealthiest native families. When she started her own operation, one young indigenous couple offered to back her venture
with an immediate cash loan of U.S. $30,000. (It was graciously de-
clined.) In 1993, the *Los Angeles Times* reported that one Otavalo-
based native merchant made over $100,000 a year.[4] While few other
families have such cash ready at hand, many have acquired significant assets. Galo's cousin Francisco (see chapter 4), for example, owns
three town homes in Otavalo, collects rental incomes from a Chinese restaurant and an export business, and runs his own sweater-

3. The quotes come from Amable Herrera (1909: 256) as cited in Chavez (1982: 37),
his translation.
4. *Los Angeles Times Magazine*, 14 November 1993.

complement his cool expressionless eyes as he ambled the sidelines. Braids are out. The majority had combed their long silky hair and bound it . . . with a simple loop of elasticized cloth, preferably worn low on the ponytail.

The older men went the other way. While we drank our beers with Santo [in a private house converted to a tavern], five stout, middle-aged fellows tumbled into our room, shouting at the top of their lungs. Their ponchos, blue, clean and pressed; white pants spotless. They spoke/yelled in Spanish. We asked Santo where they were from. He said Peguche. "*Ellos son otro cualidad; son mas alto*" ["They are of another quality; they are taller"]. He could tell from their clean clothes, the fact that they spoke Spanish (occasionally, when they settled down, they spoke a bit of Quichua), and their look he said.

My description dwelt on the men; yet women, too, sported the newest styles. Eschewing the plain black or blue *anakus* of their mothers, teenage girls wore *anakus* made of imported, dark Italian and Spanish fabrics of muted pinstripes and subtle plaids. Many left their shawls at home and wore oversized sweatshirts or loose, Patagonia-style fleece jackets. The most impressive women were those driving around the field in their own new trucks with a few friends in the cab. Neither the accumulation nor the conspicuous consumption of wealth is limited to one gender or another.

The phrase "conspicuous consumption," coined by Veblen in *The Theory of the Leisure Class* (1994 [1899]), has become a cliché. As Bourdieu (1984: 31) puts it, such behavior is seen as a "naive exhibitionism . . . which seeks distinction in the crude display of ill-mastered luxury." The term implies that consumption stems from both envy of the rich and desire to show oneself superior to the poor. In its shorthand way, the phrase neatly captures the inextricable bond between social position and material display. Yet anthropologists have been largely dissatisfied with the notion, especially the reduction of consumption to simple matters of status. The notion of "conspicuous consumption" may help to understand why people put on their best clothes to come to a soccer game. Veblen's emphasis on emulation, however, cannot explain how native teenagers shape fashion to define an identity distinct from their parents, other native groups, white-mestizo Ecuadorians, and grunge-clad youth in the United States where some of these traders pick up their clothes. Not surprisingly, the flourishing of recent consumption studies in anthropology has begun with a rejection of Veblenesque ideas of conspicuous consumption.[7]

Criticism of Veblen, however, misses his key insight. He underscores how the constitution of an elite group does not happen merely through the accumulation of economic capital. Distinctive modes of ownership and connoisseurship turn economic advantage into social privilege. Without acknowledging Veblen, Bourdieu makes this idea central to his analysis of class, taste, and distinction in France. He writes,

> Social class is not defined by a property (not even the most determinant one, such as the volume and composition of capital) nor by a collection of properties (of sex, age, social origin, ethnic origin— proportion of blacks and whites, for example, or natives and immigrants—income, educational level) . . . but by the structure of relations between all pertinent properties. (1984: 108)

He goes on to demonstrate how the acquisition of taste for art, music, furnishings, and entertainment objectifies the relations among these properties. By discriminating among the world of goods, people distinguish among each other and naturalize their position in a class-divided society. Orlove (1994: 121) describes this relationship between person and thing as "performative" in which "objects create identities, rather than marking or affirming them."

Furthermore, as Veblen also noted, cultivating material tastes matters most in larger, industrializing societies with growing geographic and economic mobility. As society becomes more anonymous, neighbors have less personal and direct knowledge of each other's activities and rely more on material signs. Five decades of widespread commercial migration have brought these conditions of anonymity to Agato, Ariasucu, Quinchuqui, and the other native communities of Otavalo. In the absence of regular personal contact along the paths, at water taps, or in the Saturday market, Otavaleños build their image of others' character and achievements by reading the physical signs. The body, in particular, receives a lot of attention.

---

7. Jonathan Friedman (1991, 1994) has persistently criticized Veblen's theories of emulation as being inadequate for explaining how people create a "life-space" through consumption. Campbell (1987; 1994) has outlined other motives capable of explaining consumer behavior in both sociological and psychological terms. Miller (1987), Wilk (1994), and Colloredo-Mansfeld (1994) also offer critiques of conspicuous consumption models.

◢ The New Bodies and Clothes of the Handicraft Economy ◣

"*Ellos son otro cualidad; son mas alto.*" Santo identified the drunken traders in the tavern by referring first to their bodies. Santo measures bodies using his neighbors—lean-bodied persons of short stature and angular faces—as the norm. Suffering environmental blocks to growth throughout their lives, few reach the height of 5' 6". The problems start in childhood. With meals limited chiefly to maize and other grains and lacking in protein, many children do not get the nutrients they need. Chronic intestinal parasites, endemic in communities without adequate potable water, further hamper health and development.

As adults, Otavalo's peasant-proletarians stay thin working on construction sites, in marketplaces, or among the commercial *fincas* (farms) located in the northern part of the province. Physical labor hardens muscles and thins the flesh of those who never established viable commercial careers. Later in life, myriad vague illnesses, such as locally diagnosed problems of a "hot stomach" or "cold heart," wear away at poor bodies. Dental problems can be among the worse ailments. One fifty-year-old man I visited throughout 1994 underwent the excruciating agony of losing his teeth one at a time for months on end. Some days I dropped by to find him prostrate in pain, barely able to move. Upon my arrival, he would drag himself up into a sitting position to be polite. Resting on my arm he would lean into my face, whispering his greeting and I would bend closer, straining to make out his consonant-less sounds, seeing the snapped stumps of teeth, pillowed in glistening, swollen gums. By the end of the summer, the agony had hollowed his cheeks and left his five-foot frame stooped.

A combination of more disposable income and government investments has improved health and dental care for many. At rural clinics, doctors and nurses now immunize children and treat the worst cases of parasite infections. Meanwhile teenagers spend some of their earnings to obtain metal fillings and caps for decaying teeth. Down in Otavalo, people take care of less-threatening problems, too. Many get their eyes checked and buy glasses when necessary. Such corrective lenses are still a novelty in rural areas. In fact, many view them with disdain. Galo's sons José and Luis often speculate whether acquaintances of theirs really needed glasses or just acquired some clear-lens spectacles to show off.

While access to dental and medical services has strengthened bodies, the rich diet of trading families may have raised stature the most. With more income, people have provided their families with vegetables and fruit. When Santo told me that a blender offered "a different life" than an indigenous one (chapter 3), he was referring specifically to the fresh tree tomato and orange juice drinks that families can enjoy with these appliances. Milk has also become more common. In the early 1970s, a boy in Ariasucu once demanded that his parents give him milk with a meal. The request was so extravagant that he became nicknamed *"Leche"* (milk) and is still called that to this day. Now, small shops along the main road in Quinchuqui, Agato, and La Compañia regularly stock and sell liter bags of milk to their customers. Protein, too, has become more available. Evening meals in many indigenous homes now smell of frying eggs or fish and occasionally of roasted chicken.

The new cuisine has resulted in big bellies on men, wide girths on women, and children who are six inches taller than their parents (see Meisch 1995: 448 for a fuller description). In my own experience, I find that my height (6 feet, 2 inches) makes me a bit of a freak in the countryside where I tower over others. Yet, in Otavalo, young men are more my size. In fact, the young man who traveled to California to tour with the Grateful Dead (chapter 3) had made a strong impression on me even before I learned about his occupation simply because we saw eye to eye as we walked along.

Otavaleños now take the physical changes that come with money for granted. Rural people only comment on physiques that deviate from the expected correlation between weight and wealth, saying things like "although he is rich, he is not fat" or "he is rich, but he is thin, thin. He is still a good person." The latter comment hints at the animosity that has developed between the wealthy and those who have missed out on the tourist boom. Sometimes, this rancor fuels collective anger like that manifested in the bus route skirmish. More frequently, hostility takes the form of vicious rumors about individuals. People claim that a theft or betrayed partner underlie a merchant's fortunes. Worse, they speak of visits to *brujos* (witches) and supernatural pacts that provide the profits that have made someone fat.

Where locals feel resentment, foreigners have become excited by the new bodies of the handicraft economy. Some *gringas* (North American or European women) take a fancy to the physiques of indígenas, particularly young men. As one woman from the United States told Lynn Meisch (1995: 449), "These guys are so sexy! Long hair, high cheek bones, white teeth, well-built, nicely dressed, friendly . . .

Sometimes I just like to sit and look at them. They're Madison Avenue Andean Indians." From *"indio sucio"* (dirty Indian) to Madison Avenue, Otavaleños have moved a long way from the humble and rustic image of old.

Male fashion accentuates the rising generation's willingness to take on worldly styles. When I interviewed teenage girls about boys' consumption, respondents claimed that boys want to dress like white-mestizos: *"wanbracuna mishu pantalonata munan"* ("Boys want mestizo pants"). However, with their long hair, hats, and careful discriminations among Western clothes, boys still consider their look as being clearly indígena, even while being "very modern." In my own view, I clearly saw their styles as distinct from other young men in Ecuador or abroad. For example, outfits based on baggy jeans and loose shirts exhibit the relaxed style favored by youths in the United States, yet there is nothing sloppy about them. Despite the casual dress, many young men preserve an air of formality with the collared shirts, hair bound in a ponytail, and spotless versions of their fathers' narrow-brimmed fedoras. The uniqueness of their outfits comes partly from the way they combine elements from the different regions of the "handicraft archipelago"—jeans from the United States, windbreakers from Bogotá, hats fashioned in a local style—and partly from a distinct sensibility that unites these different elements through a shared taste for the clean, bright, and well-groomed.

Although more conservative, girls, too, pick up both *mishu* and, perhaps more interestingly, male fashion elements. As one thirty-five-year-old woman noted about her neighbor's teenage daughters: *"de la cintura por arriba sacosta munan, wanbrashina. Umalla rin"* ("from the belt up [girls] want sweaters, like boys. They go bareheaded"). Certainly, teenage girls often wear the feminine cardigans used by white-mestizo women. However, many others prefer the U.S.-style sweatshirts or fleece pullovers favored by boys. And like boys, more and more have given up wearing anything on their heads except during special events. Their allegiance to *anakus* and embroidered blouses insures that girls' outfits remain gender-specific. However, the similarities between male and female clothing fit other mergings in gender roles. In more and more weaving and textile-dealing tasks, young women cross over into formerly male occupations (see chapter 5). The androgynous elements in clothing express the growing interchangeability between male and female commercial work.

For both genders, the desire to show one's most stylish clothes intensifies during family fiestas. At baptisms, godparents spend a substantial sum acquiring little white shirts, pants, shoes, jackets, and caps for their godchildren. During confirmations, adolescent girls don pristine white blouses and *anakus*, dressing like immature brides to receive their first communion, while boys often get their first full-sized double-faced, navy blue poncho. And at weddings, parents or godparents of the *novios* (bride and groom) buy or rent special accessories to enhance the couple's appearances. Galo's preoccupation with showing his neighbors that "he knows how to do a wedding" led to a substantial investment in his daughter's wedding clothes.

On the day of the wedding, the crowning element of Celestina's nuptial wear was a rented veil, a great flowing, confection of lacy polyester muslin. As *padrinos*, we were expected to help Celestina get dressed on the morning of the wedding. After she put on most of her clothes and had her hair wrapped in a spotless white hair ribbon, she came to us for help with the veil. We had no clue. I was about to suggest she put the elastic strap under her chin as if it were worn like the pointy, conical birthday hats of my childhood. Fortunately, an aunt walked in and set her up properly (the strap went around the crown of her head). The saga of the veil then became worse.

As the *padrino*, I had to walk Celestina down the aisle. So for the hours prior to the service, I stayed with her trying to ease her nervousness. We shared a cab from her house to the church. Waiting in the taxi for the service to begin, I made sure that no one (we had one or two small cousins in the car with us) sat on the veil and continued to make small jokes to distract Celestina (by this point, I conceived of myself as Ariasucu's biggest ever maid-of-honor). Things took a turn for the worse when a gaggle of aunts showed up and started to converse loudly outside the car. Suddenly Celestina dissolved into tears.

"What happened?" I asked. She replied, "My aunt said, 'Celestina's veil is ordinary.'"

I had had enough of the veil at this point. I said, "The veil is not important. It is not important. It is better to have simple things. You are beautiful. Do not worry about the veil. Your mother picked simple flowers and your veil goes with them." Wrong thing to say. Now I had managed to insult both the veil and the flowers. Soon we had aunts and grandmothers pressed against the windows hissing instructions at us: "Don't cry," "Don't get tears on the veil," "Blow on your hands and rub your eyes to clear the tears." Celestina concentrated on the last task, restoring some composure. She then turned to me, cradling the veil in her arms, asking, "have I cried on the veil? Is the veil good?"

"The veil is good," I answered.

If anything represented Bourdieu's "ill-mastered luxury," that veil was it. Yet, Celestina and I were the only ones who lacked the mastery. The aunts knew how it should be worn and where it ranked in the hierarchy of veils. As a young bride, Celestina realized that the frilly shroud mattered. By the time her sister and younger cousins would be married, she herself would have developed a "veil aesthetic" and be able to direct them. So proceed most new consumption matters. Throughout Otavalo, Celestina's peers develop a strong implicit sense for what shoes are in, how hair should be worn, and when dark glasses are needed. They control their new luxuries. Indigenous fashion does not mindlessly imitate cosmopolitan white-mestizos, American or European products, nor even one single group of return migrants and commercial elite. Rather style synthesizes multiple influences with bits and pieces of regional traditions.

Indigenous observers nonetheless criticize a younger generation's preoccupation with new clothes and consumer goods. Some see young people becoming more like white-mestizos. Others complain about rich young traders' shallow commercialism, a trait glorified in a popular new folklore song in 1996. In the lyrics, a young man explains to his girlfriend that he would love her only as long as she had a car. Galo's sons loved the song. They bought a bootleg tape of it and played it over and over, laughing as they explained the words to me. A writer from Peguche has complained that such materialism has turned the newly rich into "indios plasticos," detached from the native values of their home communities (Terán 1991; see Meisch 1996a). Yet for all the concern about teenage purchasing practices, the older generation's spending may pose a greater challenge to the indigenous ethos that they ostensibly mean to uphold.

◢ The Leisure Class Displaces the Homeland ◣

At first glance, wealthy dealers' consumption affirms the significance of Otavalo and the rural environs. They spend their earnings to make regular trips to Imbabura from their expatriate homes. Fiestas of all kinds, from the public celebrations of Carnival to family weddings attract healthy investments of time and money from returning migrants, who splurge on a nephew's baptism or a neighbor's new house party. Whether at a fiesta or just running errands, the men frequently wear their formal white clothes, *alpargatas* (sandals) and blue poncho while women sport *anakus*, blouses and shawls. In fact, they dress more "traditionally" than those who stay at home to earn their living from their looms and land do. These latter go about their business in blue jeans, sweaters, and rubber boots. Finally, in a far greater expenditure than clothes, many sink their savings into new homes built on the farmland inherited from their parents.

Such commitment to place distinguishes Otavaleños from white-mestizo migrants to the United States and elsewhere, at least according to one man who journeys often to Boston, New York, and other East Coast U.S. cities. He said, "*Mishucuna* (white-mestizos) go and work in restaurants. They live there. They go and stay. They go and stay. *Runacuna* (indigenous people) do not travel like that." Native businessmen always return to their wives and children and land, he said.

Yet he qualified his connection to the land. *Runacuna* can no longer live off of their fields, he said. "Now the poor *runa* goes to (the United States, to Europe, to Asia) to sell his sweater," he explained. Earlier, the grandparents could make a living here in Imbabura; they had a lot of land, planted grains and kept oxen. Such bounty, such *"llashac alpacuna"* [heavy amounts of land], however, now belonged to a golden past. Today's *runacuna* are *"waglishca"* [damaged] living among divided fields. They lead an "orphan's" life. His comments reflected the sentiments of fellow merchants. Two other successful dealers also explained to me how lucky their grandparents had been because they could live from the abundant fruits of their fields. Both dealers, a 27-year-old woman who had spent much time in Italy and a 33-year-old man who lived in Bogotá with his wife and two kids, considered themselves worse off than past generations. The poor condition of Ariasucu's subsistence parcels deprived them of the chance to farm.

The wealthy merchants who still try to farm often do so half-heartedly. I once joined in the cornstalk *minga* hosted by Bernardo Santillan, who, as he kept reminding me, had traveled sixteen hours by bus from his market stalls in Cuenca in order to participate. I had a hard time seeing why he bothered. Early in the afternoon, Bernardo gave up lifting the bundles of dusty, withered stalks. He had grabbed a stick and went to hunt mice hidden in the month-old rows of drying sheaves. After poking around for a while, he flushed his quarry. As a tiny mouse scurried through the stubble for cover, Bernardo gave chase, flicking his switch wildly, and yelling at us to get a nearby cat. The mouse went to ground; the cat fled in panic; and Bernardo exhausted himself. He spent the rest of the time standing around and chatting. Meanwhile, working alone, an older, poor compadre took

Drawing 25: Stacked Cornstalks

up his shovel and whacked the misshapen stack into a more present-able form (drawing 25).

Like other returning migrants, Bernardo valued the *minga* more for its social aspects than practical benefits. He did not worry about getting any real work done. By the 1990s, in fact, the countryside had become a place of leisure for textile dealers, not labor. They came home to catch up with others and take a break from the stress and tedium of selling. I frequently met the Euro-traveling Maria wandering the paths, bored, looking for someone to visit. When I asked her where she was going, she replied "*dar la vuelta*" (she was out for a stroll). For Ariasucu's small textile-dealing class, the sector was a scenic spot, valued because it is, in Maria's words "*mas tranquilo*" ("more peaceful") than the cities where they earn a living.

Their houses reflect the new priorities of rest and relaxation.

These are vacation homes, not the productive hearths of agricultural households (cf. Fletcher 1997). The American traveler who pointed out to me that indigenous people always come home did not even put a kitchen into his new house. They stood their gas oven in the attic, a space that is so short that no one can stand fully upright. To stir the soup, his wife stands on the top step of the stairs leading to the attic and reaches over her head to stir the pot with her ladle. In a similar vein, other merchant architecture does not incorporate open hearths, *corredors* for milling maize and preparing grains, or even spaces dedicated to cooking. When migrants return home they improvise by locating a small gas stove somewhere inside the house. If they have to stay for more than a month, they build a cooking shed out back. Ironically, those families forced by circumstances to return for extended periods often find themselves living primarily in an improvised structure behind their impressive new homes (cf. H. Moore 1986).

In constructing their houses, migrants demonstrate a remarkable insensitivity to arable land. The American traveler for example, paved a wide path from the dirt road to his house, taking half a maize field out of production. The Colombian couple had eliminated two thirds of their largest field with a house design that included a large, enclosed patio. And Maria's brother, who spends more time in Italy than she, has built a large home on his field opposite his parents' house. During the last phase of construction, he displaced his parents' oxen corral with the walls of a garage, which would one day shelter the car he hoped to own. Ironically, after eliminating the hearth and trampling cornfields, some of these families then memorialize their farming past. They hung old planting sticks on their wall or placed a grindstone in the corner of their patio as a decoration. I found it incongruous to go from homes adorned with these souvenirs to Santo's house where the blades of his hoes shone through the crusted mud of recent use and Maria's grindstone was slick from freshly milled maize.

Around Ariasucu, people often describe the commercial traders with words borrowed from the racial discourse of clean and dirty lives. Jaime Cuyo, a man who has been to Europe himself and had some commercial success, puts it this way, "life is already changing. It is different. It is cleaner." These few rich migrants have secured the *limpiu kawsay*, the clean, advantaged life that eludes so many rural people. Santo believes that, more than adopting the *mishu's* comfortable life, they have also picked up white-mestizo arrogance and prejudice. He told me, "They go to Europe and sing about *runa kawsay* [native life] and working together. But in reality, it is different. They come home and buy cars, build *wasi limpia* [clean houses]. They live like *mishus*. They say *'indio'* and *'runa mapa'* [dirty indígena] to people who live in the country and work the earth."

Once again, metaphors of dirtiness aggravate class differences, as some of the wealthy reject poor indígenas with caustic remarks about their soiled appearance. In related fashion, several successful dealers tell me that the poor only have their own drunkenness and laziness to blame for the rundown condition of upper Ariasucu. In this talk, the rising merchant class borrows Ecuador's racist discourse to divide invidiously their own community. Instead of recognizing a common ethnicity, they dehumanize the poorest as "irrational" for failing to escape a livelihood they have already dismissed as "damaged." Appropriating this racist logic, wealthy traders cut the moral lines tying themselves to their neighbors and minimize any claim the poor may have on their capital and contacts (cf. Scott 1985).

In one small and important way, however, indigenous use of racist terms differs from mestizo use. Rich, corpulent, finely dressed indígenas express their contempt in Quichua. "Dirty Indian" becomes *"runa mapa"* (Quichua) not *"indio sucio"* (Spanish). Thus, their disparagement of their country cousins does not mean a repudiation of Quichua language and culture. These rich textile dealers are still proudly indígena, if not proud of all indígenas.

Money and class difference, therefore, threaten to do what migration alone has not: radically diminish the social power of Imbabura's productive soil. Enjoying greater capital and transnational contacts, rich merchants circulate among Quito, Cuenca, Tulcan, and Ibarra with only the briefest social stops in Otavalo. While professing allegiance to Imbabura, they have lost interest in the agrarian economy that carries on there. The centralized archipelago described in chapter 4 dissolves. Living internationally, cosmopolitan textile migrants wrestle with the significance of Otavalo's hinterland for their collective identity and sense of self (cf. Hannerz 1990).

In his analysis of diasporas, James Clifford (1994) describes the impossibility of being both "native" and diasporic. He claims that "diasporas are caught up with and defined against (1) the norms of nation-states and (2) indigenous claims by 'tribal' peoples" (Clifford 1994: 307). While agreeing that indigenous groups do experience displaced conditions—travel, trade, migration, dwelling for long periods of time away from home, etc.—he argues that they ultimately are not diasporas because "their sense of rootedness in the land is precisely what diasporic peoples have lost." His distinction fits the image wealthy migrants have of themselves. Precisely their return from abroad makes them true Andean natives, as opposed to the white-mestizos who remain in their new countries—or so they want to believe.

The homeland of Otavalo's merchant diaspora, however, increasingly is not one of sweat, mud, and marginal grain yields of current peasant life, but is a more romantic and imaginary place of healthy animals, productive fields, and ample foods. Repudiating the present, merchants reconnect themselves to this lost homeland through spending on brand new ponchos and shawls, rural houses, and family fiestas. Their largest monuments—big, "clean" houses built amongst their maize fields—move them furthest from the values of subsistence production. Thus, in Otavalo, the "loss" of a native people's agrarian homeland comes not from the exodus of people, but the influx of a new material culture.[8] Through consumption styles, merchants "re-imagine" their community to be more dispersed and less bound to the physical demands of the country than it actually is for others.

The merchants' reconstitution of Otavalo as the "lost" homeland of a trade diaspora returns us to problems of imagination and community formation. In the wake of Anderson's seminal work, other authors have touted imagination's importance in a new global order. Appadurai (1990: 5) writes there is "something critical and new in the global cultural processes: the imagination as a social practice. No longer mere fantasy . . . the imagination has become an organized field of social practices, a form of work and a form of negotiation between sites of agency." He could have gone further. Imagination gains its power by moving from personal mental images and narratives and taking material form. By fixing their vision of the future in commodities, architecture, and public space, commercial migrants can convince others of its inevitability (cf. Wilk 1994). Yet-to-be-purchased cars become more real than an oxen team when half-built garages go up in place of a livestock corral. The daily consumer practices of a few usher in a new "clean" reality, even as it remains out of reach for most local residents.

◢ Two Ecuadors . . . Both Quichua ◣

During my time-allocation study in 1994, I spent much time walking around upper Ariasucu. Trying to speed up my visits to participants, I discovered a handy shortcut that took me from one cluster of houses, up along a *zanja* (stone dike), past two abandoned houses, to

---

8. Kirshenblatt-Gimblett (1994) makes a similar point that the creation of a diaspora does not have to follow the physical displacement of a people.

a second cluster. Of all the old buildings in the sector, these abandoned homes poignantly illustrated for me the decline of rural economy. A *lechera* post used to support one the rafters had sprung back to life, sending a spray of branches through the tile roof. At the end of the study, I went back there to spend some time on my own and draw it (drawing 26).

In my first fieldwork season in 1991, I used to draw in public places as a way to initiate conversations with others. Drawing offered a chance to meet new people, who often detoured from their errands to look over my shoulder, comment on the sketch, and ask me what I was doing (Colloredo-Mansfeld 1993). By late 1994, however, I chose subjects in Ariasucu's sleepy corners. Having become enmeshed in a network of compadres and others to whom I owed (or from whom I was owed) favors, I now sought refuge. At first, this old adobe building on the edge of an unused path offered peace and quiet. Then two young boys discovered me. They charged up to where I sat, clambered on my back, and puzzled over what I was trying to draw. After a bit, they lost interest and darted off into a freshly plowed field, poked around for any interesting insects that may have been dug up,

Drawing 26: Tree Growing through Roof

and then they wrestled themselves through a bushy hedge and disappeared.

The next day I returned to finish my sketch. Before long, the same two boys came back. After they checked on my progress, they jogged back down the hill and promptly returned with their mother. We greeted each other and she came up and sat beside me. After silently observing my hand scratching in the tiles and darkening the shadows under the eaves, she told me that her father had built this house and lived there for the last years of his life. She herself only lived in it a few years with him before getting married and moving to a house 200 meters down the path. The tiles and beams had not yet been salvaged, she said, because she still used the building to lock up her pigs if she left Ariasucu for longer than a few hours. She also kept plows and some infrequently used planting tools here. The structure was not as abandoned as I thought.

She hung out for about fifteen minutes before excusing herself to go fix dinner. Moments later, she returned carrying a beige, black-rimmed enamel plate heaped high with raw barley. She asked, *"ushangi?"* ("Can you take it?"). *"Diuslpagui"* ("thank you"), I answered, pulling my backpack around. She tipped the grain into the bag and said goodbye. I thanked her again as I watched her back recede down the hill. In retrospect, I do not think her gift related to the subject of the drawing but rather the act. Unlike many others who encouraged me to draw certain houses, objects, or activities (and unlike one angry woman who thwarted my attempt to draw a house) she offered no judgment either way on my art. Rather, I think she saw me, for a brief moment, as her neighbor and this sketching as my labor; like her, I was bound to this spot by my work. Amid those hidden fields and old houses, our livelihoods intersected, and she consecrated this moment with that plate of food.

A "golden age" of subsistence farming may have passed, but small, gracious gestures of agrarian life still prevail throughout Otavalo. While lost upon many merchants, agriculture remains vital, both economically and socially, for a large segment of the population. Gifts of grain, cooked maize and beans, and soup are the coin of family bonds and neighborliness among those with little cash. These exchanges invest the *yanga kawsay* (humble/fruitless life) of the countryside with dignity, restoring humanity to those mired in a morass of underemployment and marginally rewarded agricultural labor.

In 1990s Ecuador, however, Quichua culture has outgrown its rural sectors. Like over 1 million other Ecuadorians, thousands of native Otavaleños have joined the flood of transnational migrants. Also like other Ecuadorians, those indígenas who have stayed at home enjoy new consumer goods made available through Ecuador's closer integration into the global economy. In Otavalo, this combination of migration, consumption, and higher incomes fosters a new, more consumerist native culture. In the past, both conservative indígenas and like-minded anthropologists have dismissed such commodity-buying as dubious imitation of white-mestizo culture and values. However, a new generation of fat, car-driving, poncho- and *anaku*-wearing, Quichua-speaking merchants has shown that owning commodities does not mean becoming "white." Quichua culture does not just gather around a smoking hearth; sometimes it thunders down the Pan American Highway in a Ford truck with new folklore music blasting out the windows. If anything, more than two Quichua cultures exist in Otavalo today. Between poor peasant-proletariat and rich global textile dealer are thousands of people like Celestina buying furniture and renting veils, trying to establish their own balance between farming and dealing, country and town, Otavalo and elsewhere.

The new affluence calls for a more critical understanding of class culture within subaltern societies. In a situation with important parallels, Gates (1993) describes the dilemmas that an affluent black elite poses for African-American culture.[9] Its presence has created a "complicated truth: that for black America, these are the worst of times . . . and the best of times" (1993: 249). Further, he points out that black intellectuals have never made their peace with the black bourgeoisie, "a group that is typically seen as devoid of cultural authenticity, doomed to mimicry and pallid assimilation" (Gates 1993: 250). Gates could well be describing the circumstances of modern Otavaleño society. Never before have subsistence resources been so at risk and provided so little for communities historically dependent on their fields. Nor has there ever been such an accumulation of capital and material prosperity within a native Andean group in Ecuador.

The rise of cocky young merchants in jeans, Raybans, and ponytails may repel some who long for a "truer Andean culture," where land and maize reign as *the* cultural resources and reciprocal mores unite people with each other and the *Pachamama* (mother earth). Yet, even with the real problems of materialism and class-based, racially expressed arrogance, Otavalo's commercial class offers signs of hope. *Indios plasticos*, "ordinary" veils, and other ill-mastered

9. I have pilfered the title of this section from Gates's article, "Two Nations . . . Both Black" (1993).

luxuries all signal a new chapter in the expansion of Quichua culture in a politically important way. Terence Turner (1995) makes a similar point about the urban-based leaders of the Kayapo people in Brazil. He writes,

> While their level of personal spending and lavish style appeared to go beyond any reasonable requirements of communal business, it should not be overlooked that these young leaders, in their guise as successful and wealthy Brazilian men about town, came to fulfill an important and unprecedented symbolic function in the evolving pattern of inter-ethnic relations . . . Probably for the first time in the history of Amazonian native peoples, individual members of indigenous communities succeeded in establishing themselves on an equal footing with the Brazilian regional elite. (1995: 106)

Otavalo's merchant elite moves toward similar equal footing. And, unlike the Kayapo, they have achieved this by building on traditional livelihoods that remain connected to older communities, not just the cities in which they live. These links create a tangled legacy. On the one hand, indigenous production and exchange itself grows complicit in perpetuating the poverty of the poorest peasant-artisans. On the other hand, because the rising middle class live in the same places and circulate through the same markets as the poor, they stay aware of (and indeed periodically suffer) the predicaments that underdevelopment inflicts upon the peasant/working class. The "two Ecuadors" emerging in Imbabura are not the mutually cut-off realities dividing inner-city, underclass from suburban, middle-class black Americans (Watts 1993).

Yet, even if the textile economy has not categorically divided Otavaleño society into opposing classes, in either the structural or social senses, it could head that way. The burdens of participating in Otavaleño society mount. In the urbanized/suburbanized future of Otavalo, a clearly marked indigenous identity could become the property of the middle class. Only those with steady and higher than average incomes will consistently wear ponchos and *anakus*, celebrate baptisms and weddings with feasts of milled-corn soup, pork, and guinea pigs, insist on bilingualism in the schools, and invest in the other more costly trappings of indigenous life. Meanwhile, working-class Otavaleños will make do with mixtures of cheaper mestizo garb and indigenous clothing, attend abbreviated family fiestas, speak *"chawpi shimi"* (half Quichua-half Spanish), and depend on subsistence plots that have been reduced to kitchen gardens.

Should such a polarized world emerge (and the signs are already there), Otavaleño textile entrepreneurs would share some of the blame—as would misguided development policies, discriminatory educational practices, and the enduring racism of many workplaces. Indeed, against these other ills, the lopsided successes of textile merchants do not appear so bad. As with black Americans, Quichua speakers throughout the Andes "need more success individually and collectively, not less" (Gates 1993). To offer the hope of real change, this economic success must find its counterparts in expanded political accomplishments of indigenous leaders, the artistic achievements of musical groups who have found success in Europe, and the professional attainments of a small cadre of native educators, linguists, and legal professionals. The past five decades of economic gains make these other successes all the more possible—and necessary, if Quichua culture is to continue as a rich form of expression, knowledge, and power.

▰ EPILOGUE ▰
Consumption and Cultural Concentration in the Andes

Starting out almost ten years ago, I received implicit warnings from colleagues against doing work in Otavalo. Studying in Otavalo had become clichéd; too much had already been done, they suggested. Besides, praise from national commentators about "rational" Indians and the patronage of tourists made Otavalo culturally suspect, or at least too much of a special case for understanding Quichua culture. Others worried that the successful market and extra cash in the economy had changed things *a lot* (that is, too much) in recent years. Good, I thought. I did not intend to study "authentic" native culture, per se. Rather, I wanted to research consumption as a social field of action. The warnings reinforced my sense that Imbabura would be a dynamic place for such work.

In the course of my fieldwork, I came to appreciate all of Otavalo's cultural "contaminations." I liked spending an afternoon hanging out with teenagers, drinking cokes and watching Bugs Bunny cartoons. Bumping into someone in La Compañia who had spent time selling crafts in Venice, California, was a relief. This man could relate to my world and knew something of my other life. I even liked interviewing informants who had worked with other anthropologists because they proved very quotable. (I do concede a limit to my tolerance. When the troop of Scandinavian dancers showed up in their traditional costumes at our godchildren's wedding, I did feel put out.)

And yet, despite my "hard-nosed" attitude toward change, I found myself gravitating to Antuca's and Manuel's house. I liked relaxing in the cool shade of its deep *corredor*, chatting with Santo, watching his mother twist together bundles of freshly harvested barley in preparation for hand threshing, and listening to the rhythmic "thwap, thwap" of his father working on a backstrap loom. Worked out on materials of stone, wood, leather, and wool, life here had a different sound. Paced by the couple's careful skills, it slowed down too, offering the tranquility that wealthy expatriate dealers long for on their trips home but rarely enjoy. Having done my surveys, interviews, and observations, I realized that few households still worked like this and could imagine none in Santo's generations who would continue to do so. So, despite my celebration of what was being made in Otavalo, I became more nostalgic about what was being lost. Reproducing itself with Coca-Cola, Adidas, and Sony, Quichua culture demonstrated remarkable creativity. It also seemed to be paying a price in growing "Americanization" or "globalization": the adoption of consumerist tendencies and "branded" identities.

One of the goals of this book, however, is to show how uneven such cultural change can be. Americanization, as Roseberry (1994) argues, is not a unilineal process. He points out three historical factors that interrupt the very idea of a uniform, transformative process in Latin America. First, since long before the United States or even Spain exerted influence, the peoples of Latin America have woven their own histories with episodes of contact, exchange, and alliance with other societies. Engagement with modern capitalist markets and consumer commodities thus comes not as a contact between "two autonomous cultures but the intersection of at least two—and often more—historical processes, each of which was developing in contradictory and uneven fashion" (Roseberry 1994: 86).

Second, cultural groups, whether marked as nations or local ethnicities, contain social hierarchies, rival economic sectors, and conflicts between individuals and corporate groups. Furthermore, contact can be mediated through consumer goods, religious faiths, books, movies, individuals, or transnational firms. The encounter, then, extends through time, varies across space, and engages different sets of social actors (cf. Kearney 1996). Third, the cultural meanings emerging from contact with an Americanized global order reflect two levels of power: (1) the power differences between the United States or the European Union and a country like Ecuador and (2) power differences among groups within Ecuador. Roseberry uses Blanca Muratorio's (1980) work on Protestant conversion in Andean Ecuador to demonstrate that what might appear to be capitulation to external United States forces is in fact a complex part of local history. In this case, Quichua peasants convert to the Protestantism of the North American Gospel Missionary Union, in part, to maintain their ethnic identity against the pressure of Roman Catholic, white-mestizo culture. The conversion "simultaneously represents a form of accommodation (the adoption of a foreign set of forms) and of resistance (to the Ecuadorian state and Catholic Church)" (Roseberry 1994: 120).

Given such complexities, Roseberry argues that the analysis of

change must move beyond a preoccupation with Americanization—
with the cultural and economic power of the United States or the
institutions of the global economy—to examine geographically specific historical process. Rather than thinking in terms of a collision
between an economic superpower and local culture, we must address
the narrower question: How do national societies internalize hege-
monic external forces within particular contexts of power to produce
cultural meanings and identities? That is, we need to explain "Mex-
icanization" or "Peruvianization," not Americanization. The shift in
emphasis recognizes the power of local agency without separating
national histories from global process.

As the materials presented in this book suggest, this argument
could be pushed back further, from nation to region, from national
society to ethnicity. However deeply enmeshed they are, the process
of "Otavaleño-ization" runs a separate course from that of "Ecuador-
ianization." Understanding the specific nature of Otavaleño-ization
returns us to the questions raised at the outset of the book: What
(and whose) values guide Otavaleños' economic development? Second, how do Otavaleños use a proliferating material culture as a
medium to reconcile conflicting values and produce their cultural
enterprises?

By speaking of values rather than "models" or "schemas," I draw
attention to the moral nature of the principles structuring economic
activity. As matters of morality, they go to the very core of the self
and constitution of society. Moral rules are supreme among rules,
Robert Edgerton (1985: 42) writes; they "can build self-esteem when
they are followed consistently but when they are broken, the result
can be self-loathing." Such prescriptions are enduring, but they are
not divorced from historical circumstances. Rules gain meaning
within concrete situations and the consequences of either compli-
ance or violation materialize within the settings of everyday life. As
the scope for accumulation expands with new markets or the fortunes of traditional occupations decline with deteriorating subsistence resources, values become shaded with new meanings.

Proving to be continuously adaptable and painfully resilient, the
pernicious morality of hygienic racism has shaped national development and defined what it means to be a good citizen. The rural white-
mestizo elite and urban middle classes measure their virtues by the
standards of a hispanicized culture and despair that "dirty Indians"
will never progress to their level. As the nineteen-year-old-son of a
hacienda owner put it: "The Indian who has overcome his origins,

besides being educated, is an Indian who bathes."[1] This racism poisons interethnic social relations and skews national development policies. Designing programs to organize native communities and clean up indigenous homes, provincial authorities have in the past ignored the development priorities of rural peoples. Even as social and material realities change, new signs of contamination are identified, from the cholera-harboring potential of peasant hearths to the narco-trafficking possibilities of handicraft bundles ready for international shipment. Consequently, indigenous wealth never achieves that same status as white-mestizo earnings and their culture never gains full legitimacy. Despite their money (and however often they bathe), native entrepreneurs rarely enjoy the full equality of Ecuadorian citizenship.

Such discrimination has not precluded significant indigenous success and this success has arrived with its own ideological explanation. As they build up their inventory "little by little" and fix up their houses, indigenous textile operators "objectify" (Miller 1987) their entrepreneurial principles. Within workshop settings, a new discipline takes shape, as do new subjects and sharpened ideals. Manufacturers have brought agrarian life indoors, moved from general skills to specialization, and jacketed flexible routines into regular schedules. Well-to-do proprietors note the signs of their own hard work and innovativeness in their full storerooms and furnished homes, often contrasting their gain with a neighbor's poverty. Faulting "humble" peasants for their drinking and laziness, they say the poor "*no son racionales*" (are not rational). Thus, the perhaps inevitable ironic twist. Asserted as a rejection of the backward Indian stereotype, entrepreneurial ideals nonetheless echo of the same racial bias. Not that making money is somehow a non-Indigenous, white-mestizo activity. Rather, the effort to protect relative wealth against the moral claims of poor relatives forces the indigenous middle class to repeat the insidious, logical contortions as other privileged groups.

Struggling peasant artisans reject rationality-based explanations of their plight. Poverty stems not from a lack of labor but from labor spent in vain. Low-paid jobs, intensely competitive craft markets, and declining subsistence resources all rob indigenous people of the

---

1. Quoted on the occasion of the 500-year anniversary of Columbus's first voyage to the New World on 12 October 1992, in *Hoy*, a daily newspaper published in Quito and Guayaquil. Citation found in Meisch (1994), her translation.

potential for bettering their lives. Their precariousness reaffirms the importance of older subsistence values. For many, even the relatively well-off, being a good *runa*, a good indigenous man or woman, means continuing to farm and to invest in and to honor obligations of mutual assistance with family, neighbors, and compadres. Both the necessities and the virtues of defensive economic strategy must occasionally supersede market opportunity. When the subsistence ethic requires work on "humble" tasks and with "worthless" things, the gaps between native people and the wider circuits of national society take shape in the exhausted possessions of a peasant home. Reflecting the economic toll of underdevelopment, such *yanga cosas* (simple/worthless things) have great discursive power. Men and women can use them, talk about them, and pass them on in ways that reaffirm the imperatives of subsistence obligations.

The useful, "useless" things of peasant homes return us to the topic of the material world's role in social process, especially in the institutionalization of social relations. Operating in overlapping economic and moral realms, the objects of Otavalo's social world assume double values. Handicraft inventories have both commodity exchange values and the power to communicate rational ideals. Humble goods appear as spent exchange value and a communicative instrument of subsistence ethics. Taken whole, indigenous goods are devalued in the context of national development models as they precipitate the racist ideologies of many white-mestizos. Inextricably moral and economic, all these objects are essential to both white-mestizo and indigenous efforts to naturalize economic change within established social conventions.

Chapters 4 and 5 explored in detail how Otavaleños use material culture to stabilize the social relationships of two evolving activities. While the cases are quite different—the formation of households and networks in a transnational context and the commercialization of *faja*-weaving—the circumstances are broadly similar. Both draw on long-established traditions of textile manufacture and exchange and both must reconcile the same moral contradiction: accumulating profits by using the skills, knowledge, and labor of those to whom one holds reciprocal obligations. Further, in both cases, consumption practices play a pivotal role. Migrants use goods to save their earnings, set the direction of future economic activity, affirm their connection to their parents' household, begin the formation of their own, and, not least, to show off their accomplishments. In *faja* workshops, consumer goods become instruments of social reorganization. Modern appliances and electronics streamline domestic life, reducing food preparation and cooking, and extending the hours people are prepared to sit in their looms.

Consumption in its more sensual forms makes the cultural ideals of these social relations come alive. The "serving culture" of fiestas offers an experiential frame for notions of reciprocity and respect. Handing out food and drink, receiving one's own allotment in return, consuming and then repeating the cycle encodes moral principles in shared sense of timing, turn-taking, and satiation. Textile dealers or workshop proprietors can recreate the feeling of such occasions in the course of other pursuits. In *faja* workshops, for example, loom owners borrow culinary, spatial, and temporal codes from many places—fiestas, *mingas*, domestic routines, and urban occupational sites—in order to sustain the social life of their operations. Consumption's regularity and immediateness embeds new economic forms in the experiential details of prevailing social conventions, mitigating, at least momentarily, the social disruption of Otavalo's increasingly stratified economic institutions.

Otavalo-ization thus speaks of the expansive development of Imbabura's indigenous society in a transnational economy. With "mass-produced," hand-woven, polyester *fajas*, luxurious *anakus* made of European fabric, and dishes of garlic-roasted guinea pigs, maize, and potatoes, this Andean world contains much that is unique. Yet, the case for local distinctiveness can be pushed too far. I do not want the details of Otavaleño life to obscure the global forces that helped to produce them. While recognizing that native peoples have their own rich histories, the links among cases, especially those of "enhanced" indigenous cultures that find some measure of success in world markets for their products or services, need to be made explicit (Stephen 1991b). Otavaleño-ization in Ecuador, relates to Kuna-ization in Panama (cf. Tice 1995), Maya-ization in Amatenango del Valle, Chiapas, Mexico (Nash 1993b), and, Zapotec-ization in Oaxaca, Mexico (Stephen 1991a), among other cases in Latin America (Korovkin 1998).

The Otavaleño case clarifies four factors that produce organizational continuities. First, economic success does not end the struggle against the racism or ethnic discrimination of a dualized society in which nationalist ideologies devalue economic and social forms that fail to conform to particular sets of modern ideals. Second, some advantage in location or resources that is exploited at a pivotal moment of economic integration may result in big, long-term payoffs for a selected occupation, community, or ethnic group. In Ecuador, for example, other native Andeans have long had economic and cultural attributes similar to Otavaleños: a rich tradition of textile manufacture, business acumen, and ethnic distinctiveness. Yet by exploiting the legacy of the *casimir* trade and their Quiteño contacts in the 1940s and 1950s during the time of Mision Andina and the development of Imbabura's infrastructure, Otavaleños have leveraged their textile skills into a dominant position within the tourist handicraft trade.

Third, within the group, the large payoffs offered by an expanded market ultimately reduce the range of occupations people pursue. Talented women and men shun subsistence work and neglect mundane occupations—clerical work, teaching, municipal employment, etc.—for a chance at achieving the highest possible status and wealth within their social sphere. Celestina is not the only one in her community who gave up further schooling for early entrance into the textile market. Others continue to do so, even as evidence mounts that only a few will make it while many suffer prolonged periods of deprivation in Tulcan, Bogotá, and Amsterdam while working for their chance at the big time.[2] Fourth, as production becomes more specialized and fragmented, consumption grows in cultural importance. On the one hand, people invest in and update traditional material culture to find new ways of expressing individual and collective identity. Such expressions matter more as migration and urbanization split up once relatively cohesive social worlds. On the other hand, consumption and material displays become more important for personal stature, which, in turn, matters for developing social networks.

Taken together, these four conditions contribute to a process that might be called cultural concentration. As the market unevenly elevates the amount of cash circulating within society, the basic means of social participation, from rituals to architecture to outfits, become more expensive. While many keep pace with the rising costs associated with their distinctive culture, some work harder for less of the social trappings that a previous generation had. The result of new affluence, therefore, is not a uniformly enhanced culture but potential for a new division. On one side are those expressing a creative indigenous culture and using distinctive cultural forms to intensify the bonds of their community. On the other side are those "quick-change artists" (Kearney 1996), shifting among multiple cultural contexts according to economic opportunity and social

2. Frank and Cook (1995) have examined in detail this potentially wasteful narrowing of careers in economies marked by highly competitive markets with big payoffs accruing to a small group of winners.

circumstances and developing a more splintered cultural identity. The signs of such a dualized world already appear in Otavalo.

◢ One Final Story ◣

"What is the third world?"

Maria's question caught me by surprise. We were hanging out on the unfinished roof of her brother's new house. It was a tall, raw structure of concrete blocks and protruding iron reinforcement bars. Only half-listening, I had been taking in the view. It seemed that the whole of the *cantón* (county) of Otavalo unfolded out from this spot. Rising up and away behind us was the community of Ariasucu and *Tayta Imbabura's* grassy shoulders and deep gullies. Down through the eucalyptus trees to the east lay Lake San Pablo, broad, blue, and fringed by the swampy pastures of densely settled communities like La Compañia, Pucará, and San Rafael. Above the south side of the lake, the Pan American Highway cut a neat line across the flanks of Mount Mojanda's rolling green slopes. Turning to the west, I had a view of the smoking cement factory that sprawled on a ridge above Otavalo and, beyond that, Mount Cotacachi's snowy peak poked through a cloud.

Maria, too, had not been saying much. She had been staring down at where a cobbled road intersects a busy dirt path just a few yards from the house. At the moment, the last few passengers were getting off the creaking red cooperative bus parked below us. Some older women grabbed the chrome handrail and swung down off the bottom step into the rutted path. Maria observed them as they bent forward, shrugged their *kipis* (large shawls containing their load) up onto their backs, and pushed the corners of the shawls into knots with their gnarled knuckles. With her eyes narrowed and head cocked, Maria contemplated throwing a bucket of water on them.

It was Carnival. In Ecuadorian fashion, Maria and residents from all over Ariasucu celebrated by waging a month-long water fight. Staying inundation, she brought us both back into the conversation, repeating her question, "What is the third world?"

I did not know what to say. Many things that I once might have used to distinguish First World from Third no longer served that purpose. Because of the international expansion of the craft trade, jet travel and faxes or other communication technology were now a part of Otavaleño occupations and routines. On the other hand, when Otavaleños travel to Berlin, New York, or Los Angeles, their experiences were often grim. One local man had been knifed in the apartment buildings where he stayed in Queens. Others had become sick living off of the local food—pizza, canned soups, and pasta. And, as Otavaleños went about their business of selling handicrafts or playing music, they saw people eking out a living in the United States by collecting trash out of garbage cans.

Maria knew much of this. She had been to Europe twice with her brothers. (She called her brother's new house a "souvenir" from Italy, because profits from his sales trip paid for it.) She enjoys a better diet, more free time, and a safer, more comfortable home in Ariasucu than in Italy. "It is more peaceful here," she said, explaining why she returned to raise her daughter in this rural community. However, she also wanted her daughter to learn English and become a competent handicraft dealer. Thus, she pulled the girl out of the local school and enrolled her in one down in the town of Otavalo. Maria had arranged her life to take advantage of multiple places—native communities, provincial market centers, and European cities.

Thinking about how her life spanned what I thought to be First and Third Worlds, I chose my words carefully. Drawing on a stereotype I was losing confidence in, I said, "When people use the term, they usually are talking about places where people do not have water, where many babies die when they are small, where people do not have electricity."

I paused. She stared intently at me as I added, "Many people would think upper Ariasucu is the Third World." This amazed and upset her. "Really?" she asked, "In upper Ariasucu they do not have electricity? Are you sure?"

Now I was astonished. How could she know the best places to sell handicrafts in Milan and not know the living conditions of her neighbors—those women with their *kipis* who live 500 meters up the path from her?

No longer united by poverty or a common agrarian livelihood, native Otavaleños sometimes seem to be going their separate ways. Yet growing gaps in shared knowledge coexist with new areas of common bonds, from bus cooperatives to radicalized community *mingas* to the "nativized" forms of national fiestas like Carnival. If their artifacts and rituals seem to be concentrating opportunities and benefits in the hands of people like Maria, the process is far from complete. With Imbabura's peasant-artisans materializing their values in water pipelines, bus routes, architecture, fiesta cuisine, and fashions, Otavalo still contains much that provides a strong and fluid connection between globe-trotting Maria and the *kipi*-carrying women—in addition to the arc of water Maria finally flung their way.

◢ REFERENCES CITED ◣

Alexander Rodriguez, L.
1985   *The Search for Public Policy: Regional Politics and Government Finances in Ecuador 1830–1940.* Berkeley: University of California Press.

Allen, Catherine
1988   *The Hold Life Has: Coca and Cultural Identity in an Andean Community.* Washington, DC: Smithsonian Institution Press.

Allen, Catherine, and Nathan Garner
1995   "Condor Qatay: Anthropology in Performance." *American Anthropologist* 97 (1): 69–82.

Almeida Vinueza, José
1981   "Cooperativas y comunidades ¿integración u oposición de dos formas de organización campesino? Reflexión en torno a un caso." In *Campesinos y haciendas de la sierra norte,* edited by M. Cristina Farga Hernandez and José Almeida Vinueza, pp. 147–349. Otavalo: Instituto Otavaleño de Antropologia.
1993   "El levantamiento indígena como momento constituvo nacional." In *Sismo Etnico en el Ecuador,* pp. 7–28. Quito: CEDIME and Ediciones Abya Yala.

Anderson, Benedict
1991   *Imagined Communities,* revised edition. New York: Verso.

Andrade, Susan
1990   *Vision Mundial: Entre el Cielo y La Tierra: Religión y desarrollo en la sierra ecuatoriana.* Quito: Abya-Yala and CEPLAES.

Annis, Sheldon
1987   *God and Production in a Guatemalan Town.* Austin: University of Texas Press.

Appadurai, Arjun
1986   "Introduction: Commodities and the Politics of Value." In *The Social Life of Things: Commodities in Cultural Perspective,* edited by Arjun Appadurai, pp. 3–63. Cambridge: Cambridge University Press.
1990   "Disjuncture and Difference in the Global Cultural Economy." *Public Culture* 2 (2): 1–24.
1996   *Modernity at Large: Cultural Dimensions of Globalization.* Minneapolis: University of Minnesota Press.

Aquirre Beltran, Gonzolo
1970   "Prologo: El indio y la reinterpretación de la cultura." In *Antologia de Moises Saenz.* Mexico D. F. Ediciones Oasis.

Bakhtin, M.
1981 *The Dialogic Imagination,* translated by C. Emerson and M. Holquist. Austin: University of Texas Press.

Bakewell, Liza
1998 "Image Acts." *American Anthropologist* 100 (1): 22–32.

Barth, Fredrik
1981 "On the Study of Social Change." In *Process and Form in Social Life: Selected Essays of Fredrik Barth,* pp. 105–19. Boston: Routledge and Kegan.

Barsky, Osvaldo
1988 *La Reforma Agraria Ecuatoriana,* 2d ed. Quito: Corporacion Editora Nacional.

Baudrillard, Jean
1981 *For a Critique of the Political Economy of the Sign.* St. Louis, MO: Telos Press.

Bauer, Ranier Lutz
1992 "Changing Representations of Place, Community and Character in the Spanish Sierra del Caurel." *American Ethnologist* 19 (3): 571–88.

Becker, Marc
1999 "Citizens, Indians, and Women: The Politics of Exclusion in Ecuador." Paper presented at the annual meeting of the Conference on Latin American History, Washington, DC, January 1999.
forthcoming "Comunas and Indigenous Protest in Cayambe, Ecuador." *The Americas* 55 (4).

Belote, Jim, and Linda Belote
1977 "The Limitation of Obligation in Saraguro Kinship." In *Andean Kinship and Marriage,* edited by Ralph Bolton and Enrique Mayer, pp. 106–16. Washington, DC: Special Publication of the American Anthropology Association, No. 7.

Belote, Linda, and Jim Belote
1981 "Development in Spite of Itself: The Saraguro Case." In *Cultural Transformations and Ethnicity in Modern Ecuador,* edited by Norman E. Whitten, Jr., pp. 450–76. Urbana: University of Illinois Press.

Berman, Marshall
1981 *All That Is Solid Melts Into Air.* New York: Simon and Schuster.

Bernstein, H.
1979 "African Peasantries: A Theoretical Framework." *Journal of Peasant Studies* 6: 421–43.

Béteille, André
1990 "Race, Caste, and Gender." *Man* 25 (3): 489–504.

Bonacich, Edna
1973 "A Theory of Middlemen Minorities." *American Sociological Review* 38: 583–94.

Bonilla, Adrian
1993 *Las sorprendents virtuds de lo perverso: Ecuador y narcotrafico en los 90.* Quito: Flacso-Sede Ecuador.

Bourdieu, Pierre
1977 *Outline of a Theory of Practice.* Cambridge: Cambridge University Press.
1984 *Distinction.* Cambridge: Harvard University Press.
1990 *The Logic of Practice.* Stanford: Stanford University Press.

Bourque, L. Nicole

1997 "Making Space: Social Change, Identity, and the Creation of Boundaries in the Central Ecuadorian Andes." *Bulletin of Latin American Research* 16 (2): 153–67.

Bouissac, Paul, Michael Herzfeld, and Roland Posner, eds.

1986 *Iconicity: Essays on the Nature of Culture: Festschrift for Thomas A. Sebeok on his 65ᵗʰ Birthday.* Tübingen, Germany: Sauffenburg Verlag.

Briggs, Charles L., and Clara Mantini Briggs

1997 "'The Indians Accept Death as a Normal, Natural Event': Insitutional Authority, Cultural Reasoning, and Discourses of Genocide in a Venezuelan Cholera Epidemic." *Social Identities* 3 (3): 439–69.

Broad, William J.

1980 "The Osage Oil Cover-up." *Science* 208: 32–35.

Brown, Michael

1996 "On Resisting Resistance." *American Anthropologist* 98 (4): 729–49.

Brown, Paul

1987 "Population Growth and the Disappearance of Reciprocal Labor in a Highland Peruvian Community." *Research in Economic Anthropology* 8: 225–45.

Brush, Stephen

1977a "Kinship and Land Use in a Northern Sierra Community." In *Andean Kinship and Marriage,* edited by Ralph Bolton and Enrique Mayer, pp. 136–52. Washington, DC: Special Publication of the American Anthropology Association, no. 7.

1977b *Mountain, Field, and Family: The Economy and Human Ecology of an Andean Valley.* Philadelphia: University of Pennsylvania Press.

Buitrón, Aníbal

1947 "Situacion economica y social del indio Otavaleño." *América Indígena* 7:45–67.

1956 "La tecnificacíon de la industria textil manual de los indios del Ecuador." In *Estudios Antropológicos en Homenaje al Dr. Manuel Gamio,* edited by Eusebio Dávalos Hurtado and Ignacio Bernal, pp. 287–95. Mexico City: Universidad Nacional Autónoma de México, Dirección General de Publicaciones.

1962 "Panorama de la aculturación en Otavalo, Ecuador." *América Indígena* 26: 53–79.

1974 *Investigaciones Sociales en Otavalo.* Otavalo: Instituto Otavaleño de Antropologia.

n.d. *Taita Imbabura: Vida indígena en los Andes.* Quito: Impresa Mision Andina.

Buitrón, Aníbal, and Barbara Salisbury Buitrón

1945 "Indios, blancos, y mestizos en Otavalo, Ecuador." *Acta Americana* 3: 190–16.

Bulmer-Thomas, Victor

1994 *The Economic History of Latin America since Independence.* Cambridge: Cambridge University Press.

Burke, Timothy

1996 *Lifebuoy Men, Lux Women.* Durham, NC: Duke University Press.

Campbell, Colin

1987 *The Romantic Ethic and the Spirit of Modern Consumerism.* Oxford: Basil Blackwell.

1994 "Capitalism, Consumption and the Problem of Motives: Some Issues in the Understanding of Conduct as Illustrated by an Examination of the Treatment of

Motive and Meaning in the Works of Weber and Veblen." In *Consumption and Identity*, edited by Jonathan Friedman, pp. 23–46. Chur, Switzerland: Harwood Academic Publishers.

Carrier, James G., and Josiah McC. Heyman
1997   "Consumption and Political Economy." *The Journal of the Royal Anthropological Institute*, N.S. 3 (1): 1–19.

Casagrande, Joseph B.
1971   "The Indian and Ecuadorian Society." In *The Condor and the Bull: Tradition and Change in Andean Indian Culture*, edited by Joseph B. Casagrande, Andrew Cohen, and William Mangin, pp. 337–436. Washington, DC: The Peace Corps.
1981   "Strategies for Survival: The Indians of Highland Ecuador." In *Cultural Transformations and Ethnicity in Modern Ecuador*, edited by Norman E. Whitten, Jr., pp. 260–77. Urbana: University of Illinois Press.

Casagrande, Joseph B., and Arthur R. Piper
1969   "La transformación estructural de una parroquia rural en las tierras altas del Ecuador." *América Indígena* 29: 1039–64.

Chavez, Leo Ralph
1982   "Commercial Weaving and the Entrepreneurial Ethic: Otavalo Indian Views of Self and the World." Ph.D. diss., Dept. of Anthropology, Stanford University. Ann Arbor: University Microfilms International.
1985   "'To get ahead': The Entrepreneurial Ethic and Political Behavior among Commercial Weavers in Otavalo." In *The Political Anthropology of Ecuador: Perspectives from Indigenous Cultures*, edited by Jeffrey Ehrenreich, pp. 159–89. Albany, NY: The Center for Caribbean and Latin America, the State University of New York at Albany, and the Society for Latin American Anthropology.

Chavez Valdospinos, Virgilio A.
n.d.   *Paisaje y Alma de Otavalo*. Otavalo: Editorial Gallocapitan.

Chayanov, A. V.
1966   *The Theory of Peasant Economy*. Madison: University of Wisconsin Press.

Chevalier, Jacques
1983   "There Is Nothing Simple about Simple Commodity Production." *Journal of Peasant Studies* 10 (4): 153–86.

Chuquín, Carmen, and Frank Salomon
1992   *Runa Shimi: A Pedagogical Grammar of Imbabura Quichua*. Madison: Latin America and Iberian Studies Program, University of Wisconsin-Madison.

Clifford, James
1994   "Diasporas." *Cultural Anthropology* 9 (3): 302–38.

Clifford, James, and George Marcus, eds.
1986   *Writing Culture: The Poetics and Politics of Ethnography*. Berkeley: University of California Press.

Codere, H.
1950   *Fighting with Property*. American Ethnological Society Monograph 18. Washington, DC: American Anthropological Association.

Collier, George, with Elizabeth Lowery Quaratiello
1994   *¡Basta! Land and the Zapatista Rebellion in Chiapas*. Oakland, CA: Food First Books, Institute for Food and Development Policy.

Collier, John, and Anibal Buitrón
1949   *The Awakening Valley.* Chicago: University of Chicago Press.

Collins, Jane
1988   *Unseasonable Migrations.* Princeton: Princeton University Press.

Colloredo-Mansfeld, Rudolf
1993   "The Value of Sketching in Field Research." *Anthropology UCLA* 20: 89–104.

1994   "Architectural Conspicuous Consumption and Economic Change in the Andes." *American Anthropologist* 96 (4): 845–65.

1998   " 'Dirty Indians,' Radical *Indígenas,* and the Political Economy of Social Difference in Modern Ecuador." *Bulletin of Latin American Research* 17 (2): 185–205.

1998   "The Handicraft Archipelago: Consumption, Migration and the Social Organization of a Transnational Andean Ethnic Group." *Research in Economic Anthropology* 19, edited by Barry Isaac, pp. 31–67. Greenwich, CT: JAI Press.

Cook, Scott
1984   *Peasant Capitalist Industry.* Lanham: University Press of America.

Cook, Scott, and L. Binford
1990   *Obliging Need: Rural Petty Industry in Mexican Capitalism.* Austin: University of Texas Press.

Cordero Palacios, Alfredo
1957   *Lexico de vulgarismos azuayos.* Cuenca: Casa de la Cultura Ecuatoriana, Nucleo de Azuay.

Costin, Catherine, and Timothy Earle
1989   "Status Distinction and Legitimization of Power as Reflected in Changing Patterns of Consumption in Late Prehistoric Peru." *American Antiquity* 54 (4): 691–714.

D'Amico, Linda
1993   "Expressivity, Ethnicity, and Renaissance in Otavalo." Ph.D. diss., Department of Anthropology, Indiana University.

Dávilo, Mario
1971   *"Compadrazgo*: Fictive Kinship in Latin America." In *Readings in Kinship and Social Structure,* edited by Nelson Graburn, pp. 396–406. New York: Harper and Row.

de Janvry, Alain
1982   *The Agrarian Question in Latin America.* Baltimore: Johns Hopkins University Press.

1987   "Latin American Peasants." In *Peasants and Peasant Societies: Selected Readings,* edited by T. Shanin, pp. 391–404. Oxford: Blackwell.

de la Cadena, Marisol
1996   "The Political Tensions of Representations and Misrepresentations: Intellectuals and Mestizas in Cuzco (1919–1990)." *Journal of Latin American Anthropology* 2 (1): 112–47.

de la Torre, Carlos
1997   " 'La letra con sangre entra': racismo, escuela, y vida cotidiana en Ecuador." Paper presented at the meeting of the Latin American Studies Association, Guadalajara, April 1997.

DeMarrais, Elizabeth, Luis Jaime Castillo, and Timothy K. Earle
1996   "Ideology, Materialization and Power Strategies." *Current Anthropology* 37 (1):
       15–31.
Desjarlais, Robert
1996   "The Office of Reason: On the Politics of Language and Agency in a Shelter for
       'the homeless mentally ill.'" *American Ethnologist* 23 (4): 880–900.
Douglas, Mary
1966   *Purity and Danger: An Analysis of the Concepts of Pollution and Taboo.* London:
       Routledge & Kegan Paul.
1992   "Why Do People Want Goods?" In *Understanding the Enterprise Culture*, edited
       by Shaun Hargreaves Heap and Angus Ross, pp. 19–31. Edinburgh: Edinburgh
       University Press.
Douglas, Mary, and Baron Isherwood
1979   *The World of Goods.* New York: Basic Books
Duranti, Alessandro
1992   "Language in Context and Language as Context: The Samoan Respect Vocabu-
       lary." In *Rethinking Context*, edited by Alessandro Duranti and Charles Goodwin,
       pp. 77–100. Cambridge: Cambridge University Press.
1994   *From Grammar to Politics: Linguistic Anthropology in a Western Samoan Vil-
       lage.* Berkeley: University of California Press.
1997   "Indexical Speech across Samoan Communities." *American Anthropologist* 99
       (2): 342–54.
Eastman, Jorge Mario, and David Ruben Sanchez
1992   *El Narcotrafico En La Region Andino.* Bogotá: Parlamento Andino, ONU-
       UNDCP.
Ebron, Paulla A.
1998   "Enchanted Memories of Regional Difference in African American Culture."
       American Anthropologist 100 (1): 94–105.
Edgerton, Robert B.
1985   *Rules, Exceptions, and Social Order.* Berkeley: University of California Press.
Errington, Fredrick, and Deborah Gewertz
1996   "The Individuation of Tradition in a Papua New Guinean Modernity." *American
       Anthropologist* 98 (1): 114–26.
Farmer, Paul
1994   *The Uses of Haiti.* Monroe, ME: Common Courage Press.
Field, Les
1991   "Ecuador's Pan-Indian Uprising." *NACLA Report on the Americas.* Volume 25,
       no. 3 (December): 39–46.
Fields, Barbara
1982   "Ideology and Race in American History." In *Region, Race, and Reconstruction:
       Essays in Honor of C. Vann Woodward*, edited by J. Morgan Kolsser and James M.
       McPherson, pp. 143–77. Oxford and New York: Oxford University Press.
Fisher, James
1990   *Sherpas: Reflections on Change in Himalayan Nepal.* Berkeley: University of Cal-
       ifornia Press.

Fiske, John
1993 *Power Plays, Power Works.* London: Verso.
Fletcher, Peri
1997 "Building from Migration: Imported Design and Everyday Use of Migrant Houses in Mexico." In *The Allure of the Foreign,* edited by Benjamin Orlove, pp. 185–202. Ann Arbor: University of Michigan Press.
Foster, George
1965 "Peasant Society and the Image of the Limited Good." *American Anthropologist* 67 (2): 292–315.
Foster, Hal
1995 "The Artist as Ethnographer." In *The Traffic in Culture: Refiguring Art and Anthropology,* edited by George E. Marcus and Fred Myers, pp. 302–9. Berkeley: University of California Press.
Foucault, Michel
1990 *The History of Sexuality: An Introduction,* vol. 1, translated by Robert Hurley. New York: Vintage Books.
Fox, Richard G.
1991 "Introduction: Working in the Present." In *Recapturing Anthropology,* edited by Richard G. Fox, pp. 1–16. Santa Fe, NM: School of American Research Press; distributed by the University of Washington Press.
Frank, Robert H., and Philip J. Cook
1995 *The Winner-Take-All Society: Why the Few at the Top Get So Much More Than the Rest of Us.* New York: Penguin Books.
Friedman, Harriet
1978 "Simple Commodity Production and Wage Labour in the American Plains." *The Journal of Peasant Studies* 6 (1): 71–100.
Friedman, Jonathan
1991 "Consuming Desires: Strategies of Selfhood and Appropriation." *Cultural Anthropology* 6 (2): 154–63.
1994 "Introduction." In *Consumption and Identity,* edited by Jonathan Friedman, pp. 1–22. Chur, Switzerland: Harwood Academic Publishers.
Friedman, Jonathan, ed.
1994 *Consumption and Identity.* Chur, Switzerland: Harwood Academic Publishers.
Friedman, Kathie
1984 "Households as Income Pooling Units." In *Households and the World Economy,* edited by Joan Smith and Immanuel Wallerstein, pp. 37–55. Beverly Hills: Sage Publications.
Fundacion Nuestros Jovenes
1989 *El Sistem de Drogas Ecuatoriano y el Impacto de la Cocaina en el Area Andina.* Quito: Fundacion Nuestros Jovenes.
García Canclini, Néstor
1995a *Hybrid Cultures: Strategies for Entering and Leaving Modernity.* Translated by Christopher L. Chiappari and Silvia L. López. Minneapolis: University of Minnesota Press.
1995b "Una modernización que atrasa." *Journal of Latin American Anthropology* 1: 2–19.

Gates, Jr., Henry Louis
1993 "Two Nations . . . Both Black." In *Reading Rodney King, Reading Urban Upris-
      ing*, edited by Robert Gooding Williams, pp. 249–54. New York: Routledge.
Geertz, Clifford
1973 "Deep Play: Notes on the Balinese Cockfight." In *The Interpretation of Cultures*,
      pp. 412–53. New York: Basic Books Publishers, Inc.
1988 *Works and Lives: The Anthropologist as Author*. Stanford: Stanford University
      Press.
Gell, Alfred
1986 "Newcomers to the World of Goods: Consumption among the Muria Gonds." In
      The Social Life of Things: Commodities in Cultural Perspective, edited by Arjun
      Appadurai, pp. 110–38. Cambridge: Cambridge University Press.
Gelles, Paul H.
1992 "'Caballeritos' and Maiz Cabanita: Colonial Categories and Andean Ethnicity in
      the Quincentennial Year." Kroeber Anthropological Society Papers 75–76: 14–27.
      Oakland: GRT Press.
1995 "Equilibrium and Extraction: Dual Organization in the Andes." *American Eth-
      nologist* 22 (4): 710–42.
Giddens, Anthony
1979 *Central Problems in Social Theory: Action, Structure, and Contradiction in
      Social Analysis*. Berkeley: University of California Press.
1981 *A Contemporary Critique of Historical Materialism*. Berkeley: University of Cal-
      ifornia Press.
Gluckman, Max
1962 "Les Rites de Passage." In *Essays on the Ritual of Social Relations*, edited by Max
      Gluckman, pp. 1–53. Manchester: Manchester University Press.
Goldberg, David Theo
1992 "The Semantics of Race." *Ethnic and Racial Studies* 15 (4): 543–69.
Goodwin, Charles, and Alessandro Duranti
1992 "Rethinking Context: An Introduction." In *Rethinking Context*, edited by Ales-
      sandro Duranti and Charles Goodwin, pp. 1–42. Cambridge: Cambridge Univer-
      sity Press.
Goody, Jack, ed.
1958 *The Development Cycle in Domestic Groups*. Cambridge: Cambridge University
      Press.
Gose, Peter
1994a *Deathly Waters and Hungry Mountains: Agrarian Ritual and Class Formation in
      an Andean Town*. Toronto: University of Toronto Press.
1994b "Embodied Violence: Racial Identity and the Semiotics of Property in Huaquirca,
      Antabamba (Apurimac)." In *Unruly Order: Violence, Power, and Cultural Iden-
      tity in the High Provinces of Southern Peru*, edited by Deborah Poole, pp. 165–98.
      Boulder: Westview Press.
Graburn, Nelson
1976 *Ethnic and Tourist Arts: Cultural Expressions from the Fourth World*. Berkeley:
      University of California Press.

Graña, Cesar
1971   *Fact and Symbol.* New York: Oxford University Press.
Gudeman, Stephen, and Alberto Rivera
1990   *Conversations in Colombia: The Domestic Economy in Life and Text.* Cambridge: Cambridge University Press.
Guerrero, Andrés
1991   *La semantica de la dominacion: el concertaje de indios.* Quito: Ediciones Libri Mundi-Enrique Grosse-Luemern
1993   "La desintegración de la administración étnica en el Ecuador." In *Sismo Etnico en el Ecuador*, pp. 91–112. Quito: CEDIME and Ediciones Abya-Yala.
1994   "The Construction of a Ventriliquist's Image: Liberal Discourse and the 'Miserable Indian Race' in Late 19th Century Ecuador." *Journal of Latin American Studies* 29: 555–90.
Habermas, J.
1987   *The Philosophical Discourse of Modernity.* Cambridge: MIT Press.
Hale, Charles R.
1994   "Between Che Guevara and the Pachamama: Mestizos, Indians, and Identity Politics in the Anti-Quincentenary Campaign." *Critique of Anthropology* 14 (1): 9–39.
Halperin, Rhoda, and James Dow, eds.
1977   *Peasant Livelihood: Studies in Economic Anthropology and Cultural Ecology.* New York: St. Martin's Press.
Hamilton, Gary
1978   "Pariah Capitalism: A Paradox of Power and Dependence." *Ethnic Groups* 2: 1–15.
Hannerz, Ulf
1990   "Cosmopolitans and Locals in World Culture." In *Global Culture: Nationalism, Globalization, and Modernity*, edited by Mike Featherstone, pp. 237–51. Newbury Park, CA: SAGE Publications.
Harrison, Regina
1989   *Songs, Signs, and Memory in the Andes: Translating Quechua Language and Custom.* Austin: University of Texas.
Harvey, David
1989   *The Condition of Postmodernity.* Oxford: Basil Blackwell.
Harvey, Neil, Luis Hernández Navarro, and Jeffrey W. Rubin
1994   *Rebellion in Chiapas: Rural Reforms, Campesino Radicalism, and the Limits of Salinismo.* Revised Edition. Transformation of Rural Mexico Series, 5. Ejido Reform Research Project. San Diego: Center for U.S.-Mexican Studies, University of California.
Hassaurek, Friedrich
1967   *Four Years among the Ecuadorians.* Carbondale: Southern Illinois University Press.
Herrera, Amable
1909   *Monografia del Canton de Otavalo.* Quito: Tipografia Encuadernación Salesiana.
Heyman, Josiah McC.
1990   "The Emergence of the Waged Life Course on the United States-Mexico Border." *American Ethnologist* 17: 348–59.

Himpele, Jeffrey
1995 "Distributing Difference: The Distribution and Displacement of Media, Spec-
      tacle, and Identity in La Paz, Bolivia." Ph.D. diss., Department of Anthropology,
      Princeton University.
Hobsbawm, Eric
1990 *Nations and Nationalism since 1780.* Cambridge: Cambridge University Press.
Hurtado, Osvaldo
1980 *Political Power in Ecuador.* Translated by Nick D. Mills. Albuquerque: Univer-
      sity of New Mexico Press.
Isbell, Billie Jean
1974 "The Influence of Migrants upon Traditional Social and Political Concept: A Peru-
      vian Case Study." In *Latin America Urban Research*, vol. 4, edited by Wayne Cor-
      nelius and Feliciana Trueblood, pp. 237–62. Beverly Hills: Sage Publications.
1978 *To Defend Ourselves: Ecology and Ritual in an Andean Village.* Austin: Institute
      of Latin American Studies. The University of Texas at Austin.
Iturralde, Diego
1984 "Legislacion Ecuatoriana y Población Indígena." In *Politica Estatal y Población
      Indígena*, pp. 21–34. Quito: Ediciones Abya-Yala.
Jackson, Jean E.
1995 "Culture, Genuine and Spurious: The Politics of Indianness in the Vaupés, Co-
      lombia." *American Ethnologist* 22 (1): 3–27.
Jaramillo Alvarado, Pio
1949 "Prologo." In *El Indio, Cerebro y Corazon de America*, by Segundo B. Maig-
      uashca. Quito: Fr. Jodoco Ricke.
Kearney, Michael
1996 *Reconceptualizing the Peasantry: Anthropology in Global Perspective.* Boulder:
      Westview Press.
Kirshenblatt-Gimblett, Barbara
1994 "Spaces of Dispersal." *Cultural Anthropology* 9 (3): 339–44.
Knapp, Gregory
1991 *Andean Ecology: Adaptive Dynamics in Ecuador.* Boulder: Westview Press.
Kopytoff, Igor
1986 "The Cultural Biography of Things: Commoditization as Process." In *The Social
      Life of Things: Commodities in Cultural Perspective*, edited by Arjun Appadurai,
      pp. 64–91. Cambridge: Cambridge University Press.
Korovkin, Tanya
1998 "Commodity Production and Ethnic Culture: Otavalo, Northern Ecuador." *Eco-
      nomic Development and Cultural Change* 47(1) 125–154.
Kovel, Joel
1984 *White Racism.* New York: Colombia University Press.
Krasniewicz, Louise
1993 "Show or Tell." Paper presented at American Ethnological Society Annual Meet-
      ings, Santa Fe, New Mexico.
Kulick, D.
1992 *Language Shift and Cultural Reproduction: Socialization, Self and Syncretism in
      a Papua New Guinean Village.* Cambridge: Cambridge University Press.

Lambert, Bernd
1977 "Bilaterality in the Andes." In *Andean Kinship and Marriage,* edited by Ralph Bolton and Enrique Mayer, pp. 1–27. Washington DC: Special Publication of the American Anthropology Association, No. 7.
Leach, E.
1964 *Political Systems of Highland Burma: A Study of Kachin Social Structure.* London: The Athlone Press.
Leon, Luis A.
1946 "Breves consideraciones sobre la patologia del indio en el Ecuador." In *Cuestiones Indigenas del Ecuador,* vol. 1, pp. 241–62. Quito: Casa de la Cultura Ecuatoriana.
Littlefield, Alice
1979 "The Expansion of Capitalist Relations of Production in Mexican Crafts." *Journal of Peasant Studies* 6 (4): 471–88.
Long, Norman
1977 "Commerce and Kinship in the Peruvian Highlands." In *Andean Kinship and Marriage,* edited by Ralph Bolton and Enrique Mayer, pp. 153–76. Washington, DC: Special Publication of the American Anthropology Association, No. 7.
Long, Norman, and Brian Roberts, eds.
1978 *Peasant Co-operation and Capitalist Expansion in Central Peru.* Austin: Institute of Latin American Studies. University of Texas.
1984 *Miners, Peasants, and Entrepreneurs: Regional Development in the Central Highlands of Peru.* Cambridge: Cambridge University Press.
Lury, Celia
1996 *Consumer Culture.* New Brunswick, NJ: Rutgers University Press.
Lynch, Michael, and Steve Woolgar, eds.
1990 *Representation in Scientific Practice.* Cambridge, MA: MIT Press.
MacCannell, Dean
1989 [1976] *The Tourist: A New Theory of the Leisure Class.* New York: Schocken Books.
1992 "Reconstructed Ethnicity: Tourism and Cultural Identity in Third World Countries." In *Empty Meeting Grounds: The Tourist Papers,* pp. 158–72. London: Routledge.
Mallon, Florencia
1983 *The Defense of Community in Peru's Central Highlands: Peasant Struggle and Capitalist Transition, 1860–1940.* Princeton: Princeton University Press.
Malo Gonzalez, Claudio
1988 "Estudio introductorio." In *Pensamiento Indigeniste del Ecuador,* edited by Claudio Malo Gonzalez, pp. 9–98. Quito: Banco Central del Ecuador.
Mannheim, Bruce
1991 *The Language of the Inka since the European Invasion.* Austin: University of Texas Press.
Maquet, Jacques
1986 *The Aesthetic Experience: An Anthropologist Looks at the Visual Arts.* New Haven: Yale University Press.
Martínez, Hector
1963 "Compadrazgo en una comunidad indigena altiplanica." *América Indígena* 23 (2): 127–39.

Marx, Karl
1976 *Capital*, volume 1. New York: Penguin.
Masuda, Shozo, Izumi Shimada, and Craig Morris, eds.
1985 *Andean Ecology and Civilization*. Tokyo: University of Tokyo Press.
Mauss, Marcel
1990 *The Gift: The Form and Reason for Exchange in Archaic Societies*. New York: W. W. Norton.
Mayer, Adrian
1966 "The Significance of Quasi-groups in the Study of Complex Societies." In *The Social Anthropology of Complex Societies*, edited by M. Banton, pp. 97–122. ASA Monographs No. 4. London: Tavistock Publications.
Mayer, Enrique
1985 "Production Zones." In *Andean Ecology and Civilization*, edited by Shozo Masuda, Izumi Shimada, and Craig Morris, pp. 45–84. Tokyo: University of Tokyo Press.
McCracken, Grant
1988 *Culture and Consumption: New Approaches to the Symbolic Character of Consumer Goods and Activities*. Bloomington: Indiana University Press.
Meier, Peter
1978 *La situatción socio-economico de los artesanos textiles en la región de Otavalo: Resumen de una investigación empirica*. Quito: FLACSO.
1985 *Los Artesanos Textiles en la región de Otavalo*. Sarance 10. Otavalo: Instituto Otavaleño de Antroplogia.
Meisch, Lynn
1987 *Otavalo: Weaving, Costume and the Market*. Quito: Ediciones Libri Mundi.
1994 "'We will not dance on the tomb of our grandparents': 500 years of resistance in Ecuador." *The Latin American Anthropology Review* 4 (2): 55–74.
1995 "Gringas and Otavaleños: Changing Tourist Relations." *Annals of Tourism Research* 22 (2): 441–62.
1996a "Andean Communities in a Transnational Context." Ph.D. Diss., Department of Anthropology, Stanford University.
1996b "Two Amoebas Dancing the Lambada: *Artesanias* Production, Wealth and Fluid Identities in Otavalo, Ecuador." 1996 Annual Meetings of the American Anthropological Association.
Miles, Ann
1997 "The High Cost of Leaving: Illegal Emigration from Cuenca, Ecuador and Family Separation." In *Women and Economic Change: Andean Perspectives*, edited by Ann Miles and Hans Buechler, pp. 55–74. Washington, DC: American Anthropological Association, the Society for Latin American Anthropology.
Miller, Daniel
1987 *Material Culture and Mass Consumption*. Oxford: Basil Blackwell.
1994 *Modernity: An Ethnographic Approach*. New York: Berg Publishers.
1995a "Consumption and Commodities." *Annual Review of Anthropology* 24: 141–61.
1995b "Consumption Studies as the Transformation of Anthropology." In *Acknowledging Consumption*, edited by Daniel Miller, pp. 264–95. New York: Routledge.

1995c "Consumption as the Vanguard of History." In *Acknowledging Consumption*, edited by Daniel Miller, pp. 1–57. New York: Routledge.

1998a "Why Some Things Matter." In *Material Cultures: Why Some Things Matter*, edited by Daniel Miller, pp. 3–21. Chicago: University of Chicago Press.

1998b "Coca-Cola: A Black Sweet Drink from Trinidad." In *Material Cultures: Why Some Things Matter*, edited by Daniel Miller, pp. 169–87. Chicago: University of Chicago Press.

Mintz, Sidney

1985 *Sweetness and Power: The Place of Sugar in Modern History*. New York: Penguin.

Mintz, Sidney W., and Eric R. Wolf

1950 "An Analysis of Ritual Co-Parenthood (*Compadrazgo*)." *Southwestern Journal of Anthropology*. 6 (4): 341–68.

Mision Andina

n.d. *Seis Años de Trabajo de la Mision Andina en el Ecuador*. Quito: Mision Andina.

Mitchell, William

1991 "Some Are More Equal than Others: Labor Supply, Reciprocity and Distribution in the Andes." *Research in Economic Anthropology* 13, edited by Barry Isaac, pp. 191–219. Greenwich, CT: JAI Press.

Monslave Pozo, Luis

1943 *El Indio: Cuestiones de su vida y de su Pasión*. Cuenca: Editorial Austral.

Moore, Henrietta

1986 *Space, Text, and Gender*. Cambridge: Cambridge University Press.

Moore, Sally Falk

1975 "Epilogue: Uncertainties in Situations, Indeterminacies in Culture." In *Symbol and Politics in Communal Ideology: Cases and Questions*, edited by Sally Falk Moore and B. Meyerhoff, pp. 210–39. Ithaca: Cornell University Press.

1986 *Social Facts and Fabrications*. Cambridge: Cambridge University Press.

Morales, Edmundo

1995 *The Guinea Pig: Healing, Food, and Ritual in the Andes*. Tucson: The University of Arizona Press.

Muratorio, Blanca

1980 "Protestantism and Capitalism Revisited in the Rural Highlands of Ecuador." *Journal of Peasant Studies* 8 (1): 37–60.

Murra, John V.

1946 "The Historic Tribes of Ecuador." In *Handbook of South American Indians*, vol. 2: *The Andean Civilizations*, edited by Julian H. Steward, pp. 785–821. Washington, DC: Smithsonian Institution.

1972 "El control vertical de un máximo de pisos ecológicos en la economía de las sociedades andinas." In *Iñigo Ortiz de Zúñiga, visita de la provincia de León de Huánuco en 1562. Toma 2*, edited by John V. Murra, pp. 429–76. Huánuco, Perú: Universidad Nacional Hermilio Valdizán.

1985a "El Archipelago Vertical Revisited." In *Andean Ecology and Civilization*, edited by Shozo Masuda, Izumi Shimada, and Craig Morris, pp. 3–14. Tokyo: University of Tokyo Press.

1985b "The Limits and Limitations of the Vertical Archipelago." In *Andean Ecology and Civilization*, edited by Shozo Masuda, Izumi Shimada, and Craig Morris, pp. 15–20. Tokyo: University of Tokyo Press.

Myers, Greg

1990 "Every Picture Tells a Story: Illustrations in E. O. Wilson's Sociobiology." In *Representation in Scientific Practice*, edited by Michael Lynch and Steve Woolgar, pp. 231–65. Cambridge, MA: MIT Press.

Naranjo, Marcelo

1989 *La Cultura Popular en el Ecuador, toma V: Imbabura.* Quito: Centro Interamericanos de Artesanias y Artes Populares (CIDAP).

Nash, June

1993a "Introduction: Traditional Arts and Changing Markets in Middle America." In *Crafts in the World Market*, edited by June Nash, pp. 1–22. Albany: State University of New York Press.

1993b "Maya Household Production in the World Market: The Potters of Amatenango del Valle, Chiapas, Mexico." In *Crafts in the World Market*, edited by June Nash, pp. 127–54. Albany: State University of New York Press.

1994 "Global Integration and Subsistence Insecurity." *American Anthropologist* 96 (1): 7–30.

Nations, Marilyn, and Cristina M. G. Monte

1996 "'I'm Not a Dog, No!': Cries of Resistance Against Cholera Control Campaigns." *Social Sciences and Medicine* 43 (6): 1007–24.

Netting, Robert McC, Richard W. Wilk, and Eric J. Arnould, eds.

1984 *Households: Comparative and Historical Studies of the Domestic Group.* Berkeley: University of California Press.

Orlove, Benjamin

1977 "Inequality among Peasants: The Forms and Uses of Reciprocal Exchange in Andean Peru." In *Peasant Livelihood*, edited by Rhoda Halperin and James Dow, pp. 201–14. New York: St. Martin's Press.

1994 "Beyond Consumption: Meat, Sociality, Vitality and Hierarchy in Nineteenth-Century Chile." In *Consumption and Identity*, edited by Jonathan Friedman, pp. 119–46. Chur, Switzerland: Harwood Academic Publishers.

Orlove, Benjamin, and Henry Rutz

1989 "Thinking about Consumption: A Social Economy Approach." In *The Social Economy of Consumption*, edited by Henry J. Rutz and Benjamin Orlove, pp. 1–58. Society for Economic Anthropology 6. Lanham: University Press of America.

Orlove, Benjamin, and Arnold J. Bauer

1997 "Giving Importance to Imports." In *The Allure of the Foreign*, edited by Benjamin Orlove, pp. 1–30. Ann Arbor: University of Michigan Press.

Ortiz Crespo, Gonzalo

1990 "Ecuador." In *Narcotrafico: Realidades y Alternativas*, edited by Diego Garcia Sayon, pp. 33–41. Lima: Comision Andina de Juristas.

Ortner, Sherry

1984 "Theory in Anthropology since the Sixties." *Comparative Studies in Society and History* 26 (1): 126–66.

1989   *High Religion: A Cultural and Political History of Sherpa Buddhism.* Princeton: Princeton University Press.

Oxfeld, Ellen

1993   *Blood, Sweat, and Mahjong: Family and Enterprise in an Overseas Chinese Community.* Ithaca: Cornell University Press.

Pacari, Nina

1993   *"Levantamiento indígena."* In *Sismo Etnico en el Ecuador,* pp. 169–86. Quito: CEDIME, Ediciones Abya-Yala.

Park, Kyeyoung

1996   "Use and Abuse of Race and Culture: Black-Korean Tension in America." *American Anthropologist* 98 (3): 492–99.

Parsons, Elsie Clews

1945   *Peguche: A Study of Andean Indians.* Chicago: University of Chicago Press.

Peek, Peter

1982   "Agrarian Change and Labour Migration in the Sierra of Ecuador." In *State Policies and Migration,* edited by Peter Peek and Guy Standing, pp. 121–46. London: Croom Helm.

Philibert, Jean-Marc

1984   "Affluence, Commodity Consumption, and Self-Image in Vanuatu." In *Affluence and Cultural Survival: 1981 Proceedings of the American Ethnological Society,* edited by Richard F. Salisbury and Elisabeth Tooker, pp. 87–94. Washington, DC. American Ethnological Society.

Plattner, Stuart

1989   "Markets and Marketplaces." In *Economic Anthropology,* edited by Stuart Plattner, pp. 171–208. Stanford: Stanford University Press.

Poole, Deborah

1997   *Vision, Race, and Modernity: A Visual Economy of the Andean Image World.* Princeton: Princeton University Press.

Powelson, Michael

1996   "The Use and Abuse of Ethnicity in the Rebellions in Chiapas." *Blueprint for Social Justice* 49 (5): 1–7.

Powers, Richard

1998   *Gain.* New York: Farrar, Straus, and Giroux.

Ramírez, Susan

1995   "Exchange and Markets in the Sixteenth Century: A View from the North." In *Ethnicity, Markets, and Migration in the Andes,* edited by Brooke Larson and Olivia Harris, with Enrique Tandeter, pp. 135–64. Durham: Duke University Press.

Ramón Valarezo, Galo, and Elba Gámez Barahona

1993   "¿Hay nacionalidades indias en el Ecuador?" In *Sismo Etnico en el Ecuador,* pp. 187–206. Quito: CEDIME and Ediciones Abya-Yala.

Rappaport, Joanne

1994   *Cumbe Reborn: An Andean Ethnography of History.* Chicago: University of Chicago Press.

Renfrew, Colin

1986   "Varna and the Emergence of Wealth in Prehistoric Europe." In *The Social Life of Things: Commodities in Cultural Perspective,* edited by Arjun Appadurai, pp. 141–68. Cambridge: Cambridge University Press.

Riley, Kevin Jack
1996   *Snow Job? The War against International Cocaine Trafficking.* New Brunswick: Transaction Publishers.
Roberts, Bryan
1975   "Center and Periphery in the Development Process: The Case of Peru." In *Latin America Urban Research,* vol. 5, edited by Wayne Cornelius and Feliciana Trueblood, pp. 77–108. Beverly Hills: Sage Publications.
1978   *Cities of Peasants: The Political Economy of Urbanization in the Third World.* Beverly Hills: Sage Publications
Rogers, Elizabeth Marberry
1998   "Ethnicity, Property, and the State: Legal Rhetoric and the Politics of Community in Otavalo, Ecuador." *Research in Economic Anthropology* 19, edited by Barry Isaac, pp. 69–113. Greenwich CT: JAI Press.
Rogers, Mark
1998   "Spectacular Bodies: Folklorization and the Politics of Identity in Ecuadorian Beauty Pageants." *Journal of Latin American Anthropology* 3 (2): 54–85.
Rohr, Elisabeth
1990   "Acerca de las razones del triunfo de la empresa de la misión protestante en América Latina." In *Ecuador Indigena: Antropologia y Relaciones Interetnicas,* pp. 93–120. Otavalo: Ecuador.
Rosaldo, Renato
1995   "Foreword." In *Strategies for Entering and Leaving Modernity,* by Néstor García Canclini, pp. xi–xvii. Translated by Christopher L. Chiappari and Silvia L. López. Minneapolis: University of Minnesota Press.
Roseberry, William
1983   *Coffee and Capitalism in the Venezuelan Andes.* Austin: University of Texas Press.
1989   "Peasants and the World." In *Economic Anthropology,* edited by Stuart Plattner, pp. 108–26. Stanford: Stanford University Press.
1994   *Anthropologies and Histories: Essays in Culture, History, and Political Economy.* New Brunswick: Rutgers University Press.
Rubio Orbe, Gonzalo
1956   *Punyaro, estudio de antropologia social y cultural de una comunidad indigena y mestiza.* Quito: Casa de la Cultura Ecuatoriana.
Rueda Novoa, Rocío
1988   *El Obraje de San Joseph de Peguchi.* Quito: Abya Yala and TEHIS.
Saenz, Moises
1933   *Sobre El Indio Ecuatoriano y su Importancia al Medio Nacional.* Mexico: Publicaciones de la Secretaria de Educacion Publica.
Sahlins, Marshall
1972   "The Domestic Mode of Production." In *Stone Age Economics.* Chicago: Aldine.
1981   *Historical Metaphors and Mythical Realities.* Association for Social Anthropology in Oceania. Ann Arbor: University of Michigan Press.
Salisbury, Richard F.
1984   "Affluence and Cultural Survival: An Introduction." In *Affluence and Cultural*

Survival: 1981 Proceedings of the American Ethnological Society, edited by Richard F. Salisbury and Elisabeth Tooker, pp. 1–11. Washington, DC. American Ethnological Society.

Salomon, Frank

1981   "Weavers of Otavalo." In *Cultural Transformations and Ethnicity in Modern Ecuador*, edited by Norman E. Whitten, Jr., pp. 420–49. Urbana: University of Illinois Press.

1985   "The Dynamic Potential of the Complementarity Concept." In *Andean Ecology and Civilization*, edited by Shozo Masuda, Izumi Shimada, and Craig Morris, pp. 511–31. Tokyo: University of Tokyo Press.

1986   *Native Lords of Quito in the age of the Incas: the political economy of north-Andean chiefdoms*. Cambridge: Cambridge University Press.

Salz, Beate

1955   *The Human Element in Industrialization: A Hypothetical Case Study of Ecuadorian Indians*. Washington, DC: American Anthropological Association, Memoir no. 85.

Scott, James

1976   *The Moral Economy of the Peasant: Subsistence and Rebellion in South East Asia*. New Haven: Yale University Press.

1985   *Weapons of the Weak*. New Haven: Yale University Press.

Seremetakis, C. Nadia

1994   "The Memory of the Senses, Part I: Marks of the Transitory." In *The Senses Still: Perception and Memory as Material Culture in Modernity*, edited by C. Nadia Seremetakis, pp. 1–18. Boulder: Westview Press.

Smith, Carol

1984   "Does a Commodity Economy Enrich the Few while Ruining the Masses? Differentiation among Petty Commodity Producers in Guatemala." *Journal of Peasant Studies* 11: 60–95.

Smith, Gavin

1979   Socio-economic Differentiation and Relations of Production among Rural-based Petty Producers in Central Peru, 1880–1970." *Journal of Peasant Studies* 6 (3): 286–310.

1989   *Livelihood and Resistance*. Berkeley: University of California Press.

Smith, Waldemar

1977   *The Fiesta System and Economic Change*. New York: Colombia University Press.

Spyer, Patricia

1997   "The Eroticism of Debt: Pearl Divers, Traders, and Sea Wives in the Aru Islands, Eastern Indonesia." *American Ethnologist* 24 (3): 515–38.

Stark, Louise

1981   "Folk Models of Stratification in the Highlands of northern Ecuador." In *Cultural Transformations and Ethnicity in Modern Ecuador*, edited by Norman E. Whitten, Jr., pp. 387–401. Urbana: University of Illinois Press.

Starn, Orin

1994   "Rethinking the Politics of Anthropology: The Case of the Andes." *Current Anthropology* 35: 13–38.

Starrett, Gregory
1995   "The Political Economy of Religious Commodities in Cairo." *American Anthropologist* 97 (1): 51–68.
Stepan, Nancy
1991   *The Hour of Eugenics: Race, Gender, and Nation in Latin America*. Ithaca: Cornell University Press.
Stephen, Lynn
1991a *Zapotec Women*. Austin: University of Texas Press.
1991a "Culture as a Resource: Four Cases of Self-Managed Indigenous Craft Production in Latin America." *Economic Development and Cultural Change* 40(1): 101–30.
Stoler, Ann
1995   *Race and the Education of Desire*. Durham, NC: Duke University Press.
Stoller, Paul
1989   *The Taste of Ethnographic Things: The Senses in Anthropology*. Philadelphia: University of Pennsylvania Press.
1997   *Sensuous Scholarship*. Philadelphia: University of Pennsylvania Press.
Strathern, Andrew
1971   *The Rope of Moka*. Cambridge: Cambridge University Press.
Strathern, Marilyn
1994   "Foreward: The Mirror of Technology." In *Consuming Technologies: Media and Information in Domestic Spaces*, edited by R. Silverstone and E. Hirsh, pp. vii–xiv. New York: Routledge.
Stutzman, Ronald
1981   "El Mestizaje: An All-Inclusive Ideology of Exclusion." In *Cultural Transformations and Ethnicity in Modern Ecuador*, edited by Norman E. Whitten, Jr., pp. 45–94. Urbana: University of Illinois Press.
Taussig, Michael
1980   *The Devil and Commodity Fetishism*. Chapel Hill: University of North Carolina Press.
Terán, Benjamín
1991   "Indios Plásticos." *Shimishitachi* 9 (diciembre): 20–22.
Thompson, Stephen I., Susan C. Vehik, and Daniel C. Swan
1984   "Oil Wealth and the Osage Indians." In *Affluence and Cultural Survival: 1981 Proceedings of the American Ethnological Society*, edited by Richard F. Salisbury and Elisabeth Tooker, pp. 40–52. Washington, DC: American Ethnological Society.
Tice, Karin E.
1995   *Kuna Crafts, Gender, and the Global Economy*. Austin: University of Texas Press.
Tobar Bonilla, Guadalupe
1985   "Natabuela: Un caso de resistencia y adaptación cultural de la indumentaria indígena." *Cultura* 7 (21a): 243–81.
Turner, Terence
1995   "An Indigenous People's Struggle for Socially Equitable and Ecologically Sustainable Production." *Journal of Latin American Anthropology* 1: 98–121.

Turner, Victor

1967 *The Forest of Symbols.* Ithaca: Cornell University Press.

van den Berghe, Pierre

1993 "Tourism and the Ethnic Division of Labor." *Annals of Tourism Research* 19: 234–49.

van den Berghe, Pierre, and George Primov

1977 *Inequality in the Peruvian Andes: Class and Ethnicity in Cuzco.* Columbia: University of Missouri Press.

Veblen, Thorstein

1994 [1899] *The Theory of the Leisure Class.* New York: Penguin.

Villavicencio Rivadeneira, Gladys

1973 *Relaciones interétnicas en Otavalo¿una nacionalidad india en formación?* Mexico City: Instituto Indenista Interamericano, Ediciones especiales: 65.

Vincent, Joan

1986 "System and Process, 1974–1985." *Annual Reviews in Anthropology* 15: 99–119.

Wagner, Roy

1986 *Symbols that Stand for Themselves.* Chicago: University of Chicago Press.

Wallis, Brian

1984 "What's Wrong with This Picture? An Introduction." In *Art after Modernism,* edited by Brian Wallis, pp. xi–xvii. New York: The New Museum of Contemporary Art.

Walter, Lynn

1981 "Social Strategies and the Fiesta Complex in an Otavaleño Community." *American Ethnologist* 8 (1): 172–85.

Warren, Kay B.

1998 *Indigenous Movements and Their Critics: Pan-Maya Activism in Guatemala.* Princeton: Princeton University Press.

Watanabe, John

1992 *Maya Saints and Souls.* Austin: University of Texas Press.

Waters, William F.

1997 "The Road of Many Returns: Rural Bases of the Informal Urban Economy in Ecuador." *Latin American Perspectives* 24 (3): 50–64.

Watts, Jerry G.

1993 "Reflections on the Rodney King Verdict and the Paradoxes of the Black Response." In *Reading Rodney King, Reading Urban Uprising,* edited by Robert Gooding Williams, pp. 236–48. New York: Routledge.

Weber, Max

1978 *Max Weber: Selections in Translation.* Edited by W. G. Runciman, and translated by E. Matthews. Cambridge: Cambridge University Press.

Weiner Annette

1992 *Inalienable Possessions.* Berkeley: University of California Press.

Weismantel, Mary

1988 *Food, Gender, and Poverty.* Philadelphia: University of Pennsylvania Press.

1989a "Making Breakfast and Raising Babies." In *The Household Economy: Reconsidering the Domestic Mode of Production,* edited by Richard Wilk, pp. 55–72. Boulder: Westview Press.

1989b "The Children Cry for Bread: Hegemony and the Transformation of Consumption." In *The Social Economy of Consumption,* edited by Henry J. Rutz and Benjamin Orlove, pp. 85–100. Society for Economic Anthropology 6. Lanham: University Press of America.

1995 "Making Kin: Kinship Theory and Zumbagua Adoptions." *American Ethnologist* 22(4) 685–709.

1997 "Time, Work Discipline, and Beans: Indigenous Self-Determination in the Northern Andes." In *Women and Economic Change: Andean Perspectives,* edited by Ann Miles and Hans Buechler, pp. 31–54. Washington, DC: American Anthropological Association, the Society for Latin American Anthropology.

Weismantel, Mary, and Stephen Eisenman

1998 "Race in the Andes: Global Movements and Popular Ontologies." *Bulletin of Latin American Research* 17 (2): 121–42.

Whitaker, Morris D., and Duty Greene

1990 "Development Policy and Agriculture." In *Agriculture and Economic Survival: The Role of Agriculture in Ecuador's Development,* edited by Morris D. Whitaker and Dale Colyer, pp. 21–42. Boulder: Westview Press.

Whitten, Norman

1981a ed. *Cultural Transformations and Ethnicity in Modern Ecuador.* Urbana: University of Illinois Press.

1981b "Introduction." In *Cultural Transformations and Ethnicity in Modern Ecuador,* edited by Norman E. Whitten, Jr., pp. 1–40. Urbana: University of Illinois Press.

1985 *Sicuanga Runa: The Other Side of Development in Amazonian Ecuador.* Urbana: University of Illinois Press.

Whitten, Norman, Dorothea Scott Whitten, and Alfonso Chango

1997 "Return of the Yumbo: The Indigenous Caminata from Amazonia to Andean Quito." *American Ethnologist* 24 (2): 355–91.

Wilk, Richard

1989a "Beyond the Black Box." In *The Household Economy: The Domestic Mode of Production Reconsidered,* edited by Richard Wilk, pp. 23–52. Boulder: Westview Press.

1989b "Houses as Consumer Goods: Social Processes and Allocation Decisions." In *The Social Economy of Consumption,* edited by Henry J. Rutz and Benjamin Orlove, pp. 297–322. Society for Economic Anthropology 6. Lanham: University Press of America.

1994 "Consumer Goods as a Dialogue about Development: Colonial Time and Television Time in Belize." In *Consumption and Identity,* edited by Jonathan Friedman, pp. 97–118. Chur, Switzerland: Harwood Academic Publishers.

Wolf, Eric

1955 "Types of Latin American Peasantry: A Preliminary Discussion." *American Anthropologist* 57 (3, part 1): 452–71.

1957 "Closed Corporate Communities in Mesoamerica and Java." *Southwest Journal of Anthropology* 13 (1): 1–18.

1966 *Peasants.* Englewood Cliffs, NJ: Prentice-Hall, Inc.

1986 "The Vicissitudes of the Closed Corporate Peasant Community." *American Ethnologist* 13: 325–29.

1990 "Distinguished Lecture: Facing Power–Old Insights, New Questions." *American Anthropologist* 92 (3): 586–96.

1994 "Perilous Ideas: Race, Culture, and People." *Current Anthropology* 35 (1): 1–12.

Zamosc, León

1993 "Protesta agraria y movimiento indígena en la sierra ecuatoriana." In *Sismo Etnico en el Ecuador*, pp. 273–304. Quito: CEDIME and Ediciones Abya-Yala.

1994 "Agrarian Protest and the Indian Movement in the Ecuadorian Highlands." *Latin American Research Review* 29 (3): 37–68.

1995 *Estadística de las áreas de predominio étnico de la sierra ecuatoriana*. Quito: Ediciones Abya-Yala.

Zuniga, Neptali

1940 *Fenomenos de la Realidad Ecuatoriana*. Quito: Talleres Graficos de Educación.